Colección Támesis

SERIE A: MONOGRAFÍAS, 287

# SERGI BELBEL AND CATALAN THEATRE

## TEXT, PERFORMANCE AND IDENTITY

By the late 1970s, internationally known performance groups such as Els Joglars, La Fura dels Baus or La Cubana had precipitated a decline in text-based Catalan theatre, reversed in the mid 1980s with the appearance of a younger generation of playwrights led by Sergi Belbel. Influenced by contemporary European rather than Spanish or Catalan drama, his work was very different from the realist idiom favoured by playwrights of the Franco generation.

But playwriting is only one aspect of Belbel's work as a theatre practitioner. He also has a highly successful career as a director of Spanish, Catalan and foreign plays (a number of which he himself has translated), and, since 2006, he has held the position of Artistic Director of the National Theatre of Catalonia.

This study examines these three key aspects of his career, as well as Ventura Pons's film adaptations of his plays. Finally, it considers the reception of his plays in several countries, analysing his evolving relationship with critics at home and abroad.

DAVID GEORGE is Professor of Hispanic Studies at Swansea University.

DAVID GEORGE

# SERGI BELBEL AND CATALAN THEATRE
## TEXT, PERFORMANCE AND IDENTITY

TAMESIS

First published 2010 by Tamesis, Woodbridge

ISBN 978–1–85566–220–9

Tamesis is an imprint of Boydell & Brewer Ltd
PO Box 9, Woodbridge, Suffolk IP12 3DF, UK
and of Boydell & Brewer Inc.
668 Mt Hope Avenue, Rochester, NY 14620, USA
website: www.boydellandbrewer.com

A CIP catalogue record for this book is available
from the British Library

The publisher has no responsibility for the continued existence or
accuracy of URLs for external or third-party internet websites referred to
in this book, and does not guarantee that any content on such websites is,
or will remain, accurate or appropriate

This publication is printed on acid-free paper

Typeset by Pru Harrison, Hacheston, Suffolk
Printed in Great Britain by
CPI Antony Rowe Ltd, Chippenham and Eastbourne

# CONTENTS

Per a Mària Antònia, que m'anima sempre

# LIST OF ILLUSTRATIONS

# ACKNOWLEDGEMENTS

I have accumulated numerous debts of gratitude in the preparation of this book. Xavier Puchades kindly made available to me his University of Valencia doctoral dissertation. Anton Pujol allowed me to see a draft of his 'Ventura Pons y la crónica de un territorio llamado Barcelona'. Julio Huélamo, Berta Muñoz, Pedro Ocaña and Gerardo del Barco were helpful and welcoming at the Centro de Documentación Teatral in Madrid. The Centro allowed me to view recordings of Madrid productions of Belbel's play, while similar facilities were made available to me by Lídia Giménez at Serveis de l'Espectacle Focus, S.A. in Barcelona and by Amparo Valera at the Teatre Nacional de Catalunya (TNC). Belbel's secretary Txiqui Vanaclocha generously made available to me numerous press reviews and other useful visual material. I am most grateful to all the theatre practitioners who agreed to my interviewing them, and who provided much helpful material for Chapter 2. Sergi Belbel himself was always willing to provide information, and to discuss issues surrounding his writing, his directing and his Artistic Directorship of the TNC. Filmmaker Ventura Pons was similarly generous with his time, and I shall be eternally grateful to him for welcoming me at the shooting of his latest film adaptation of a Belbel play. Much valuable information on the productions and reception of Belbel plays in Germany and Denmark was provided by Belbel's German translator Klaus Laabs and Copenhagen-based director Simon Boberg respectively.

A number of colleagues at Swansea University contributed in various ways to the preparation of the book. Dr Katharina Hall evaluated German reviews with me, and  students on the MA in Translation with Language Technology (MATLT) provided translations of them. Dick James of the Department of Media Resources assisted in providing technical support prior to the interviews I conducted in Spain. John London made available to me an article on the reception of Belbel in Germany, while Australian director Scott Gooding sent me information on his productions of two Belbel plays in that country.

Maria Delgado, Mair George, Jim McCarthy and Lourdes Orozco all provided invaluable feedback on the various drafts of the book. Ellie Ferguson, Commissioning Editor of Tamesis Press, calmly and helpfully fielded my questions and solved the inevitable problems. The book was completed with assistance from the AHRC's Research Leave Scheme, for which I am most grateful. And finally my warm thanks go to the School of Arts and Humanities of the University of Swansea for assistance with the production costs of the volume.

# INTRODUCTION

'A complete creative artist, without whom it is impossible to understand contemporary Spanish theatre'.[1]

By the end of the 1970s, Spanish theatre faced an uncertain future. The political crossroads that was the end of the Franco dictatorship and the transition to democracy was reflected in the theatre. The censorship with which playwrights had battled under the previous regime was no longer the challenge, and, in any case, the social realism that had been *de rigueur* in Spanish and Catalan playwriting of the 1960s and early 1970s was now out of fashion in international theatre. Collective creation was in vogue, and the performance art and street theatre that had developed during the 1960s in Europe and North America had, to an extent, supplanted text-based theatre.

By this time the collective ethos had taken root in Spain, especially in Catalonia, and such companies as San Francisco Mime Troupe and Théâtre du Soleil had their Catalan counterparts in internationally renowned performance groups, including Els Joglars and Comediants, while the performance group of the rock age, La Fura dels Baus, was about to break new boundaries and attract new audiences. Their world was far removed from the dominant mode of text-based theatre of the late Franco period. Els Joglars' shows were as anti-Franco as the plays of social realists like Josep M. Benet i Jornet or Jordi Teixidor, but the

---

[1] 'Un creador completo, sin el que no es posible entender el teatro español contemporáneo' (Pedro Villora, 'Belbel, *En la Toscana*', *El Mundo*, 6 March 2008; http://www.elmundo.es/papel/2008/03/06/madrid/2340900.html, accessed 31 July 2008). English translations of Catalan and Spanish quotations appear in the main body of the text. The originals are reproduced in footnotes, unless they are very short, in which case they will appear in parentheses in the main text after the English translations. Titles of newspaper reviews will also be translated if they are of relevance to the argument being pursued.

idiom was radically different. Words were often replaced by mime, movement and, especially in the case of La Fura, music. Their early shows, performed in locations as varied as a morgue and a garage, were an assault on their audiences' senses, and a world away from the well-made play in a proscenium-arch theatre.

The success of the groups went a long way towards ensuring that text-based Catalan theatre had been largely marginalised by the early 1970s. The realist idiom of the latter would have seemed passé to younger audiences, who found their desire for new theatrical forms satisfied in the performance groups, while the lack of a theatre infra-structure was another factor in this process. Catalan playwrights had laboured under a double handicap during the Franco years. Like their counterparts in the rest of Spain, they were subject to censorship laws, but they also suffered from the difficulty of getting plays in the Catalan language performed, at least in mainstream theatres. Catalan theatre was largely kept alive during these difficult years in the independent sector. The Agrupació Dramàtica de Barcelona (ADB) did sterling work in the 1950s and early 1960s to stage plays by young Catalan play-wrights, while the Escola d'Art Dramàtic Adrià Gual (EADAG), founded in 1960 by, among others, Ricard Salvat, introduced Brechtian techniques to the Catalan stage and was particularly noted for its epic productions of poetic texts by such writers as the poet Salvador Espriu.[2]

By the early 1980s a more solid theatre infrastructure had begun to be established in Spain. The Centro Dramático Nacional de Madrid (CDN) was founded in 1978, with the mission to 'disseminate and consolidate the various currents and tendencies of contemporary playwriting, with special attention to contemporary Spanish play-wrights'.[3] In Catalonia a prototype National Theatre, the Centre

2 On the ADB, see Jordi Coca, *L'Agrupació Dramàtica de Barcelona: intent de Teatre Nacional Català, 1995–1963*, Monografies de Teatre, 9 (Barcelona: Edicions 62/ Institut del Teatre, 1978); on EADAG and other theatres from the independent sector, see Ricard Salvat Ferré, 'Les aportacions del Teatre Viu, l'EADAG i la Companyia Adrià Gual dels anys cinquanta i seixanta', *Assaig de Teatre: Revista de l'Associació de 'Investigació i Experimentació Teatral*, 37 (2003), 111–22; and Enric Ciurans, *El Teatre Viu, una resistència cultural* (Barcelona: Associació d'Investigació i Experimentació Teatral, 2009).

3 'difundir y consolidar las distintas corrientes y tendencias de la dramaturgia contemporánea, con atención especial a la autoría española

Dramàtic de la Generalitat de Catalunya (CDGC), was founded in 1981, with its headquarters at Barcelona's Teatre Romea. The Teatre Lliure had been established in 1976 in the working-class district of Gràcia in the city, and acquired an international reputation for its productions of Catalan and foreign plays and in particular for the collaborations of director Lluís Pasqual and designer Fabià Puigserver.

In short, by the early 1980s, several elements were in play within the Catalan theatre scene, reflecting to an extent similar tendencies within the rest of Spain and, more widely, the Western world. Performance art was dominant (and much more so in Catalonia than in Madrid, for example), while, in Gabriele and Leonard's words, the 'general absence' ('ausencia general') during the early 1980s of plays by the playwrights who were active during the Franco years 'seems to suggest a preference on the part of audiences for a less politicised theatre and a desire to forget the past'.[4] In Catalonia Benet i Jornet was almost alone among his social realist peers in finding favour in post-1980 Spain, but, crucially, only after he had completely changed his playwriting style.[5]

By the time a young Sergi Belbel first came to prominence in the mid-1980s he faced the changing panorama that I have outlined. He shared a theatre aesthetic with other Spanish writers of the so-called Bradomín Generation, which included Yolanda Pallín, Juan Mayorga, and his fellow Catalan Lluïsa Cunillé. The Marqués de Bradomín Prize – which gave the Generation its name – was awarded annually from 1985 to 1994 to the best play written by a Spanish dramatist under the age of thirty and was one of the factors that helped to form that younger generation of post-Franco playwrights. In Ragué-Arias's words, 'the Sala Beckett workshops, the Marqués de Bradomín prize for writers under thirty years old, the alternative theatre festivals, have

actual' (from the CDN's website, http://cdn.mcu.es/qs.php?leng=es, accessed 17 June 2009).

4 'parece sugerir una preferencia del público por un teatro menos politizado y un deseo de olvidar el pasado' (Candyce Leonard and John P. Gabriele, 'Fórmula para una dramaturgia española de finales del siglo XX', in *Panorámica del teatro español actual*, ed. John P. Gabriele and Candyce Leonard, Serie Teatro (Madrid: Fundamentos, 1996), pp. 7–21, p. 10).

5 For details of Belbel's direction of *Desig*, one of the emblematic plays by the 'new' Benet, see Chapter 2, pp. 81–85.

contributed to the creation of a generation. The obvious head of this generation was Sergi Belbel, winner of the first Marqués de Bradomín prize, today an internationally recognised author who is also an excellent director.'[6] According to Ragué-Arias, characters in the plays of the Bradomín Generation are often abstract, traditional dramatic structures disappear, there is an absence of an obvious plot, juxtaposition is common, and dialogue is replaced by monologue (p. 238).

Of course, not all these characteristics are present in Belbel's plays. However, his early works represent a complete break with the Franco generation of Catalan (and more broadly, Spanish) playwrights. A scenic structure replaced the well-made, three-act format, characters were often unnamed, settings non-specific, and a delight in language was evident. In short, this was writing for its own sake, with no obvious social or political purpose.[7] The dominant influence was no longer Brecht but other, very different and more recent, European playwrights. The writer/director José Sanchis Sinisterra was a key guiding light for the young Belbel, who worked with him in the former's Samuel Beckett-inspired Teatro Fronterizo (Frontier Theatre). This group was founded in Barcelona in 1977, and found a fixed space in the newly created and appropriately named Sala Beckett in Barcelona's Gràcia district in 1988.[8] Manuel Aznar Soler's description of

---

[6] 'los talleres de la Sala Beckett, el premio Marqués de Bradomín para menores de 30 años, las muestras de teatro alternativo, han contribuido a crear una generación. La cabeza visible de la misma es Sergi Belbel, el ganador del premio Marqués de Bradomín en su primera convocatoria, un autor reconocido internacionalmente hoy y que es, además, un excelente director escénico' (María-José Ragué-Arias, *El teatro de fin de milenio en España (de 1975 hasta hoy)*, Ariel Literatura y Crítica (Barcelona: Ariel, 1996), p. 227). The prize was awarded to Belbel for his first play *Calidoscopios y faros de hoy* (1985), and he won the 1987 Ignasi Iglésies prize for *Elsa Schneider*.

[7] That said, to a greater or lesser degree many of Belbel's plays are political in a broader sense. This issue will be discussed more fully in Chapter 1.

[8] For further information on the Sala Beckett see Enric Gallén, 'Catalan Theatrical Life', in *Contemporary Catalan Drama*, ed. David George and John London, Anglo-Catalan Society Occasional Publications, 9 (Sheffield: Anglo-Catalan Society, 1996), pp. 19–42, p. 37; and Sharon G. Feldman, 'The Sala Beckett and the Zero Degree of Theatricality: From Lluïsa Cunillé to Carles Batlle', in *Catalan Theatre, 1975–2006: Politics, Identity, Performance*, ed. Maria M. Delgado, David George and Lourdes Orozco, special issue of *Contemporary Theatre Review*, 17:3 (2007), 370–84.

Sanchis's 'constant willingness to experiment, carried out with a theoretical rigour most unusual in Spanish theatre'[9] could equally be applied to Belbel's early work. The influences on this early theatre reflected his wide reading, particularly of foreign plays. A student of French Philology, he was steeped in French theatre, from such classical writers as Molière and Racine to more recent figures like Bernard-Marie Koltès. Belbel's plays seem to have much more in common with pre-Civil War playwrights, which would include Lorca and Genet, or with post-war European and North American writers like Beckett, Koltès or Mamet than with his immediate Catalan predecessors. Beckett's influence is felt particularly in the disturbingly enigmatic nature of many of Belbel's plays and in their spare, suggestive language, while the colloquial register of the theatre of David Mamet is reflected in such works as *Carícies* and *Després de la pluja*. The Austrian Peter Handke is another early influence, particularly in his questioning of the nature of the actor–audience relationship and the scenic, non-linear structure of his plays, as is the East German Heiner Müller, for what Puchades describes as his 'subjective drama which emerges from the dramaturgy of a narrative text'.[10]

By the mid-to-late 1980s Belbel had absorbed such influences, and created what was recognised as his own individual style. His early plays had such an impact on the Catalan stage that the term 'Operation Belbel' was coined to define a certain style of playwriting adopted by the new generation of Catalan dramatists. It was more abstract and less specific than that of his predecessors, and, in 1989, an article in the Catalan daily *Avui* could carry the title 'Catalan Theatre is Called Sergi Belbel'.[11] His reputation has spread far and wide, within and beyond Europe. According to his German translator, Klaus Laabs, the only two Spanish playwrights who are widely known outside specialist theatre

---

[9] 'permanente voluntad de investigación, realizada con un rigor teórico muy poco frecuente en el teatro español' (Introduction to José Sanchis Sinisterra, *Ñaque/ ¡Ay, Carmela!* (Madrid Cátedra, 1993), pp. 9–101, p. 11).

[10] 'drama subjetivo creado a partir de la dramaturgia de un texto narrativo' (Xavier Puchades, 'Renovación teatral en España entre 1984–1998 desde la escritura dramática; puesta en escena y recepción crítica' (unpublished doctoral dissertation, University of Valencia, 2005), p. 80, note 122).

[11] Anon., 'El teatre català es diu Sergi Belbel', *Avui*, 4 January 1989, p. 34. Other members of the so-called Belbel Generation are Lluïsa Cunillé, Jordi Galceran and Joan Casas.

circles in Germany are García Lorca and Belbel.[12] The German press review of Belbel's *Forasters* (as *Wildfremde*) in Mannheim states that Belbel 'is probably the most famous contemporary Spanish author'.[13]

Belbel's friend and the leading Catalan playwright of the post-Civil War period, Josep M. Benet i Jornet, traces Belbel's impact on Catalan theatre to *Minim.mal Show* (1987): 'if we are to be fair, we would recognise that, after *Minim.mal Show*, and despite, if you will, its modesty, nothing could be the same again for our theatre'.[14] In an interview I conducted with him in September 2008, Benet recalled how Belbel emerged onto the Catalan theatre scene in the mid-1980s via the Teatro Fronterizo and the Universitat Autònoma's Aula de Teatre (Theatre Seminar), of which Belbel was a founder member and where, under the guidance of Jordi Castellanos, he had begun his theatrical activity, combining a knowledge of established theatre forms with more experimental currents and dance theatre productions. What Belbel also did in those early plays, said Benet, was to bring to the Catalan stage a taste of such leading figures from the European theatrical scene as Beckett and Pina Bausch. Benet sees similarities with the work of the artist and writer Joan Brossa (1919–98), although he feels that this prime representative of the post-Civil War avant-garde was not a major influence on Belbel who, at that time, had read little Catalan drama. The early influences, said Benet, were writers he had discovered through Sanchis or through his own knowledge of the theatre beyond Catalonia.[15]

Benet also acknowledged the importance of Belbel's work as a translator, thus confirming his status as a multifaceted theatre practi-

---

12  In conversation with me in Berlin in May 2009.

13  Reinhard Wengierek, 'They kiss and then they clobber each other', translation of 'Sie küssen und sie kloppen sich', *Welt.de*, 24 January 2006. Review translated by Chloë Driscoll and Josephine McCrossan, two students on the MA in Translation with Language Technology (MATLT) at Swansea University.

14  'Si hem de ser justos reconeixerem que després de *Minim.mal Show*, i malgrat, si voleu, la seva modèstia, ja no res podia tornar a ser igual per al nostre teatre' (Josep M. Benet i Jornet, 'Per situar-nos', in Miquel Górriz and Sergi Belbel, *Minim.mal Show*, Teatre 3 i 4 (Valencia: Eliseu Climent, 1992), pp. 9–16, p. 12).

15  Benet added that, despite the innovative quality of his early work, Belbel in no way despised established Catalan theatre.

tioner. Indeed, he was the first Catalan since Adrià Gual (1872–1943) to dedicate himself full-time to the theatre. In addition to his playwriting and his translating, he is a respected director, with a wide and varied repertoire of plays from Catalonia and beyond, from the seventeenth century to the present day. He has also taught at Catalonia's theatre academy, the Institut del Teatre, an important venue for the training of young theatre practitioners and, since 2006, he has been Artistic Director of the National Theatre of Catalonia (Teatre Nacional de Catalunya, or TNC).

My aim in this book is to consider three aspects of Belbel's work – his playwriting, his directing and his work as Artistic Director of the TNC – thereby conveying a sense of the breadth of his activity. Chapter 1 examines his development as a playwright from the late 1980s to the present day. Chapter 2 – entitled 'Performance and Practitioners' – is concerned with his directing, both of his own plays and those of a wide variety of Catalan and foreign playwrights. This chapter will make extensive use of interviews I have conducted with a number of practitioners who have been involved in selected productions directed by Belbel, and will assess both his working methods and their results in productions selected to reflect a variety of styles and periods.

Although the focus of Chapter 3 is not primarily Belbel's plays but Catalan filmmaker Ventura Pons's adaptations of them, it will complement Chapter 1 by highlighting contrasts between three plays discussed there and their cinematic versions. Chapter 4, 'Belbel and the Critics', will offer another angle on Belbel's plays as it analyses their reception in a number of theatre venues at home and abroad. Making extensive use of theatre reviews in Catalonia, Spain and beyond, it will attempt to understand and account for what is a surprisingly varied set of critical and audience responses. Chapter 5 is dedicated to the most recent development in Belbel's portfolio, his artistic directorship of the TNC, and will attempt an evaluation of his task in this inevitably contentious and politically sensitive position.

Questions to be posed in the study include: Why did Belbel write in such a radically different style from that of the previous generation of Catalan dramatists, whose work was characterised by realism? How important was Belbel's own knowledge of contemporary European playwrights such as Beckett, Koltès and Heiner Müller, and how might he be positioned within a wider European tradition? How has his work been received in Germany and Denmark, and how does this compare

with its reception in his native country? In which directions has
Belbel's writing evolved since the early years? Why has he anchored
his later plays in more recognisable settings? Has it been an advantage
to him to direct his own plays? How has direction influenced the
quality and reception of these? To what extent has Belbel's directing
(as opposed to his dramaturgy) contributed to the development of the
careers of other Catalan playwrights and to what extent has it allowed
Josep Maria Benet i Jornet to reshape his career?

# 1

# Belbel the Playwright

A striking feature of Belbel's plays is that they defy easy categorisation, for he has written in a number of different dramatic forms. Some of these belong to what one might term popular theatre or paratheatre, including the student review, the musical, television soap and crime drama. He often parodies these and other forms,[1] while, in his sometimes stylised versions of them, he belongs to an avant-garde tradition whose most obvious exponent in twentieth-century Spain is Ramón del Valle-Inclán, and in Catalonia, Joan Brossa. Neither can his plays be categorised easily as comedies or tragedies, and he frequently moves between the comic and the serious, often within individual plays. Xavier Puchades terms the process the 'constant struggle between the comic Belbel and the tragic Belbel; the playful Belbel and the social Belbel',[2] a combination appreciated by German reviewers of his plays. Simon Boberg, Belbel's Danish director, feels that Belbel belongs principally in the tradition of the French *comédie*, which, in Boberg's view, is a key factor in his popularity in Denmark, a country that is attracted to this style of theatre.[3] The dramatic forms and language of the plays convey a broad critique of contemporary society, not in a narrow sense of contemporary Catalonia or Spain, but of what might broadly be termed Western society. The plays' characters are essentially middle-class or – particularly in the early works – classless, in the sense that their social status is not always evident. The subjects of the plays are

[1] For Belbel's parodies of various dramatic and paratheatrical forms, see Xavier Puchades, 'Renovación teatral en España entre 1984–1998 desde la escritura dramática; puesta en escena y recepción crítica' (unpublished doctoral dissertation, University of Valencia, 2005), p. 213.

[2] 'lucha continua entre el Belbel cómico y el Belbel trágico; el Belbel lúdico y el Belbel social' (p. 177).

[3] In conversation with me in Copenhagen, 11 May 2009.

not limited to contemporary society, however, and broader concerns such as sexuality and death characterise many of them.

This chapter aims, through an analysis of representative texts, to trace Belbel's development as a playwright since the mid-1980s. These texts have been chosen to illustrate what I consider to be the principal stylistic and thematic features of his œuvre. The objective is not to provide an exhaustive analysis of his plays, nor to consider other genres in which he has written, notably the television soap and the novel in dialogue form, as, to date, his output in these areas is scant. I attempt to achieve a chronological balance, although I devote more time to his most recent plays as they have received less critical attention than those that belong to the pre-2000 period. An analysis of the theatrical language of Belbel's plays precedes a consideration of their main thematic concerns. The emphasis in this chapter is on the play as literary text rather than on performance, which is covered more fully in Chapter 2. Although I provide detailed analysis of just one Belbel play in that chapter, further consideration is given to the more practical, performance aspects of Belbel's plays in Chapter 4, in which productions of a selection of them in several countries are examined through the eyes of theatre critics.

## Theatrical language and structure

One of the salient characteristics of Belbel's theatre is that he is continually experimenting with both language and dramatic form. The complexity of the identity question – which involves mainly personal, but also national, gender and cultural identity (see pp. 45–50 below) – is perhaps one reason for this, but there are others, not least his fascination with what might be called the mechanisms of how a play is shaped and written. He juxtaposes the quotidian, or banal, with the philosophical, in a way that reflects his setting one dramatic form against another as he probes their possibilities and limitations. His language is sometimes playful and humorous, and at others disconcerting and surprising, as he strives to create a sense of shock, which can have multiple purposes. As far as staging is concerned, Belbel's use of space, lighting, music, movement and mime all contribute to his experimental, essentially metatheatrical approach.

It is in his early plays that the experimentation is most noticeable, especially in *Minim.mal Show*. Minimalism is a feature of all aspects of the play, including language, use of the stage, and details about the characters. This is perhaps the area in which the influence of Beckett – at its strongest during this period of Belbel's writing career – is most apparent. The tone is evident from the Dramatis Personae, which is playfully headed 'Personatges (?) (!)' ('Characters (?) (!))'; p. 19). The characters are totally minimalist, with just letters to identify them. However, characteristics of individuals do emerge as the play progresses. C and Y seem to be the gentle, romantic ones, while B, X and especially A are violent and X is brassy. In the Dramatis Personae, A, B and C are referred to as 'Ells' ('They' – Male), and X and Y as 'Elles' ('They' – Female). We are given practically no information on their past, and the relationships between them are never made clear. The notion of sometimes nebulous links between characters is developed in other plays such as *En companyia d'abisme*, *Carícies* and *A la Toscana*. All the scenes of *Minim.mal Show* bear titles, many of which are tantalisingly and playfully idiosyncratic (see Appendix, pp. 195–6). Perhaps the most significant for a word-merchant like the early Belbel are the Sil·logisme scenes. Some common characteristics of individual types of scene do emerge (as with a chair moving in the Pòdium sequences), but the audience would find it difficult to make the links.

Several other Belbelian characteristics are present in the play, as the author forges a theatrical language that has come to be associated with him. This reinforces the minimalism evident in the Dramatis Personae, and characters sometimes speak in incomplete sentences. It is also often mocking, with sudden, disconcerting shifts of register. Ironic humour is present throughout, but Belbel never lets his audience settle. Examples include the unexpected, unprovoked violence in the Conseqüència sequence (p. 33), or the sudden death of Y and A in the L'Escena sequence (p. 53), the shock heightened by the contrast with their previous kissing. Such incidents seem to anticipate a similar technique in *Carícies* and other plays.

Another kind of typically Belbelian surprise in *Minim.mal Show* is sexual, for instance in the Discòpula scene, in which a male character reads a newspaper and a woman files her nails while both simulate sexual intercourse by uttering 'guttural sounds, sighs, etc., while at all times holding their respective poses, without touching each other, without looking at each other, he reading and she filing her nails'.[4] The

---

[4] 'sons guturals, sospirs, etc., i sempre sense desfer les poses respectives, sense tocar-se, sense mirar-se, ell llegint i ella llimant-se les ungles' (Miquel

sense of metatheatre present in this scene is repeated at other points in the play, with the introduction of the idea of 'voyeurs' (p. 21), for instance, while at others the impression is given of theatre students working, as in 'Bolero (!)', where it looks as if the actors are measuring their steps and studying the composition of the bodies and the space (p. 37). The strong awareness of the presence of the audience, and the ironic attitude towards them, that surface on several occasions in the play, are rather reminiscent of the Autor's position in García Lorca's *La zapatera prodigiosa* (*The Shoemaker's Wonderful Wife*, 1924–26). For instance, the final stage direction of one of the play's longest scenes, the theatrically entitled L'Escena, in which C observes the deaths of Y and A, indicates that the characters should act without ever forgetting the presence of the audience' (p. 53). A second metatheatrical level emerges at this point, as B mysteriously enters without being seen by the observer C while simultaneously observing the audience.

Part of Belbel's metatheatrical exploration in *Minim.mal Show* is his use of mime and movement. The foot movement in the third Bolero suggests dance, while the play reflects – and seems to offer an ironic commentary on – drama school teaching. In some ways, this play reveals the influence of Catalan performance groups, in particular Els Joglars. Mime and clowning play a crucial role in this parallel. The clown motif appears in the play, specifically in L'Escena (p. 52), which recalls Els Joglars's leader Albert Boadella's use of mime in *Àlias Serrallonga* (1974) and also more generally the clown, Harlequin or puppet master. At another point in the play the characters explain things by pointing at a kind of a parchment or board, which is once again reminiscent of *La zapatera prodigiosa*. The reference to a whistle in the final stage direction of the first Síncope ('*A whistle blows – one of those that says "play it again"*'[5]) also connects with the circus/ clowning element of the play.

Clowning, of course, is a paratheatrical genre in which comedy or farce and tragedy are never far removed from each other, especially – but not exclusively – in the Romantic and Symbolist periods. Although the overall tenor of *Minim.mal Show* is humorous, the comedic mask

---

Górriz and Sergi Belbel, *Minim.mal Show*, Teatre 3 i 4 (Valencia: Eliseu Climent, 1992), p. 73).

   [5] '*Sona un xiulet – dels de "repetició de la jugada"*'.

does hide the presence of serious themes, which are developed more fully in Belbel's later work. For example, in a particularly provocative and thought-provoking scene (Pentàgon) the contrast between the words and the gestures which is suggested in other scenes is made specific here: '*At that precise moment they all adopt a static, rigid, bored attitude and posture, in contrast with the banality of the conversation we are hearing.*'[6] Then the actions become more complicated and sexual, including one of the men touching one of the women, and another mechanically masturbating. There is a notable contrast between the intimate, sexual nature of the action and the banal conversation. The final scene (Pista, p. 84) has the characters all separate ('*Isolated, islands*'),[7] each doing their own thing, such as picking up a nail file. Beneath the humour, this seems to be a commentary on the isolation and loneliness of modern life, in which each person is an island, communication is impossible, and language frequently takes the form of a dialogue of the deaf (as on pp. 47, 51).[8]

Language is intuitive in *Minim.mal Show*, as it is in another early play, *En companyia d'abisme*. But more than this, language is uncertain, confusing, and often wounding in the latter work, with doubt over whether things have been said, and who has said them, and a combination of everyday words that confuses the spectator: 'MAN: I thought so./ YOUNGER MAN: And I thought that you thought so.'[9] In addition to the doubt over their identities that was mentioned earlier (p. 11) it is also unclear whether or not they have met previously. In a demand that seems to anticipate Benet i Jornet's *Desig* (1991), the younger man says 'confess that we have suddenly met', to which Man replies: 'I have waited for you for so long'.[10] This discrepancy gives rise to a semantic discussion, which illustrates a recurring feature of early Belbel, namely

6 '*En aquest precís moment, tots adopten una actitud i una postura estàtica, rígida, avorrida, contrastant amb la banalitat de la conversa que es va sentint*' (p. 81).

7 '*Aïllats, illes*'.

8 In this respect, the parallel with French dramatist Bernard-Marie Koltès's *Dans la solitude des champs de coton* is striking.

9 'HOME: M'ho imaginava./ HOME MÉS JOVE: I jo m'imaginava que t'ho imaginaves' (p. 28).

10 'confessa que ens hem trobat de sobte', and 'Feia tant de temps que t'esperava' (p. 29). These words anticipate Man's mention of 'a new meeting' ('retrobament', p. 33).

that words are confusing, their meaning is constantly shifting, and therefore not to be trusted:

> MAN: 'To meet suddenly', 'surpised to meet', 'not knowing anything previously', 'chance meeting', 'nothing set out' … but what does all that mean?
> YOUNGER MAN: And what does 'ambiguous' mean? And 'bored'? And 'most strange'?
> MAN: Forgive me, but 'most strange' is only the superlative of 'strange' […].[11]

Another exchange between the two men (p. 31) questions the meaning of words (in this case, among other aspects, verb tenses) and, in Delgado and George's words, 'the shifting nature of the dialogue works to comment on the unreliable nature of language and the manner in which it both facilitates and impedes communication'.[12]

*En companyia d'abisme* is a constant word game between the two men, but the game becomes physical and painful when one of them moves. The language is sometimes extremely violent too, as in the following speech by the Younger Man:

> To be able finally to throw myself on you and spit you out, tread on you, smash your face, beat you up, shove my knee into your stomach, my foot into your testicles, make you bleed, break the veins in your neck with my hands, break the bones in your legs, destroy you.[13]

As in two of Belbel's best-known plays, *Carícies* and *Després de la pluja*, verbal battles and a dialogue of the deaf are illustrative of a

---

11 'HOME: 'Trobar-se de sobte', 'sorpresa de trobar-se', 'no saber res abans', 'atzarosa trobada', 'res de plantejat' … però què vol dir tot això?/ HOME MÉS JOVE: I què vol dir 'ambigua'? I 'avorrida'? I 'estranyíssima'?/ HOME: Perdona, però 'estranyíssima' és només el superlatiu d'estranya' […]' (p. 29).

12 Maria M. Delgado and David George, 'Sergi Belbel', in *Modern Spanish Dramatists: A Bio-Bibliographical Sourcebook*, ed. Mary Parker (Westport, CT/London: Greenwood, 2002), pp. 75–85, p. 78.

13 Per poder finalment llançar-me damant teu i escopir-te, trepitjar-te, trencar-te la cara, apallissar-te, clavar-te el meu genoll al ventre, el peu als testicles; fer-te sagnar, rebentar-te les venes del coll amb les mans meves, petar-te els ossos de les cames, destrossar-te (p. 41).

general lack of communication and understanding between people, although on some occasions this causes pain while at others it is a source of relief. For instance, at one point in *En companyia d'abisme* the younger man says: 'It's strange ... speaking and receiving no reply', but soon adds: 'in the company of no-one, that's paradise. And that silence.'[14] Even though his companion calls him stupid and tells him to shut up, the question as to whether solitude and silence are actually superior to company and talking has been posed. The contradictions become even more apparent when the younger man states soon afterwards: 'Please, I can't stand your silence.'[15] Words are mysterious and strange: for instance, what exactly is the abyss of the title – does it perhaps have a similar function to that of Godot in the Beckett play? In short, in order to understand *En companyia d'abisme*, it is pertinent to remember Belbel's training as a linguist; he is a man who is fascinated by words but yet mistrusts them.[16] As a translator, he is strongly aware of the nature of words and of the difficulty of tying them down. In his review of the publication of Samuel Beckett's first volume of letters, Peter Conrad's observation that, 'as he travels, he [Beckett] is constantly translating, aware that any word is a dubious, untrustworthy translation of a feeling', could equally apply to many of Belbel's plays.[17]

Several features of these early plays that mark Belbel as an experimenter in language and staging recur throughout his playwriting career, although their nature and purpose change over time. They are a product of his essentially anti-naturalist concept of theatre, and include the juxtaposition between linguistic registers, which is often linked – sometimes humorously – with the desire to shock (the audience, or another character), a fascination with dramatic structure, and the pres-

---

14 'És curiós ... parlar i no rebre resposta' (p. 50), and 'en companyia de ningú, això és el paradís. I aquest silenci' (p. 51).

15 'Si et plau, no suporto el teu silenci' (p. 55).

16 See David George and John London, 'Avant-garde Drama', in *Contemporary Catalan Drama*, ed. David George and John London, Anglo-Catalan Society Occasional Publications, 9 (Sheffield: Anglo-Catalan Society, 1996), pp. 73–101, p. 91. Feldman refers to Belbel's 'ongoing preoccupation with the theatrical word' (Sharon G. Feldman, *In the Eye of the Storm: Contemporary Theater in Barcelona* (Lewisburg: Bucknell University Press, 2010, p. 165).

17 Peter Conrad, 'But You'll Have to Wait for Godot', *Observer*, review section, 24 May 2009, p. 20.

ence of metatheatre. *Després de la pluja*, for example, contains numerous examples of juxtaposition between a colloquial and an almost literary register, which forms one element of the play's ability to disconcert its audience. As in other plays by Belbel – we have seen examples in *En companyia d'abisme* – some of the dialogues in *Després de la pluja* are more like monologues.[18] These scenes sometimes give rise to delightfully but disturbingly absurdist discussions, where motifs are juxtaposed and/or interwoven in unusual or conflicting ways. The tensions that punctuate the play occasionally surface in the form of verbal tirades, such as that of the Dark-Haired Secretary against the Red-Haired Secretary in Scene 6, or the extraordinarily violent and vulgar outburst by the Female Managing Director in Scene 11.[19]

The style and tone of the play are a mixture of humour and seriousness, and of profundity and banality. The Red-Haired Secretary's almost philosophical angst, as she ponders the meaning of life, is calmed by a sexual adventure with the down-to-earth Runner, the size of whose sexual organ is first mentioned by the Blonde Secretary and then witnessed by the audience after the Red-Haired Secretary orders him to drop his pants. The juxtaposition between intellectual and carnal activity is highlighted in a large number of scenes, offering, like the plays of Jean Genet, a contrast in linguistic registers, and deflating a number of the characters' grand ideas.[20] Similarly, the contrast between the banal language of preparing ordinary, uninspiring meals, and

---

[18] In an interview Belbel makes a similar point about *Carícies*, when he speaks of 'a lack of communication since, instead of engaging in dialogue, at some points in the play they speak in monologues' ('un punt d'incomunicació perquè, en lloc de dialogar, en certs moments monologuen') (Andreu Sotorra, 'Sergi Belbel reprèn per quarta vegada la direcció d'una obra pròpia amb *Carícies*', *Avui*, 24 February 1992, p. 21).

[19] The scene will be examined in more detail later in the chapter, pp. 34–35.

[20] The actress Laura Conejero, who played the part of the Blonde Secretary in the Catalan production of the play, highlighted what she perceives as the intellectual quality of Belbel's plays in an interview I carried out with her in February 2009. When I asked her about the dialogues' seeming more like monologues at times, she made the point that two characters may be speaking in two parallel lines, but that when the lines suddenly cross, the meeting is explosive.

sudden outbursts of violent language or actions, is present in two scenes of *Caricies* (Scenes 1 and 8), while in *A la Toscana*, at the critical moment in which Marta the 'nurse' has told Marc in brutal detail of his terminal illness (in Marc's dreams, one assumes), Joana the 'doctor' is furious when she receives a call on her mobile from her 'husband' asking her how to make a bouillabaisse (p. 15).[21] In *El temps de Planck* the contrast is between the quotidian and the poetic, in a manner not dissimilar to that employed by Joan Brossa, as Maria attempts to give her father soup that her mother has just prepared, saying: 'Enough/ Eat your mother's soup/ and later we'll speak about the soup of the Universe.'[22] Food is also about consumption, and the repeated presence of consumption and excrement in Belbel's plays suggests an element of the carnivalesque, which reinforces their dominant anti-naturalism.

[21] In this scene (Scene 4) Marc and Joana are in a doctor's surgery, but (in Marc's mind) Joana is the doctor and Marta the nurse. They are discussing Marc's terminal illness and the experimental treatment he is to receive, which is not devoid of risks. Joana speaks of the irreversible nature of his illness and Marta describes the horribly painful death he will suffer, with or without the treatment. This, she claims, will produce tensions in his family and she urges him to avoid their prolonged suffering by not undergoing the treatment. Joana, on the other hand, advises him to accept it, which presents Marc with a dilemma it is not easy for this tortured spirit to resolve. For plot details of this and the other plays discussed, see the Appendix.

[22] 'Prou/ pren-te el caldo de la mare/ i parlem després del caldo de l'Univers' (Sergi Belbel and Òscar Roig, *El temps de Planck*, Col·lecció Columna Romea (Barcelona: Fundació Romea, 2002), p. 69). In my interviw with them in January 2009, the composer Òscar Roig and costume designer Mercè Paloma commented on the work as a whole and this scene in particular. According to Roig, the relationship between text and music is subtle and difficult in what, musically at least, is Belbel's most complex work. Roig said that Belbel wrote it without knowing which sections would be songs, which would have words spoken over the music, and which would have music as a kind of background: he decided on that once he had finished writing it. As it is written in verse, any part of the play could be sung, but if it were all sung, it would last for approximately nine hours. He confirmed that the type of music he wrote for individual parts of the work depended on the content of each particular section. For Roig, *El temps de Planck* is a mixture of the most insignificant daily actions and great philosophical concerns, while Paloma supported his view by referring to the song in the work that deals with the soup and the universe.

In Scene 10 of *Després de la pluja*, what may be considered to be a
typical secretarial discussion about the opposite sex is juxtaposed with
the intellectual ramblings of the Red-Haired Secretary. Just as
contrasting linguistic registers are set against each other, and intellectual and physical activities are intertwined, so are fantasy and reality
often difficult to separate in *Després de la pluja*.[23] For instance, the
Brown-Haired Secretary recounts the sexual activities of an unhappily
married wife with her lover in a neighbouring building. The other
secretaries believe she is making the whole thing up, but Belbel never
resolves the question one way or the other. Scene 3 opens with the
Runner observing a helicopter, and then commenting: 'Some day, one
of those blasted machines will crash into a building.'[24] Immediately,
the sound of a helicopter crashing is heard. In Scene 6, the Runner
recounts the accident to the Dark-Haired Secretary with a sense of guilt
that it was his psychic powers that caused the crash. The play's mixture
of humour and seriousness is disconcerting, and the audience is never
quite sure which register they are observing or what is believable.[25]

A similarly disconcerting dichotomy between humour and seriousness is evident in *Sóc Lletja*, where sexuality and dysfunction and the
star system are treated with the black humour that characterises this
play. This, of course, is not explored in a naturalistic style, but in a way
that is reminiscent of Valle-Inclán's *esperpentos* – with its well-
established Spanish tradition of black humour. Black humour and the
'sudden shock' element are both present in *La sang*, but here they take
on a more potent social dimension. The characteristic Belbel element
of surprise is strong in the play and increased by the calm,
matter-of-fact way in which the Young Woman speaks. Shock is
usually provided by the discovery of one of the amputated parts of the

[23] The difficulty of separation is also typical of other Belbel plays, in
particular, as has been observed, in *A la Toscana*.

[24] Sergi Belbel, *After the Rain*, trans. Xavier Rodríguez Rosell, David
George and John London (published with Klaus Chatten, *Sugar Dollies*),
Methuen Drama (London: Methuen, 1996), pp. 85–178, p. 113; 'algun dia, un
trasto d'aquests xocarà contra un edifici' (Sergi Belbel, *Després de la pluja*,
Teatre Català Contemporani: Els Textos del Centre Dramàtic (Barcelona:
Editorial Lumen/Generalitat de Catalunya, 1993), p. 56).

[25] Puchades refers to the 'contrasting mixture of registers' ('mezcla
contrastada de registros') in Belbel's work (p. 189).

Woman's body, often in a disconcertingly casual manner by people who have nothing to do with the kidnap.

Although the use of language is less obviously experimental in Belbel's latest plays,[26] he none the less continues to demonstrate an interest in its power to shock, and, in particular, in the unreliability of that ubiquitous form of modern communication, the mobile phone. This object has become a kind of leitmotiv in Belbel's two latest plays: *Mòbil* (as the title makes clear) and *A la Toscana*. In the former, the mobile phone is frequently a source of frustration, as people find themselves leaving voicemails for those to whom they wish to speak, and listening to messages not intended for them left on other people's mobiles. The mobile phone is a hindrance to communication, and is no substitute for face-to-face contact.[27] It is a similarly frustrating means of non-communication in *A la Toscana*, but here the issue is much more complex. Sometimes one is unsure of whose phone is ringing, or to whom the voice at the other end belongs. At one point a mobile is heard ringing. The other three characters onstage ALL hear it, and rummage in their pockets to see if it is theirs. But it is Joana's, which is in the coffin with her (p. 38) following her 'death', as has been imagined by Marc. The caller is simply Joana's Voice, but it turns out to be Marc's mother, who asks him why he let her die. This is one example of the almost surrealist imagery that appears in the play. Other examples include the final stage direction of Scene 2:

> Joana gets out of the bath. Marc starts to cry. He looks at himself in the mirror again. He is angry with himself. He sticks a finger in the

---

[26] For Puchades, Belbel's work as a director and as a writer of television scripts is a factor 'that contributed to a smoothing out of the more *avant-garde* or *hermetic* side of his previous work' ('que contribuyeron a limar el lado más *vanguardista* o *hermético* de su teatro anterior') (p. 202; italics the author's). In my interview with her, the costume designer Mercè Paloma expressed the view that Belbel was more radical in his early theatre than in his more recent plays, while Benet i Jornet spoke to me of what he sees as the evolution from the early experimental works to ones that fit more easily into what might broadly be termed a 'classical' canon.

[27] In Belbel's words, 'here technology is a kind of mask behind which we hide' ('la tecnología aquí es pues una especie de máscara tras la que nos ocultamos') (José Henríquez, 'Sobre el difícil género de la comedia', *Primer Acto*, 315:4 (2006), 14–16, p. 16).

hole in his head and, in anger, begins to empty his brain, which falls in pieces into the washbasin.[28]

The metaphorical equivalent to this literal unpicking of the brain is, of course, precisely what psychiatrists do. Another example of quasi-surrealist imagery occurs when Marc again reacts violently to Joana's threat to leave him, and grabs her by the throat (p. 30). He then despairs at what he has done, tries to kiss her, but she has something in her mouth. It is her mobile, which rings again, and which Marc tries to remove with his own mouth. A huge beetle then comes out of her mouth, she opens her eyes and says 'Marc [...] you are dead.'[29] Such instances perhaps warn the spectator to beware of declaring too categorically that Belbel's language is less striking or interesting in his later work than in his early plays.

Belbel displays just as much fascination with structure as he does with language and linguistic registers. Whether it be the overlapping arrangement of scenes in *Carícies*, the repetition of scenes with important elements changed or added in *Tàlem* and *Morir (un moment abans de morir)* [30] – and the reversal of the order of scenes in the former – the circular structure of *La sang* and *Forasters*, or the increasingly frenetic switching between the two chronological periods in the latter, Belbel's plays are marked by a sense of imaginative care in their construction. Although they are all organised in scenes, their ordering is by no means haphazard, and is sometimes highly complex.[31] Two plays in particular – *Tàlem* and *A la Toscana* – resemble a puzzle. But, whereas the earlier play was judged to have lacked an obviously 'deeper' social purpose,[32]

---

[28] 'Joana surt del bany. Marc es posa a plorar. Torna a mirar-se al mirall. S'enfada amb ell mateix. Es fica un dit al forat del cap i, enrabiat, comença a buidar-se el cervell, que cau a trossets sobre la pica del lavabo' (p. 8).

[29] 'Marc [...] Estàs mort' (p. 30).

[30] For further details on the structure of this play, and its adaptation by Ventura Pons, see Chapter 3, pp. 98–102.

[31] Despite holding certain reservations about *Morir (un moment abans de morir)*, Gallén's view is that, in this play and in *La sang*, 'Belbel continues to demonstrate [...] how he is a master of technical skills' ('Belbel continua mostrant-nos [...] el seu inestimable mestratge en el domini tècnic') (Enric Gallén, 'Pròleg', in Sergi Belbel, *La sang*, El Galliner/Teatre, 168 (Barcelona: Edicions 62, 1998), pp. 7–18, p. 13).

[32] As will be illustrated in Chapter 4, the first-night critics – particularly,

in *A la Toscana* the puzzling structure illustrates the confusion over identity and Marc's befuddled mental state. There are a number of examples of shock and surprise in a play that constantly keeps its audience guessing.

In Scene 12 Joana's Voice shouts to Marc to wake her up and put down the phone. This reinforces the possibility (likelihood?) that Marc is imagining that Joana is his mother, and it is possible that we are dealing with an Oedipus complex here, which would be appropriate in a play in which the question of an individual's psyche is central. Then Joana tells Marc that she has killed herself, as she loved him too much and could not stand watching him falling apart and making her fall apart. She says she preferred to end it at a good moment in their relationship, just before they stopped being happy. Marc declares that he loves Joana and wants to die with her. This is a romantic cliché undermined by Jaume and Marta's comments as they watch like spectators at a melodrama, in a scene that recalls characters' observing each other and the audience in *Minim.mal Show*. The conversation in question is: 'JAUME: Even though it's a lie … it's nice, isn't it?/ MARTA: Yes. Very. Very.'[33] There are clear parallels between pairs of ideas here: dream/waking, imagination/reality, fiction/reality, theatre/real life, banality/seriousness. The boundaries between each pair are constantly blurred, in another illustration of the mixture of styles that characterises much of Belbel's theatre.

A further example of careful construction is the repetition of Scene 1 in Scene 23. Whereas in the former Joana and Marc were in bed, slowly undressing each other, with occasional kisses, in the latter they are in a restaurant, and there are more pauses in the dialogue. The return to Tuscany is anticipated, although this does not actually occur until the Epilogue. Joana and Marc have just had breakfast, and she gets up and kisses him, and tells him to make the most of the two hours he has left. Her mobile rings and Joana (offstage) tells him not to bother picking it up as they will leave a message (all p. 70). Marc then listens to the message (pp. 70–71), which is what he said to Joana in an

---

but not exclusively, the London ones – criticised the play for its lack of thematic interest. It is essentially a play about the theatre itself – the nature of farce – whereas certain critics seemed to want it to be about something else.

[33] 'JAUME: Tot i ser mentida … és bonic, oi?/ MARTA: Sí. Molt. Molt' (Sergi Belbel, *A la Toscana* (Barcelona: Proa), 2007, p. 40).

earlier scene, in which his febrile mind imagines how he rescues Joana,
Marta and Jaume after World War Three has broken out and they are
trapped in a bomb shelter (p. 45). Marc then plays it back to Joana, but
she says she does not recognise the voice, which is exactly what she
said earlier to Jaume about Marc. She says it must be the wrong
number, but Marc, puzzled, asks her if it is not his own voice (p. 71).
Joana denies that he would ever say something like that, smiles and
goes into the room. Marc remains onstage, with a serious expression.

The dramatic structure of his more recent plays reveals a Belbel less
preoccupied with the ludic element than with aspects of the human
psyche, or with social issues, perhaps confirming a general trend in his
work. It is difficult to account for this shift, the causes more likely to be
personal than social or indicative of broader trends. As has been
observed, the individual psychological element predominates in *A la
Toscana*, while the socio-political aspect is especially marked in *La
sang*. The opening stage direction of this second play provides specific
instructions on the doubling of parts, which reinforces the sense of
similarity between terrorist and 'normal' society. The three pairs of
doubled characters are: Man/Timid Man, Girl/Lost Girl, Young
Woman/Young Messenger (Woman), specifically *'in order to preserve,
in the three cases, the ambiguity of whether it is a single character who
is disguised or two different characters'*.[34] One single actor should play
the parts of the remaining male characters, and one single actress those
of the remaining three female parts. Apart from anything else, one may
note the balance and symmetry here, a further indication of Belbel's
concern with form, or with what might be termed the architecture of
the play. This is further enhanced by its circular nature, which is
emphasised by the stage direction of the final scene: *'The closed interior of the first scene'* (p. 43).[35]

Blood is another structural device in *La sang* that links the terrorists
with the so-called ordinary members of the public. Two examples occur
just after the reception of packages containing amputated parts of the

[34] Sergi Belbel, *Blood*, trans. Marion Peter Holt, Estreno Contemporary
Spanish Plays, 25 (New Brunswick, NJ: Estreno, 2004), p. xvi. The original
quotation is *'per tal de mantenir, en els tres casos, l'ambigüitat de si es tracta
d'un sol personatge que es disfressa de dos personatges diferents'* (*La sang*, p.
26).
[35] *'Espai tancat de la primera escena'* (p. 87).

Woman's body that have been sent by post to so-called ordinary members of the public. At the end of Scene 2, the Boy, who has not yet looked into the package that contains the finger, has blood on his own fingers, which emanates from a head wound caused by a falling pinecone. In Scene 3, the policeman has bitten his tongue and blood starts to pour from it just after they have opened the second package containing the ear, and he is covered with blood at the end of the scene. The sense seems to be that everyone is affected/contaminated by terrorism and violence, which may be as haphazard as biting one's tongue or having a pinecone fall on one's head.[36] This is all heightened by the apparently slim and purely random links between the ordinary people who discover the packages and the terrorists themselves. In this play Belbel questions what it means to be 'ordinary'.

Similarly, the constant switching between the two time frames in *Forasters*, which speeds up towards the end of the play and which possibly suggests that the 1960s could be a flashback in which characters recall or re-live their past, is part of a reflection on and a questioning of a changing society. The change in purpose of the dramatic structure parallels a decline in the type of metatheatre that was so prominent in a play like *Minim.mal Show*. Characters selfconsciously involve their audience in this early play, as they do in others written before the late 1990s. *Sóc Lletja*, for instance, is strongly metatheatrical, appropriately in a play that considers the public persona of society's icons. For example, Lletja says to them that she feels humiliated by the men, and wonders what to do: 'Carry on with the play? Ignore them? Stand up to them?'[37] The actors' awareness of the audience is seen again when, after the three young men have disappeared as if by magic (p. 16), Lletja stands looking at the spectators intensely. At

---

[36] Ragué-Arias takes a rather different line on the connection: 'In each scene there is a character who bleeds as a result of a trivial incident; it is the blood that serves as a contrast with the real tragedy of the terrorist kidnap' ('En cada escena hay un personaje que sangra por un trivial incidente; es la sangre que sirve como contraste con la auténtica tragedia de la sangre del secuestro terrorista') (Maria-José Ragué-Arias, *¿Nuevas dramaturgias?: los autores de fin de siglo en Cataluña, Valencia y Baleares* (Madrid: Instituto Nacional de las Artes Escénicas y de la Música, 2000), p. 196).

[37] 'Continuar la comèdia? Ignorar-los? Plantar-los cara?' (Sergi Belbel, Jordi Sànchez and Òscar Roig, *Sóc Lletja*, El Galliner/Teatre, 158 (Barcelona: Edicions 62, 1997), p. 14).

the start of Scene 7 she again speaks to the audience, saying that she
has lost again. This direct metatheatrical contact with the audience (*à
la* performance groups) is absent from Belbel's more recent plays, and
seems to coincide with a far smaller presence of humour than in a
number (but not all) of his earlier plays.

## Thematic concerns and motifs

Having established certain characteristics of what might be called
Belbel's dramatic language, I move now to examine what could broadly
be termed the thematic concerns of his plays.[38] In many ways, as has
already been observed, it is not possible to separate content from form in
an author who sets such store by the careful patterning of his work.[39]
Nevertheless, it will be helpful to focus on three specific and recurring
concerns – social and literary satire, sex and violence, and more philosophical issues, including mortality, time and various forms of identity, in
particular personal and occasionally racial – both for their centrality to
Belbel's writing and because they highlight how difficult it is to separate
the contemporary and immediate from the more general and timeless
issues in his plays. There are a number of overlaps between the three
thematic areas, as well as nuances that reflect the author's trajectory.

### *Social and literary satire*
Although Puchades is probably correct to say that 'Koltès's assertion
that "I have never had political ideas in my plays" could equally be
applied to Belbel,'[40] it does not diminish the fact that, as with Koltès's
dramas, his plays deal head-on with difficult social issues.[41] Some of

---

38 One should be careful about claiming that Belbel deals with certain
'themes' in his plays. As he said in an interview, 'when you start to write
theatre, the concept of dealing with a theme does not stimulate me' ('quan et
poses a escriure teatre, el concepte de tractar un tema no m'estimula')
(Francesc Bombí-Vilaseca, 'L'escriptura surt quan trobes que la forma va
lligada amb el contingut', *Avui* (Cultura), 25 November 2004, pp. x–xi, p. x).

39 The title of Bombí-Vilaseca's interview with Belbel, 'L'escriptura surt
quan trobes que la forma va lligada amb el contingut' ('Writing Works Out
when Form and Content are Linked'), neatly illustrates the point.

40 'Belbel podría hacer suyas estas palabras de Koltès: "je n'ai jamais eu
d'idées politiques dans mes pièces" ' (p. 72).

41 Gabriele and Leonard detect a similar tendency in the new generation of

these are covered elsewhere in this chapter, including sexuality, racism, the broken family, immigration and terrorism. In general, Belbel treats these issues more overtly in the later plays, and with rather less humour than in the earlier ones. Correspondingly, the early plays tend to have a greater concentration than the later ones on what might be termed social mores, or human foibles. Two of the best examples of this kind of satire are *Minim.mal Show* and *Sóc Lletja*. The former mocks the excesses of comsumerist society in several areas. The first scene (Passarel·la), for instance, sends up the idea of the catwalk. In Galeria the ironic mocking is applied to postmodernism and modish fashion (p. 58), while Nessuno has C singing 'Nessun Dorma' (and this is prior to the 1990 World Cup). Nessuna is a female equivalent to Nessuno, and the artificiality and theatricality of the action, as well as the ironic humour, are emphasised by the opening stage direction of the scene: '*A, B, X and Y come on stage (what a crowd!), and move around looking for "their place". They each place themselves on a corner of the stage and lie down. All dead.*'[42] C then appears, observes the 'battlefield' 'camp de batalla', and sings 'Lili Marlene', but with slight alterations to the words. In fact, the whole song is a series of names joined together: some, such as Offenbach, are composers, others are philosophers (for example, Kierkegaard), and there are writers and practitioners or choreographers who have influenced Belbel and his Catalan contemporaries (Peter Handke, Brecht, Pina Bausch, Botho Strauss). This collage cabaret is a quite delicious way to satirise the seriousness of theatre criticism, while at the same time representing a break with the social realism that characterised the Franco generation of playwrights in Catalonia.

Various literary genres – including realism and postmodernism – are the target of Belbel's humour in this play, while both the stereotypical

Spanish playwrights that emerged in the early 1980s: 'although they do not lack social commitment, they are less concerned with political issues' ('sin carecer de compromiso social, les importa menos la cuestión política') (Candyce Leonard and John P. Gabriele, 'Fórmula para una dramaturgia española de finales del siglo XX', in *Panorámica del teatro español actual*, ed. John P. Gabriele and Candyce Leonard, Serie Teatro (Madrid: Fundamentos, 1996), pp. 7–21, p. 13).
   [42] '*Entren A, B, X i Y (¡quina colla!), i es mouen per tot l'escenari mentre busquen "el seu lloc". Es situen cada un en un punt de l'escenari i s'estiren damunt el terra. Tots morts*' (p. 75).

romantic encounter and the use of sex to shock – so prevalent in the
liberalisation of the first decade of the post-Franco era in Spain – are
mocked. Each Síncope is a satire of B's not meeting Y: a frustrated
amorous encounter. These are wordless scenes, with the action indicated in brief stage directions. The ironic treatment of the nervousness
associated with the frustrated encounter is illustrated in the following
quotation, which is the complete Síncope (4):

> *(B and Y come onstage at the same time. They do not see each other.*
> *They reach the chairs. She thinks: 'oh!, he's gone'. And she sits*
> *down just as he sits down to wait for her. He twitches nervously, sees*
> *that she hasn't come and decides to leave. They both get up at the*
> *same time and exit.)*[43]

The Pòdium scenes provide an example of Belbel's satire of the use of
sex for shocking or titillating effects, with the revealing of a provocative part of the body (female breast and thigh, male chest and
buttocks): this may well be a satire of the *destape* – or sexual liberation
– associated with the immediate post-Franco period. In Puchades's
words, 'in a way, we are dealing with a fragmented striptease, or an
ironic reading of the physical fragmentation of the Beckettian character'.[44] The 72 pieces of Brossa's *Strip-tease i teatre irregular*, in which
the author 'elevates striptease from the sordid to the surreal',[45] also
comes to mind. The final revelation is of male genitalia, but among the
other characters this provokes not shock but indifference (p. 83).
Following their lovemaking in the humorously titled 'Discòpula' scene,
the couple greet each other, and then the audience. This is another
example not only of Belbel's delight in wordplay, but also of
metatheatre, in which sex is presented as a purely mechanical act, with
an element of Monty Pythonesque humour.[46]

---

43 *(Entren B i Y alhora. No es veuen. Arriben a les cadires. Ella pensa:*
*'¡oh!, ja ha marxat'. I s'asseu al mateix moment en què ell s'asseu per*
*esperar-la. Ell: tics, nervis, veu que no hi arriba i decideix de marxar. Tots dos*
*s'aixequen alhora i surten.)* (p. 71).

44 'de algún modo, se trata de un *strip-tease* fragmentado, o una irónica
lectura de la fragmentación física del personaje beckettiano' (p. 98).

45 John London, 'The Theatrical Poetry of Joan Brossa', in *Joan Brossa,*
*Words are Things: Poems, Objects and Installations*, Exhibition Catalogue
(London: Riverside Studios, 1992), pp. 20–23, p. 22.

46 For further details on sexuality in Belbel's plays, see pp. 28–39.

Another play that satirises aspects of contemporary society is *Sóc Lletja*, a musical, jointly authored with Jordi Sànchez and with a libretto by Òscar Roig.[47] Our obsession with stardom features strongly in this play, especially in the person of Samuel Guasch, 'a total artist (model, actor, cinema director, novelist, singer)',[48] who possesses the huge ego often associated with the media star. One of the features of the play is the self-centred emptiness and flamboyance of the male characters. This is especially true of Samuel, who is absurdly boastful of his sexuality. Like the vain film director Antonio Valdivieso in La Cubana's *Cegada de amor* (1989), Guasch is obsessed with how he looks rather than what he is.[49] The glorification of the human body that one associates with stardom comes under the microscope in this darkly humorous musical. Equally, the theme of the putrid body, treated humorously in *Sóc Lletja*, links to the foul-smelling breath found in *Carícies* and *Forasters* and is set against the whole fetishisation of the body.

The beautification of the body in a society obsessed with physical appearance is often achieved through plastic surgery. Dr Blanes is prepared to perform it on Lletja, as a purely commercial transaction.[50] The commercialism is emphasised by the Nurse when Samuel comes to Dr Blanes for treatment. When he asks who will remove his bandages,

[47] Belbel's view, expressed in a 2000 interview, is that, while he is not fond of musicals, it is an unexplored genre in Catalonia: see Pep Tugues, 'Sergi Belbel i *El temps de l'lunk* [*sic*]', http://www.teatral.net/entrevista/belbel-plank.html, accessed 20 October 2008.

[48] 'un artista total (modelo, actor, director de cine, novelista, cantante)' (Puchades, p. 212).

[49] Puchades writes: 'As Massip points out in his review of the play, the actor who played Samuel, Joel Joan, did a self-parody of the good-looking, heart-throb character for which he was known in a Catalan TV soap called *Poble nou*. When the play premiered in Madrid, the actor was well-known there for his part in a series on Spanish television called *Periodistas*' ('Como señala Massip en su crítica a la obra, el actor que interpreta a Samuel, Joel Joan, hacia [*sic*] una autoparodia del personaje de "guaperas" por el que se le conocía en la serie de televisión catalana *Poble nou*. Cuando la obra se estrena en Madrid, el actor es conocido por otra serie televisiva nacional, *Periodistas*') (p. 214, note 491).

[50] The commercialisation that infects all aspects of society is a feature of the plays of Koltès, whose work Belbel so admires and has directed (see Chapter 2, pp. 85–88).

she replies that it will be Dr Blanes himself. If one is sufficiently rich and famous, then beauty is assured, as illustrated in Samuel's song in Scene 18, in which he sings that he will be perfect tonight, his perfection emphasised by his use of the image in the mirror (p. 88). The self-contemplation implied in gazing into a mirror is closely linked to metatheatre, while the butt of the satire could well be the type of magazine that glorifies celebrity and physical perfection. However, this is overturned when the unexpected happens. At the end of the first part of the play, having just looked at himself and announced his imminent perfection, he experiences a strange inner sensation, a feeling of shame that in the stage direction is likened to God's punishment of Adam and Eve for having tasted the apple. He panics, and covers his genitals with his arms – a clear analogy with the fig leaf. This could well be a satire of those newspaper photographs in which semi-naked women cover their breasts with their arms, or, more widely, of soft porn.

Other self-centred representatives of the star culture are an Actress, who describes herself as a 'fashionable actress' ('actriu de moda', p. 102), and a footballer. All of these 'beautiful people' are the antithesis of the protagonist of the play. Her ugliness contrasts in grotesque fashion with the sort of body beautiful that constitutes a star in our celebrity-obsessed Western world. It sets her apart not only from Samuel but from other females in the play, most notably her flatmate Clara and the Actress. Most of these stars become her victims as she engages in a redemptive orgy of violent murder. In this way, and through satire, Belbel undermines our standard concept of fame and the star. In his world there are winners and losers, although these roles are reversed when Lletja finds her purpose in life and redemption through violence.

### Sex and violence

As *Sóc Lletja*'s Samuel illustrates, sexual pleasure in Belbel's plays is basically egotistical, and sometimes connected with self-contemplation or narcissism as evidenced in the use of the mirror. Self-contemplation seems to provide Y with a certain sexual pleasure in *Minim.mal Show* (p. 45), while the most notorious instance occurs in the gay oral sex scene in *Carícies* (Scene 9), where the older man contemplates himself in a mirror, having clearly paid for sex. As in the theatre of Koltès, sex is just another form of commercial transaction in a world where anything is up for sale.

The image of the mirror in this scene links sexual gratification with identity, as it does in *Sóc Lletja*, in which the protagonist discovers both sexual pleasure and her *raison d'être* in violence (see below). Sex is a part of a person's bodily functions that contrasts with our intellectual activity, the contrast sometimes providing humour. An example is the Red-Haired Secretary's almost philosophical angst in *Després de la pluja*, which was mentioned earlier. The frank sentiments and language of the exchange between these two characters have a number of parallels in Belbel's theatre. For example, in *El temps de Planck*, Sara's down-to-earth nature is illustrated by her sexual frankness in a conversation with her youngest daughter Maria at the end of Comma Zero (14) (p. 87),[51] or in the exchange between Grandson and Granddaughter in *Forasters*, in which she counters his scorn at what he considers her trendy acceptance of her father's living with his gay partner by accusing him of hypocrisy in his addiction to internet porn.[52]

Such understanding, however, is rare in Belbel's theatre. Sexual relationships – whether hetero- or homosexual – are usually problematic, as *Carícies* and *Forasters* clearly demonstrate. The sometimes violent antipathy and lack of understanding that shock the spectator in both these plays stem basically from the existence of the family as a dysfunctional unit. In *Carícies* this takes the form of a variety of pairs of family members, to which can be added sexual relationships such as that between the father and his mistress (Scene 7), or the father and the hired male prostitute (the son from scene 10) (Scene 9). These sexual or family relationships are characterised by aggression and mistrust, with no level of the family or age group immune from Belbel's bleak portrayal of relationships in this contemporary urban environment.

In *Forasters* the family is destructive, and a source of bitterness, frustration and rottenness. The cancer suffered by the Mother and the Daughter seems to symbolise the general state of the family.[53] The

---

[51] The numbering of the scenes reflects the concept of the nanosecond (see the discussion of mortality and time, below). The first scene is numbered Zero, and this is followed by scenes numbered Comma Zero (1) to Comma Zero (42), and completed by a coda numbered U (One).

[52] Sergi Belbel, *Forasters*, Col·lecció TNC (Barcelona: Proa, 2004), p. 79.

[53] Belbel has said that the family acts as a metonym for society as a whole (interview with Bernat Salvà in *Avui*, 24 November 2008, consulted at http://www.avui.cat/article/cultura_comunicacio/47155/ventura/pons/sergi/belbel/excel·lim/tot/nomes/falta/la/gent/ho/sapiga.html, accessed 5 December 2008).

former is a particularly harsh character, her treatment of her homosexual son being especially cruel. For instance, when she orders him
never to sell the family home, she makes her feelings brutally clear: 'if
you sell this house, I'll rise up from my tomb [...] and I'll cut off your
balls and your dick, and I'll sew up your arse, you faggot'.[54] Homosex-
uality is most certainly viewed as unacceptable by the 1960s generation. The fact that he is gay is part of the trauma suffered by the Son,
who, as a young man, is unable to face up either to his sexuality or to
death. And yet, by the second time sequence, he has learned to exorcise
the demons and, interestingly, the third generation of females, in the
form of the Granddaughter, has no problems with his sexuality since,
as has been observed, she recognises the honesty with which her father
runs his sexual life. The suggestion is that Catalan society has moved
on during the three decades since the first sequence.

It is ironic that the Mother should be capable of uncovering and
expressing tenderness, as she is the person who conveys more powerfully
than anyone else the frustration, bitterness and rottenness of the family. It
is doubly ironic that the affectionate side to her character should emerge
just as her death approaches, while yet another irony is that she shows
tenderness not to her own family but to the despised immigrants who live
in the flat above. Mother helps the Neighbour, who has been physically
abused by her husband, but it is the Child – the Neighbour's son – who
really awakens her more affectionate side (see Figure 1).

The pattern of aggressive behaviour, violence and frustration occasionally tempered by an unexpected show of tenderness, which we have
observed in the Mother's character, is also a trait of *Caricies*. The
evocation in Part 2, Scene 3, of *Forasters* of the first signs of love
between the Granddaughter and the Young Man, the son of the new
generation of immigrant neighbours, is reminiscent of the sudden and

---

54 Sergi Belbel, *Strangers*, trans. Sharon G. Feldman, in *Barcelona Plays*,
trans. Marion Peter Holt and Sharon G. Feldman (New York: Martin E. Segal
Theater Center, 2008), pp. 107–231, p. 176. The original quotation is 'si et
vens aquesta casa, m'aixecaré de la meva tomba [...] et tallaré els ous i el pito
i et cosiré el forat del cul, mariconàs' (Sergi Belbel, *Forasters*, p. 97). I have
analysed elsewhere the state of the family in this play, in particular the harsh-
ness of Mother. See David George, 'Beyond the Local: Sergi Belbel and
*Forasters*', in *Catalan Theatre, 1975–2006: Politics, Identity, Performance*,
ed. Maria M. Delgado, David George and Lourdes Orozco, special issue of
*Contemporary Theatre Review*, 17:3 (2007), 398–410.

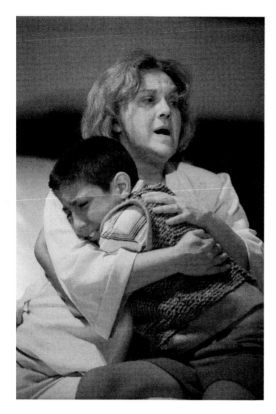

1. Anna Lizaran and
Marcel Montanyès in
*Forasters*, Teatre Nacional
de Catalunya, 2004.

unexpected gentleness of the final scene of *Carícies*, in which the
Woman bathes the wounds of the Young Man who has been physically
assaulted by his wife.[55]

Love between strangers likewise transforms a person's life and even
personality in *Mòbil*. It is through a chance encounter that love and
tenderness are found, this time between an older woman and a younger
man. It is completely unexpected, as is the development and indeed
fulfilment of Sara.[56] With sexual fulfilment there comes a calm after the
hectic nature of modern life, which is what happens in the Catalan

---

[55] Puchades sees this 'chance encounter between strangers' ('encuentro
azaroso con desconocidos') as a feature of the work of another contemporary
Catalan dramatist of the Belbel Generation, Lluïsa Cunillé (p. 131).

[56] In an interview, Belbel has said that Sara is transformed in the course of
the play from a passive to an active character, and that sex and love are the key
to communication and the best antidote to stress, fear and violence
(Henríquez, 'Sobre el difícil género de la comedia', p. 16).

version of *Després de la pluja*. In that play, as well as in *Mòbil* and *Carícies*, the relaxed encounter forms a stark contrast not only with the tensions of much of the rest of the play but also with the unhappy marital and family relationships. In Scene 27 of *Mòbil* Sara explains how her sexual fulfilment has given her an explosion of freedom and a genuine revelation. This suggestion of the explosive orgasm not only acts as a counterpoint to the literal explosion of the bombs in the airport but also fulfils an analagous function to death in *Forasters* and *El temps de Planck*.

It is in examples such as these, when tenderness and compassion replace routine sexual or even domestic relationships, that Belbel gives his audiences glimpses of how human intercourse may be transformed. Something similar happens in the original ending of *Després de la pluja*. The Brown-Haired Secretary, having previously believed herself to be sterile, is expecting a child by the Computer Programmer, who had earlier been widowed. The optimism is reinforced by the arrival of the rain, providing relief after the drought. However, Belbel was not completely satisfied with this 'happy' ending, and, in his own Spanish translation, removed it. Nevertheless, even the later version of the play, with the possibly facile ending expunged, does offer a degree of optimism regarding sexual relationships. A typically *machista* social scene is undermined, as the Secretaries get the better of their bosses. Yet this is not a feminist play, as one of the bosses is a woman with the same hang-ups as the men. The reversal is as much social as sexual, as down-to-earth, uninhibited characters like the Blonde Secretary and the Runner lack the phobias of middle-class characters, whose obsessions perhaps anticipate those of Marc in *A la Toscana*.

That said, the role reversal is in part sexual, and is also present in *Carícies*, for instance, in the first scene, in which the physical violence inflicted by the woman on the man is surprisingly greater than that he had first used on her. In Scene 7 the mistress turns the tables on her lover in a verbal replica of the physical turning of the tables in Scene 1. As they sit waiting for the train she is due to catch, and then browse in the railway station's bookshop, he displays a chauvinistic attitude when he complains that the overpowering smell of her vagina has been transferred to him and has aroused his wife's suspicions. She seems to be the submissive female victim until she suddenly recounts to him a dream in which, at the railway station, she accuses him of causing his own misfortune, before watching the train derail to the joy of all the onlookers, who support her. He now falls silent, shaken and abashed by her controlled outburst, and before the end of the scene he is in tears. Once more, the aggressor/passive partner and male/female roles have been reversed.[57]

In both *Carícies* and *Després de la pluja* the women turn out to be more dominant, resilient and varied characters than the men. This is also most certainly the case in *La sang*. The Young Woman's human side emerges when she is lecturing the Girl on her desire to hurt the Woman and says that the latter is just a poor woman like them, which may indicate the existence of a sense of solidarity amongst women, which might run counter to – and is far more human than – the unspecified ideology that ostensibly holds both the terrorist group and the ruling political class together. Her eyes then fill with tears, and she questions the validity of what they are doing, saying: 'I've had it … Oh, how will this all end …?'[58] This is perhaps an indication of hope (her humanity has not been entirely lost), but it is inconclusive, as she still carries out the amputations, and, in the final scene, she says: 'The group kills' (p. 46) ('Mata el grup', p. 92).[59] The hope is fainter than in plays such as *Després de la pluja* or even *Forasters*, and the conclusion may well be that there is no redemption and that we are all condemned.

The violence present in *La sang* is a recurring feature of Belbel's theatre, and takes several forms. In the early plays, it appears on a mostly personal level and often involves verbal abuse. It is also used to unsettle the audience in *Minim.mal Show*, in contrast to the generally humorous, even deadpan, tone of many of the scenes. Examples are the unexpected, unprovoked violence in the Conseqüència sequence, or the sudden death of Y and A (p. 33, p. 53). Violence is closely linked to the concept of the dysfunctional family or couple, particularly in *Carícies*, *Morir (un moment abans de morir)*, *Forasters* and *Mòbil*. Violent linguistic tirades are common in Belbel's theatre. In *Carícies*, as was observed above, the turning of the tables by the mistress on her lover is carried out with a devastating verbal precision that completely nonplusses and deflates him. In both Scene 1 and Scene 8, the unhappy dialogue between a young couple and between the mistress and her father respectively is characterised by an alternation between mechan-

---

57  See Sergi Belbel, *Carícies* (Barcelona: Edicions 62, 1992), p. 52.
58  'no puc més … Oh, com acabarà tot això …?' (*La sang*, p. 45).
59  For one critic *La sang* is Belbel's best play; see Iolanda G. Madariaga, 'Una fulgurante trayectoria: Sergi Belbel en la cumbre del teatro catalán', *Primer Acto*, 315:4 (2006), 8–13, p. 10.

ical, everyday dialogue and aggressive verbal outbursts. The daughter's vitriolic diatribe when she discovers halfway through the scene that her father is preparing a fish meal for her suggests that antagonism is another feature of this typically unhappy family relationship.

Similarly aggressive outbursts punctuate *Després de la pluja*, such as that of the Dark-Haired Secretary against the Red-Haired Secretary in Scene 6, or the extraordinarily violent and vulgar tirade by the jealous Executive Manageress in Scene 11, when she has learned of the Brown-Haired Secretary's promotion. The following extract illustrates the vituperative nature of her attack:

> What did you do, you fucking hole, what did you do, you rotten bitch, you shit-sucking climber, I'd like to know whose arse you licked, whose arse did you have to lick, you bitch, bitch, fucking bitch, what I've just been told about you can't be true, a vulgar, lunatic Public Relations secretary, you lunatic, stupid, hypocritical, hollow, fucking ambitious traitor, is it true that in this shitty company, in this shitty city, in this shitty world a low-class secretary can become, overnight, Assistant to the Chief Managing Director in one of the most profitable financial companies in the world, in the universe? (pp. 155–56).[60]

This speech is indicative of how the tensions of living in a modern urban environment emerge, sometimes at unexpected moments, almost like an explosion.[61] The extract also illustrates how realism of language

---

[60] 'Què has fet, filla de puta, què has fet, puta podrida, merdosa escaladora, m'agradaria saber a qui has llepat el cul, puta, puta, puta de merda, no pot ser veritat el que acaben de dir-me de tu, una vulgar secretària de Relacions Públiques llunàtica, llunàtica, estúpida, hipòcrita, falsa, ambiciosa de merda, traïdora, ¿es veritat que en aquesta empresa de merda, en aquest país de merda, en aquest món de merda una secretària de baixa estofa pot convertir-se de la nit al dia en Directora Adjunta a la Direcció General d'una de les empreses financeres de més alt rendiment de la ciutat, del país, del continent, del món, de l'univers?' (p. 127).

[61] Once more the influence of Koltès is evident. In Feldman's words, 'The typical Belbelian characters are often solitary beings, generic and anonymous, who find themselves victims, thrown into a space that is not at all hospitable. In such plays as *Carícies*, *Després de la pluja* and *La sang*, they inhabit an urban landscape of harsh, aggressive realities reminiscent of the theater of Koltès' (p. 171).

in Belbel's plays is often more apparent than real.[62] The speech is in effect quite stylised, with a deliberate – even comical – pattern to the city, country, continent, world, universe progression. As Feldman puts it, 'it is evident from Belbel's mise en scène of *Carícies*, and of other plays, that dialogues [...] are intended to be delivered at a surprisingly rapid tempo that does not resemble "normal" speech but, nevertheless, creates the impression of realism' (p. 190). At the same time, Feldman observes 'a seemingly magical ability to transform verbal detritus into lyrical poetry and a fine-tuned capacity to detect and reproduce the rhythms and syncopations inherent in ordinary daily speech' (p. 170), all of which is reminiscent of the plays of David Mamet.

The violent rant is also a feature of some of the later plays. The Mother of *Forasters*, in particular, is highly adept at using vicious language, as when she addresses her son. In *Mòbil* the hysterical nature of the women emerges in their verbal tirades, as in Rosa's language when she leaves a message on her mother's mobile explaining her sense of revulsion with men, in Scene 18 (3).[63] It is perhaps ironic that her statement of sexual independence in this message is made using foul language, and does not bring her any peace of mind, whereas her mother finds that serenity following her sexual encounter with a complete stranger, the much younger Jan.

Linguistic violence, then, is a habitual element of discourse in Belbel's theatre, and illustrates once more how language is actually a 'theme' in itself. Insults abound, and form part of our fractious modern

---

[62] In an interview I conducted with the actress Anna Lizaran in September 2008, she made the point that, although Belbel's plays are realist in the sense that they deal with everyday situations such as family relationships and love, with an everyday language, their 'craziness' means that, when an actor interprets them, they have to go somewhat beyond what one might term everyday reality. In other words, the realism is more apparent than real. What Lizaran likes about this type of theatre is that it forces one to adopt a heightened playing style, going beyond our everyday reality with the result that we desire something more when we go to the theatre.

[63] Sergi Belbel, *Mòbil* (Barcelona: Fundació Teatre Lliure, 2007), n.p. (the edition produced by the Teatre Lliure, in which the play was premiered, does not contain page numbers). In his scathing review of the play, Marcos Ordóñez refers to *Mòbil*'s having 'one swear word in every three [words]' ('un taco cada tres palabras') ('Sin cobertura', *El País* (Babelia section), 20 January 2007, p. 21).

urban environment. Although the violence is mainly verbal, it does occasionally become physical. As has been observed, this happens in the first scene of *Caricies*, when the young woman returns with interest the slight damage done to her by her partner, and inflicts on him the injuries that are tenderly cured by the neighbour in the Epilogue. However, the physical violence is much more marked in two other plays: *Sóc Lletja* and *La sang*. In the former the protagonist discovers her identity, indeed her whole *raison d'être*, through violence. When the Actress becomes a victim of Lletja in Scene 25, the stage direction (p. 107) that describes the manner of her murder highlights the extreme nature of the violence that now gives Lletja her thrills. The blood flows freely (in this aspect *La sang* seems to be anticipated), and the scene ends with the Actress's scream of terror offstage. We are witnessing a lurid crime drama, almost a Gothic horror, as Belbel uses dramatic form in a highly personal way, as if experimenting with different forms.[64] The violence becomes all the more shocking as Lletja has an orgasm after she has killed the Actress. Murder and violence provide Lletja with not only a sense of identity and purpose but also sexual gratification.

Once the pattern of violence has been established, it increases in intensity, as each of her killings is more macabre than the last. For instance, the fate of another stereotypical character from the world of fame, the Footballer, is to be sawn up by Lletja (Scene 27). This also seems to anticipate *La sang*, particularly the final scene, in which the Man saws off the Woman's head. Although in general the amputations in *La sang* are more understated than in *Sóc Lletja*, they are more shocking, as they seem closer to our 'real' world and not part of a Gothic horror show from which we can detach ourselves and at which,

---

[64] Feldman describes *Sóc Lletja* as 'a modern-day version of the "ugly-duckling" parable, which offers a surprising hybrid blend of terror, gore, comedic satire, and melodrama' (p. 196). *Sweeney Todd* comes to mind, a parallel observed by Marcos Ordóñez, who describes the play as 'a crescendo of grotesque horror à la Sweeney Todd' ('un *crescendo* de horror grotesco *à la Sweeny* [*sic*] *Todd*') (*A pie de obra* (Barcelona: Alba, 2003), p. 47). F. Corbella compares the psycho-killer element of the play with the cinema of Quentin Tarantino ('Grec 97 (I). Antes del próximo milenio', *Reseña I*, 286, September 1997). Belbel has also published a kind of Gothic horror novel entitled *Ivern*: for further details see note 79 of this chapter.

to an extent, we can laugh. Lletja carries out what other characters talk glibly about, as she explains to Pol the journalist in Scene 29: 'Have you never wanted to kill a prat who has triumphed in life because of his sexy bum while you sink in the shit?'[65] This is the revenge of the ugly losers on life's stars, and Belbel appears to be questioning the bravado and aggressive language of a modern society that is dominated by appearance and show and the cult of the celebrity.

In Scene 31, Lletja has Samuel tied up, and she gives him a moral lesson. She cuts his face, so that the contrast between the beautiful and the ugly may be lessened. Belbel also displays his usual penchant for the unexpected, shocking twist in Samuel's final words of the scene: 'Kill me. Kill me, but fuck me first, fuck me, fuuuuuuuck me!'[66] By Scene 33 Samuel has been transformed through sex with Lletja. They sing a 'Cruïlla d'Amor' ('Crossroads of Love') (pp. 127–29), and he declares: 'Now I am different. I am fulfilled', adding 'I want to die like this. But you must swear that you will retain your purity. Kill beauty wherever you find it. If you do not, from wherever I am, I will stop loving you.'[67] Sex with the ugly woman has purified him, and he urges her to carry out a cathartic cleansing by destroying beauty. In the end, she kills him accidentally. The police arrive, Lletja turns around suddenly, he jumps on top of her, the knife wounds him in the chest, and she cries 'Nooooo …!' (p. 130). He dies after the police have entered. The violence of the final scene of Sóc Lletja is the most shocking and surprising of all. Lletja has achieved fulfilment through the birth of her son. She sings a sweet lullaby to him, and then the ghost of Samuel appears to her, opens his jacket, and takes out from his chest a heart-shaped cushion and gives it to her. She then gently suffocates the baby with it, before turning to the audience and announcing 'The End' ('Fi', p. 138). Here Belbel seems to be satirising closure, reminding us of his own preference for open-ended plays as opposed to the kind of resolution demanded by the well-made play. At the same time, violence is used to shock the audience, in a manner that in some

---

[65] 'Tu no has tingut mai ganes de matar un gilipollas que perquè té el cul bufó ha triomfat a la vida mentre tu t'enfonses en la merda?' (p. 116).

[66] 'Mata'm. Mata'm, però folla'm, folla'm, follaaaaaaa'm!' (p. 123).

[67] 'Ara sóc diferent. Tinc la plenitud […] Vull morir així. Però m'has de jurar que et mantindràs pura. Mata la bellesa on la trobis. Si no ho fas, des d'allà on sigui, deixaré d'estimar-te' (p. 129).

senses recalls Edward Bond's 1965 play *Saved*. The 'in-yer-face' British theatre of the 1990s also comes to mind, as such playwrights as Mark Ravenhill and Sarah Kane used aggressive tactics to confront their audiences. The penchant observed in several Belbel plays for the violent shock as something that makes theatre visceral recalls the theatre of Antonin Artaud, as does the vomiting theme in a play like *Forasters*. The question remains of course, of how much a post-Transition Spanish audience would be shocked by the sex and violence of *Sóc Lletja* or with the sexual scenes of such plays as *Minim.mal Show* and *Caricies*.

Although, as has been stated, the extreme violence witnessed in *Sóc Lletja* is repeated in *La sang*, its purpose there is very different. The amputations inflicted on the Woman are all the more shocking as they are contrasted with the banal dialogue of everyday life. A similar effect is achieved through the lack of a clear political purpose to the terrorist violence. As will be observed later, blood is a unifying structural device in the play, and, more than that, an indication of how the whole of society is affected by terrorist violence.[68]

One of the shocking things highlighted in *La sang* is how terrorism can so seamlessly form a part of everyday life in our dehumanised society, on a level with eating and drinking and sex. Belbel was inspired to write the play by the kidnap and murder by the Basque terrorist group ETA in the summer of 1997 of the young Basque councillor from the Partido Popular, Miguel Ángel Blanco. In Belbel's own words, 'at that moment I felt we ought to be doing something ... We were all horrified, but at lunchtime we were all determined to eat: it was a case of life as usual'.[69] This is a chilling message from a play that predates 9/11 by some two years. It is possible that Belbel is suggesting that, as in *Sóc Lletja*, pretend or game violence contrasts with the real thing, which is happening in our very midst and often goes unnoticed.

A key feature of *La sang* is the contrast between everyday banality

---

68  See, for example, Puchades, p. 228.

69  'en ese momento pensé que tenía que hacer algo ... Todos estábamos horrorizados, pero cuando era la hora de comer todos nos íbamos a comer: seguíamos viviendo de la misma manera' (Sergi Belbel, Guillermo Heras, José Sanchis Sinisterra, et al., 'Perspectivas dramatúrgicas: hacia el siglo XXI', transcript of panel discussion, Sitges Teatre Internacional 1998, *Escena*, 60–61 (May–June 1999): Documentos, p. 7).

and the horrendous actions that are carried out on the Woman. Part of this is the use of calm, matter-of-fact language to describe a horrific action, for example when the Young Woman informs the Woman that they are going to amputate her finger. We can contrast the Woman's understandably hysterical reaction to this threat with the calm way in which the Young Woman and Girl contemplate it impassively. There is a constant emphasis on food, linked with other bodily necessities such as defecating and sex, and almost always contrasted with the horror of terrorist action. In the final scene, just after they have killed the Woman with a lethal injection, the Man asks how many days is it since they last had sex. He wants to go away on holiday, but the Young Woman says they have a meeting to attend. He is as selfish as the politician Husband, but she is more sensitive, although when she says that there are more important things than the two of them she is probably just referring to their group. However, the appearance of normality is deceptive, as, like Lady Macbeth, they cannot escape from what they have done. When the Man has sawn off the Woman's head (and one may note the shock produced when the unmistakable sound of the sawing through skin and neck bone is heard), he has his whole body and his hands covered in blood.

### Philosophical questions: mortality

Although a number of Belbel's plays contain a critique of contemporary society, his theatre has always demonstrated a concern with what may be termed the 'bigger' questions, which go beyond a specific time and place. In this sense, as Puchades has observed, he is an apolitical writer, although this does not in any way mean that he does not engage with contemporary society. On the contrary, as we have seen, he has much to say to a modern audience of all ages about the world in which we live. Sexuality, broken family life, violence and terrorism all feature prominently in plays whose setting is often a highly recognisable if non-specific urban environment. One of the 'bigger' questions that have increasingly preoccupied Belbel is mortality, and illness, death and their effects occupy a prominent place in more recent works such as *El temps de Planck*, *Forasters* and *A la Toscana*.[70] In the first two,

---

[70] For Puchades, death is closely linked with 'sexuality and family crisis' ('la sexualidad y la crisis familiar') (p. 257).

impending or actual death seems to provide characters with a lucidity they have previously lacked.[71] In a number of plays, Belbel deals with the moment when death occurs. For instance, the bracketed words of *Morir (un moment abans de morir)* highlight that crucial moment at which clarity becomes possible. Time is a key feature of *El temps de Planck*, as the moment of death seems to be eternally prolonged or postponed. This play sets infinity against the nanosecond, and the difference between the two seemingly opposite concepts is purely subjective.

In *Forasters*, death brings fear, but also the possibility of transcending both the fear and death itself. The Son learns to face up to the death of his sister, having run away to escape his mother's death some forty years earlier. The blinding, vertiginous image in the mirror that concludes the play's penultimate scene provides the moment of lucidity associated with death and, as in *El temps de Planck*, suggests that infinity and the split second are really interchangeable. Impending death also seems to lend the Mother a tenderness she had previously lacked, at least in her treatment of the immigrant neighbours, in particular the young lad. Having said that, the cancer suffered by Mother and Daughter is physically repulsive, and seems to symbolise the general state of the family. The key word is 'podridura' ('decay'), which the Mother uses to refer bitterly but with great clarity to her illness: 'inside I'm completely dead. Decayed. It's just a matter of the decay extending everywhere' (*Strangers*, p. 125).[72] The symbolic cancer that is destroying this Catalan middle-class family is reminiscent of the physical and moral sickness that afflicts some of Ibsen's bourgeois families. It is possible that Belbel may be posing the question as to whether anything has changed in bourgeois society in over a century. The illness suffered by Marc in *A la Toscana* is mental rather than physical. Despite the difficulty of determining the borders between reality and Marc's imaginings, there is undoubtedly a sharp contrast between his imagined illnesses and Jaume's authentic terminal illness, which serves to underline the former's self-centredness.

[71] In a 2000 interview (well before the premiere of *Forasters*), Belbel spoke of the way Planck accepts his own impending death, and wants his family to accept it too (Pep Tugues, 'Sergi Belbel i *El temps de Plank*').

[72] 'per dintre estic absolutament morta. Podrida. Només falta que la podridura s'estengui del tot' (p. 48).

## Philosophical questions: time

For an author who is so preoccupied with issues of mortality, time is naturally of central concern. The time available to humans is clearly finite, but the suggestion of some sort of afterlife or at least some meaning provided by death means that infinity is an aspect that is inevitably a possibility. Time is also intimately connected with questions of identity since, just as one character may be confused or merged with another, so one time frame is fused into another. As was observed earlier, time periods may be vast, or nanoseconds, and nowhere is this more apparent than in *El temps de Planck*. Belbel's preoccupation with time is an example of his fascination with science, as he explains in a 2000 interview in which he views science as compatible with religion or spirituality:

> Science too has its magical side. It explains how reality functions, and may be a good solution for certain anxieties; science should not be confused with materialism nor spirituality with something unscientific. This frontier does not exist. Science can be a kind of religion, more authentic and lasting, since its answers are difficult to categorise. Science is the great discovery of humankind.[73]

Many ideas on time are present in *El temps de Planck*, as in several other Belbel plays.[74] For example, in Scene Comma Zero (6), Maria speaks of the big bang in terms that anticipate the vertiginous mirror scene of *Forasters* ('what happened in Planck time/ after the big bang/ which was the origin of our Universe').[75] The explosion has sexual suggestions in Planck's expression of how he wants to experience a final orgasm before he dies at the end of Scene Comma Zero (7) (p.

[73] 'La ciència també té una part màgica. Explica com funciona la realitat, i pot ser una bona resposta a algunes angoixes; no s'ha de confondre ciència amb materialisme i espiritualitat amb quelcom acientífic. Aquesta frontera no existeix. La ciència pot ser una mena de religió, més autèntica i dura, perquè les seves respostes són difícils d'encaixar. La ciència és el gran descobriment de l'ésser humà' (Tugues, 'Sergi Belbel i *El temps de Plank*').

[74] Ragué-Arias sees a germ of Belbel's treatment of time and infinity in *La sang* (Ragué-Arias, *¿Nuevas dramaturgias?*, p. 132).

[75] 'què va passar en el temps de Planck/ després de la gran explosió/ que va donar origen al nostre Univers' (p. 42). For Feldman, 'echoes of *El temps de Planck* reverberate throughout *Forasters*' (p. 219).

52). In her summing-up of her daughters in Comma Zero (19), Sara refers to 'poor Maria/ neither present nor past nor future/ just beyond time'),[76] which seems to anticipate the Eliot-like time element in *Forasters*. The subjectivity of time is also reminiscent of *Four Quartets*. As Maria says: 'I travel at the speed of light/ My time goes faster than yours/ I stop at a point in space and observe you.'[77] This can be linked with the distortion of time, perfectly encapsulated in Maria's words at the end of Comma Zero (38): 'The total distortion of time/ and of the laws of the Universe/ whatever they may be/ When all is said and done/ Who can say if there are laws/ Inside our minds.'[78]

The sense that an individual's mind can make its own rules provides a clear connection with *A la Toscana*, in which much of what happens could simply be the product of a disturbed or a confused mind. There is sometimes vertiginous movement back and forth in time in *El temps de Planck*, between when Sara (Planck's wife) announces her first pregnancy to her husband, and his death; the first anniversary of his death (pp. 22–23); Maria's death (p. 88); post-Maria's death, when she is in a coffin (p. 125: this is reminiscent of the beyond-the-grave element in *A la Toscana*), post-Sara's death; the time when Maria was not yet born and her sisters were little girls (p. 130); when Maria was a little girl, in Comma Zero (39); and then the sudden shock and vertiginous leap in time at the start of Comma Zero (40) when both Sara and Maria are dead and Max is gravely ill, followed by another vertiginous leap in time (back this time) at the start of Comma Zero (41), to Sara's pregnancy, and the confusion in Planck's mind when he refers to himself as Maria's husband (p. 190). This leads to the question of confusion of identity at the end of the play, when there are two Marias, the second one metatheatrically greeting the audience.

These movements through time anticipate *Forasters*, in which the switching between periods and the subsequent merging of three females into one single entity speeds up as the play nears its end. Historical time is a key element of the play and intimately connected

---

76 'la pobra Maria/ ni present ni passat ni futur/ simplement més enllà del temps' (p. 109).

77 'Viatjo a la velocitat de la llum/ El meu temps corre més de pressa que el vostre/ M'aturo en un punt de l'espai i us miro' (p. 128).

78 'La distorsió total del temps/ i de les lleis de l'Univers/ siguin quines siguin/ Al cap i a la fi/ Qui pot dir que hi hagi lleis/ Dins la nostra ment' (p. 180).

with atavism. The most obvious example is that the Daughter suffers from cancer, having lost her mother to the same disease. Belbel seems to be suggesting that, no matter how hard we try to assert our own individuality, the past and our own roots are things from which we are unable to escape.[79] The reviewer of the production of the German translation of the play at the Schauspiel Leipzig Theatre comments that 'incapacity for love, mendacity, mistrust and hatred are passed on like life itself'.[80] One critic views this feature in terms of a Zolaesque determinism,[81] while Ibsen's *Ghosts* is another obvious antecedent.

[79] Belbel has said that 'we end up being like our parents even though we may deny it. It's an obsession of mine' ('acabem assemblant-nos als nostres pares encara que en reneguem. És una obsessió meva') (Francesc Bombí-Vilaseca, 'L'escriptura surt quan trobes que la forma va lligada amb el contingut', p. xi). The destructive influence of the family is strongly in evidence in *Ivern*, subtitled 'a horror story' ('una història de terror'), which Belbel originally wrote as a television script, and which has also been mooted as the script for Belbel's putative debut as a cinema director. Neither project has as yet come to fruition, but the work has been published as a kind of Gothic horror novel in dialogue form, of over four hundred pages in length. It tells the story of a family destroyed by a family curse. It was believed that the father, Àngel Ivern, had stabbed his wife and son to death, left one daughter unconscious, and then turned a shotgun on himself. After many twists and turns, amid an atmosphere of great tension and terror, it transpires that it was the surviving daughter who had stabbed her mother and brother, and who later murdered her sister. She is a schizophrenic and therefore unaware of what she has done: in some ways she is akin to Marc in *A la Toscana* and may be viewed as a precursor of this character. And it is she who utters the following words, which seem so relevant to Belbel's portrayal of the family in *Forasters*: 'Our inheritance curses us all. […] We can't escape from it. The family is the only really indestructible tyranny. The only incurable illness' ('L'herència ens maleeix a tots. […] No ens en podem escapar. La família és l'única tirania realment indestructible. L'única malaltia incurable') (Sergi Belbel, *Hivern*, Narrativa, 191 (Barcelona: Empúries, 2002), p. 395).

[80] Reinhard Wengierek, 'They kiss and then they clobber each other', translation of 'Sie küssen und sie kloppen sich', *Welt.de*, 24 January 2006. Review translated by Chloë Driscoll and Josephine McCrossan.

[81] 'With a Zolaesque determinism, which fixes the laws of inheritance, Belbel unfolds two epochs and two stages' ('Con un determinismo a la manera de Zola, el que fija las leyes de la herencia, Belbel despliega dos épocas y escenarios') (S. Doria, 'Los espejos de Belbel y la ley de la herencia' ('Belbel's Mirrors and the Law of Inheritance'), *ABC*, 24 September 2004, p. 82).

Memory is a key component of *Forasters*, becoming more and more prominent as the play develops.[82] It is often small, seemingly insignificant objects that remind the characters or the spectators of events from the past.[83] The most interesting example of the confusion of time periods is found in Scene 4 of the Second Part, immediately preceding the Epilogue, in a brilliantly spectacular theatrical moment that unites Mother, Daughter and Granddaughter in a moment of lucidity produced by death. Death is the key to an understanding of the mysteries of the universe, and, through this dazzling display of mirrors, Belbel presents the three generations of women as one single being, and the three chronological periods as one and indivisible.

Finally as far as time is concerned, one should note the circular nature of *Forasters*. It ends where it began, and the Prologue and the Epilogue frame the main action, thus illustrating how a structural device has a clearer thematic function in Belbel's more recent work than it did in some of his early plays. The context is that the Son is selling the family home to the Man, a well dressed, educated individual, who is the Child of the 1960s towards whom the Mother showed such affection. This son of immigrants has forged a career much more effectively than any member of the Catalan family, and he seems to be a more civilised human being than they are. Time has ravaged them, and they are forced to sell the house, which is now bare of all furniture. It is a scene that recalls the ending of Chekhov's *The Cherry Orchard* (1904), in which the Ranevskaya family, so languidly indifferent to changing time and sure of their own superiority, ends by being ousted from their property by a socially inferior class, represented by Lopakhin.[84] In both *The Cherry Orchard* and *Forasters* the audience witnesses the end of an era. In Belbel's play, it would appear that the

[82] A more detailed study of this feature in recent Catalan theatre is Helena Buffery, 'The "Placing of Memory"', in *Catalan Theatre, 1975–2006: Politics, Identity, Performance, Contemporary Theatre Review*, 17:3 (2007), 385–97.

[83] For further details see David George, 'Beyond the Local: Sergi Belbel and *Forasters*', pp. 404–05.

[84] Maria M. Delgado has noted this similarity. She also detects parallels between *Forasters* and Ibsen's *Ghosts*, the plays of Eugene O'Neill and, above all, *Retour au désert*, by Bernard-Marie Koltès ('Forum 2004 Barcelona: A Summer of Stagings in Spain's Theatrical Capital', *Western European Stages*, 16:3 (2004), 71–84, p. 83).

future belongs to a society that is very different from traditional Catalonia, and will be one in which several generations of immigrants play a key role. It is a play that manages to deal with issues that are of central concern to a contemporary audience, but in a way that connects its author to a broader Western theatrical and literary tradition.

### Philosophical questions: identity

Another of the 'big' issues in Belbel's theatre is identity, again one that may be both specifically Catalan and of wider import. Identity takes a wide variety of forms and is evident in his earliest plays. One may expect a Catalan writer to be concerned with the identity of Catalonia as a nation or a region, and with what Catalans call the *fet diferencial*, or what makes them distinct from the rest of Spain. However, in Belbel's plays, identity is more often personal, and related to our sense of self and self-worth rather than directly reflective of the Catalan situation. Of course, it is not easily possible to separate the personal from the political (as is clear from *La sang* for instance), but any socio-political or Catalan national identity is not, it seems to me, the main focus of Belbel's plays. We have seen how Lletja discovers her true identity through violence, which provides her with a genuine pleasure and purpose in life. On the other hand, the politically motivated violence does not seem to afford fulfilment to the terrorists who inflict it in *La sang*. Interestingly, the group to which they belong, however radical its ideology (and we know precious little about this), does not offer them any discernible sense of identity. Ironically, the political cause they ostensibly promote seems empty and meaningless, and their only sense of identity seems to be the rather humdrum existence they lead with each other.

As was observed earlier, the identity of individual characters in such early plays as *Minim.mal Show* is extremely nebulous. In *En companyia d'abisme* there is doubt over the identity of the two men. It is possible that the older man is a projection through time of the younger one, in an analogous situation with that of Lorca's *Así que pasen cinco años* (*When Five Years Pass*, 1931). In *Després de la pluja* the various Secretaries are distinguished only by the colour of their hair, and, intriguingly, there is a suggestion that they may all be disguised versions of each other:

HEAD OF ADMINISTRATION: Oh, yes. By the way, do you know who she is?

BROWN-HAIRED SECRETARY: Yes. The dark-haired one.
HEAD OF ADMINISTRATION: No. She's blonde.
BROWN-HAIRED SECRETARY: No, she's dark-haired. Dyed blonde.
(p. 134)[85]

The type of characterisation that denies individual identity and psychological or personal development is, of course, typical of avant-garde theatre, and is represented in Spain in the work of Valle-Inclán and Lorca, and in Catalan theatre by the *Poesia escènica* of Joan Brossa, and is also reminiscent of the plays of Samuel Beckett. Belbel set a trend in Catalan theatre of the late 1980s and early 1990s in that many of his characters lack proper names or obviously definable personalities, which becomes one of the features of the so-called Belbel Generation of playwrights.

Probably the most complex identity questions are found in *A la Toscana*. There are numerous parallels between Marc and Jaume, and the identities of the two women, Joana and Marta, are also confused. In my view the possibility exists that Marta and Jaume are alter egos of Joana and Marc respectively, or the fruit of Marc's confused mind. In an interview, Belbel has said that 'the spectator must look at it in its entirety, but as its creator I have to say that there is not just one Joana. There are several Joanas, and one of them is the Joana who is filtered through the labyrinth of the mental obsessions of her husband.'[86] Belbel constantly interlaces what appears to be dream and reality, and it is often very difficult to distinguish between the two, increasingly so as the play progresses. Much of it takes place in the blurred space between waking and dreaming. It is never clear to what extent the Tuscany of the title is a real place or merely a symbol of the world of illusion that Marc inhabits. Belbel specifies that Tuscany is not to be visually present until the Epilogue, when it is to take on a realistic representation.

[85] 'CAP ADMINISTRATIU: Ah, sí. Per cert, sap qui és?/ SECRETÀRIA CASTANYA: Sí. La morena./ CAP ADMINISTRATIU: No. És rossa./ SECRETÀRIA CASTANYA: No, és morena. Tenyida de ros' (p. 92).

[86] 'l'espectador ha de fer-ne un balanç global, però com a creador he de dir que no hi ha només una Joana. Hi ha diverses Joanes, i una d'elles és la Joana filtrada a través del laberint de les obsessions mentals del seu home' (From the programme note to the play, p. 12; accessed at the TNC's website, http://www.tnc.es/ca/index.html, on 28 June 2008).

Jaume's words in Scene 21 help us to understand the often complex issue of the identity of individuals, as it becomes difficult to separate their personae from that of others: 'at bottom we are all identitcal'.[87] Just as it is possible to view the two men in García Lorca's *Así que pasen cinco años* as projections through time of the same man, so we are never really sure whether the two men in *En companyia d'abisme* are really different facets of the same man, the three generations of women in *Forasters* are all part of an indivisible female, and Marc and Jaume, and Joana and Marta, are really different representations of a single male–female relationship.[88]

In *Forasters* the identity issue is more social than in *A la Toscana*. It is to an extent specific to contemporary Catalonia, in which extensive immigration from Africa, South America and Eastern Europe has prised apart the North–South binary. The play seems to question what it means to be a Catalan, and to suggest that Catalan identity cannot be limited to the traditional concept of the middle-class, Catalan-speaking family. Belbel has denied that the play is an attack on traditional Catalonia, but does admit that his own experience, as the son of Andalusian immigrants, being called a 'xarnego' as a young boy affected him deeply.[89] Migration is a fact, Belbel seems to be saying, and indeed the central family in the play are descendants of immi-

---

87 'en el fons tots som idèntics' (p. 96).

88 Speaking a propos of *Forasters*, in a joint interview with film-maker Ventura Pons on the occasion of the premiere of the latter's film version of the play (see Chapter 3), Belbel declared that 'the tragedy of today is DNA' ('la tragèdia dels nostres dies és l'ADN') (Interview with Bernat Salvà in *Avui*, 24 November 2008, consulted at http://www.auvi.cat/article/cultura_comunicacio/ 47155/ventura/pons/sergi/belbel/excel·lim/tot/nomes/falta/la/gent/ho/sapiga.html, accessed 5 December 2008). As for *En companyia d'abisme*, Puchades's view is that 'the Man is the projection of the Young Man's future, and the Young Man of the Man's past' ('el Home es proyección del futuro del Jove, y el Jove del pasado del Home') (p. 67).

89 'Xarnego' ('charnego' in Castilian Spanish) is a word used by Catalans to refer (usually derogatively) to immigrants from southern Spain. In an interview conducted after the TNC season of *Forasters* Belbel revealed that, although he did not understand that term as a child, it caused him to feel humiliated, and subsequently to reflect on the humiliation of that whole post-Civil War generation (Bombí-Vilaseca, 'L'escriptura surt quan trobes que la forma va lligada amb el contingut', p. x).

grants, albeit internal immigrants within Catalonia. At the same time, as Feldman says:

> Although Belbel does not name Barcelona explicitly in the text, there are several aspects of the context that are reminiscent of the multicultural and multiethnic conditions that have underpinned the evolution of the city, as well as Catalunya, Spain and Europe, throughout the twentieth and twenty-first centuries. (p. 222)[90]

adding: 'Belbel's plot creates an upstairs/downstairs dialectic in which the two worlds collide and then intermingle and overlap within the same urban building' (p. 223). Belbel himself has said that the real outsiders are not the immigrants but the Catalan family, and that, 'in my plays, the one who is nearest is often the most distant'.[91]

In my view, the essence of *Forasters* is not political or social comment (although these elements are, of course, present in the play), but an exploration of wider issues. Begoña Barrena, it seems to me, has fallen into a trap when, in the conclusion to her review of its Barcelona production, she writes of the play's 'very politically correct aims, in these days of mixed race and ethnic diversity, but too tendentious and sweetened'.[92] Her fellow Barcelona critic Francesc Massip is, I feel,

---

[90] However, a certain amount of caution should be exercised, since, as Buffery reminds us, *Forasters* was devised as part of the *European Convention's* 'Theatres of Europe: Mirror of Displaced Populations' project (2002–04; italics mine) ('The "Placing of Memory" in Contemporary Catalan Theatre', p. 392). Having said that, as Carles Batlle argues, *Forasters* is one of a new wave of Catalan plays that are more firmly located in a specific place (namely contemporary Barcelona) than those written in the previous decade. *Forasters*, Batlle writes, 'without stating so explicitly, clearly takes place in Barcelona' (Carles Batlle i Jordà, 'Contemporary Catalan Theatre: Between the Desert and the Promised Land', in *Catalan Theatre, 1975–2006: Politics, Identity, Performance, Contemporary Theatre Review*, 17:3 (2007), 416–24, p. 423). This would contrast with the case of *Carícies*, of which Puchades writes: 'Belbel tries to avoid the temptation of linking the city in *Carícies* with Barcelona and of making the play naturalist or localist' ('Belbel trata de evitar cualquier tentación de relacionar la ciudad de *Carícies* con Barcelona y convertir la obra en naturalista o costumbrista') (p. 148).

[91] 'a les meves obres, sovint el que està més a prop és el que està més lluny' (Interview with Bernat Salvà in *Avui*, 24 November 2008).

[92] 'intenciones políticamente correctísimas, en estos tiempos de mestizaje

nearer the mark by showing a keen appreciation of the dramatic whole of the play's internal structures and its production: 'internal rhymes in a cabalistic scene of brilliant synergies. It is all worked out to the last detail, from the lighting to the disturbing background music, so as to move the fiendish theatrical machinery at a precise pace.'[93]

While identity certainly possesses a social dimension in *Forasters*, this is not as marked as in the earlier *La sang*. As was mentioned above, the doubling of parts serves to underline the similarities between terrorists and so-called normal society and the blurring of their identities, especially in the case of the politician. For him, the terrorists are not like 'us' (p. 81), but his mistress, in her outburst, says that 'THERE'S NO TERRORIST, NONE AT ALL, YOU'RE TO BLAME FOR EVERYTHING' (*Blood*, p. 42).[94] She empathises with his wife (Woman) (possibly through a feeling of guilt), a sentiment reinforced by the blood image on p. 41 (*Blood*; *La sang*, p. 83) and by her grotesquely chewing the nail on the big toe of the severed foot (*Blood*, p. 42, *La sang*, p. 86). The sense of 'them and us' is connected to the man–woman contrast once more in the final scene in the conversation between the Woman and the Man. She emphasises the similarity between her son and the Girl, but the Man fails to see the connection. All he can say is: 'Blood, no', and she replies: 'No?' (p. 48).[95] The Woman underlines what extreme situations do to 'respectable' people (she is a teacher, someone who educates future generations): the 'there but for the grace of God' idea, which is linked with the sense that we are all the same, terrorists and non terrorists alike.

There is – typically of Belbel's plays – a sense of hope in this final scene, when, in the very last words of the play, the Girl addresses the dead Woman, and tells her that, one day, she will call at her house and ask for her son: 'He'll come, he'll look at me and say he doesn't know me at all. (*Pause*) It doesn't matter, he'll have looked at me and I'll see

y diversidad étnica, pero demasiado tendenciosas y edulcoradas' ('Ejercicio de estilo', *El País*, 18 September 2004, p. 41).

[93] 'rimes internes en una cabalística escènica de fulgents sinergies. Tot està mil·limètricament calculat, des de la il·luminació a l'inquietant fons sonor, per fer moure l'endimoniat engranatge teatral al ritme precís' ('Enmirallats', *Avui*, 18 September 2004, p. 52).

[94] 'NO HI HA TERRORISTA, TOTA LA CULPA ÉS TEVA' (*La sang*, p. 85).

[95] 'La sang, no […] ¿No?' (p. 94).

him' (p. 54).[96] The hope implied here is reinforced by the final image of the play, that of the face of the Girl resembling the Virgin Mary's.[97]

## Concluding remarks

Several characteristics of Belbel's dramatic writing have been observed in this chapter. Some of these have recurred throughout his career to date, which lends a certain consistency to his creative output. They include a depiction of fractured relationships, and a preoccupation with death, time and the workings of a disturbed mind. His use of surprising, sometimes shocking, language suggests influences on his work that include Mamet and Beckett. His more recent plays display a greater sense of social context, with less abstract settings. However, neither his characters nor his geographical locations are specific, not even in plays that have a stronger social dimension, such as *La sang* or *Forasters*. As was indicated in the Introduction, this style influenced a whole genera-tion of Catalan playwrights, and led to what was known as 'Operation Belbel'. This characteristic style was not popular with everyone, and Valencian playwright Manuel Molins voices what for him is its nega-tive aspect, namely that it has led him to play safe and to write in a formulaic fasion.[98] Molins seems to be echoing a much earlier Belbel review, namely Marcos Ordóñez's of *En companyia d'abisme*:

> I see the creatures of *En companyia d'abisme* as little laboratory animals, well made but empty. It must be said that Sergi Belbel is a sensitive and intelligent man, but maybe too young or perhaps his interests are spread too wide for him to fix his gaze on life around him, from which he might distil a play that speaks to others and not just to himself.[99]

---

96 'Ell apareixerà, em mirarà i dirà que no em coneix de res. (*Pausa*) Però tant se val, ell m'haurà mirat i jo l'hauré vist' (p. 104).

97 Puchades sees a parallel between the ending of this play and *Sóc Lletja* (p. 230).

98 Molins expressed his opinions in a 2006 interview with the Associació d'Actors i Directors Professionals de Catalunya (AADPC), which appears on their website, http://www.aadpc.cat/aadpc/ca/publicacions/revista-entreacte/ arxiu/155/hartile.html, accessed 19 June 2009.

99 'Veig les criatures d'*En companyia d'abisme* com a bestioles de laboratori, ben fabricades però buides. Sergi Belbel és, em consta, un home

As will be observed in Chapter 4, other press reviewers of Belbel's work, particularly in Catalonia and the UK, have drawn attention to this supposed lack of serious content in Belbel's plays, but, as I have tried to demonstrate in this chapter, such a view is too simplistic. It is often difficult to separate content from form, as they are inextricably linked. The content is sometimes almost hidden, and it is also essential, it seems to me, to take account of his evolving output and the articulation of concerns that are often not expressed through the vocabularies of social realism, and the possibilities of political theatre that goes beyond Brechtian paradigms.

sensible i culte, però potser sigui massa jove o potser el seu interès és massa dispers perquè pugui fixar la seva mirada en la vida al seu voltant i destil.lar-ne una peça que parli als altres i no exclusivament a si mateix' (Marcos Ordóñez, *Molta comèdia: Cròniques de teatre, 1987–1995* (Barcelona: La Campana, 1996), pp. 79–80, p. 80). This is a collection of press reviews of plays, by Ordóñez, who is probably Spain's leading theatre critic.

# 2

# Performance and Practitioners

Belbel has directed almost forty plays between the late 1980s and the mid-2000s, including many of his own, and works by Catalan, Spanish and European playwrights both contemporary and from previous centuries. He is responsible for the translations of some of the plays, especially by French and Italian authors. In this chapter, having argued for his directing to be labelled author's theatre, I present an overview of his directing career and the spaces in which he has directed. I explore his team ethos, making extensive use of interviews I have conducted with practitioners who have worked regularly with him.[1] An analysis of the preparation process will help us to understand what Belbel prioritises as a director, and, finally, a detailed scrutiny of the results of the process in selected productions will allow a judgement to be made on how the ethos is translated into practice.

## Belbel and author's theatre

Belbel's close involvement with texts as either writer or translator strongly suggests a sense of his as author's theatre. In a 2005 interview, carried out after his appointment as Director of the TNC, he made a statement that suggests that the work of the director and the playwright

---

[1] I have interviewed the following practitioners: actors Jordi Banacolocha, Anna Lizaran, Laura Conejero and Lluís Soler (on 17 September 2008, 19 September 2008, 2 February 2009 and 13 February 2009 respectively); costume designer Mercè Paloma; stage designer Max Glaenzel (22 January and 28 January 2009 respectively: I interviewed Mercè Paloma together with her husband, the composer Òscar Roig; Max Glaenzel's wife and fellow scenographer Estel Cristià was present at his interview); the composer Albert Guinovart (on 23 January 2009); the playwright Josep M Benet i Jornet (in September 2008); and the translator and Assistant Artistic Director of Madrid's Teatro de la Abadía, Ronald Brouwer (on 6 February 2009).

are inextricably linked, and that the former has a duty of care towards the latter:

> The twentieth century has done a lot of harm to playwrights with the appearance of the figure of the director, and with the importance that he has been given. It seems that the director and the author have entered into competition with each other. The time has come to have the author enter the theatre again and for the functions of author and director to be merged. I will try, therefore, to look out for the author figure, with the idea of integrating him into stage practice.[2]

These are clearly the words of a man who considers that directors' theatre in the twentieth century has not served playwrights well. It is surely significant that Belbel sees himself first and foremost as a writer: 'I have always thought that I am an author who directs and not a director who writes. The work of an author is a lot more thankless than that of a director. There is no comparison. A director has company and is protected'.[3] Throughout his directing career he has consistently attempted to be faithful to what he understands to be the individual playwright's 'intention'. Four of the interviewees mentioned Belbel's respect for the text, the costume designer Mercè Paloma attributing this to his being a writer himself. The composer Òscar Roig confirmed that the text is sacred for Belbel, while Josep Maria Benet i Jornet, four of whose plays Belbel has directed, also supported this view. For the actor Jordi Banacolocha, Belbel is perhaps too respectful and should cut more frequently. He described how the director would look at a text

---

[2] 'El segle XX ha fet molt de mal als dramaturgs amb la irrupció de la figura del director escènic, i amb la importància que se li ha donat. Sembla que director i autor hagin entrat en competència. Arriba el moment de fer que l'autor torni a entrar al teatre i que les funcions de l'autor i del director es fusionin. Intentaré vetllar molt, doncs, per la figura de l'autor, amb la idea d'integrar-lo a la pràctica escènica' (Interview with Andreu Sotorra, published in *El Temps*, 31 May 2005, consulted at http://www.andreusotorra.com/teatre/entrevista118.html, accessed 27 March 2009).

[3] 'Yo siempre pienso que soy un autor que dirige y no un director que escribe. Es mucho más ingrato el trabajo del autor que la [*sic*] de director. No se puede comparar. El director está acompañado, protegido' (Interview with Lourdes Orozco, in *Teatro y política: Barcelona (1980–2000)*, Serie Debate, 12 (Madrid: Publicaciones de la Asociación de Directores de Escena, 2007), pp. 300–07, p. 303).

again and again, and then invariably decide against cutting because some of the meaning would be lost.

## From minimalism to maximalism: Belbel's spaces

Belbel's first directing experience came within the Aula del Teatre as a student at the Autonomous University of Barcelona. Here he directed plays by Heiner Müller, Racine, and Georges Perec, as well as Beckett's *Footfalls* at Barcelona's Sala Beckett. He directed the Spanish version of *Minim.mal Show* at a converted fish market in Zaragoza, the Teatro del Mercado. These ventures were followed by several more in the early 1990s at Barcelona's Teatre Romea, under the auspices of the Centre Dramàtic de la Generalitat de Catalunya, where he also directed works by other writers including Benet i Jornet (*Desig*, 1991) and Guimerà (*La filla del mar*, 1992).[4] The late 1990s saw him continue to direct at the Romea, including his own plays and *The Merchant of Venice*. Other venues in which he directed in this period are the Sala Beckett, the Teatre Grec (Greek Theatre, a huge open-air space that regularly houses Barcelona's summer theatre festival), and theatres in other towns in Catalonia.

The last ten years have seen Belbel continue to direct in a variety of venues, but recently he has gravitated towards the Teatre Nacional, of which he became Artistic Director in 2006. He has directed in all three of its spaces, from the smallest (the Sala Tallers) to the huge stage of the Sala Gran. Most of his productions in the latter have been of other playwrights (he is contracted to direct a play annually while he remains Artistic Director of the TNC), and the challenges and achievements of his productions in this space will be analysed later in this chapter.

My discussions with members of the team who regularly work with Belbel shed interesting light on the issue of the spaces in which he has directed. Jordi Banacolocha's view is that Belbel's own plays are written for small spaces, where the audience is close to the action, surrounding the stage (i.e. theatre in the round). When he directs a play

---

4 The Centre Dramàtic de Catalunya acted as a kind of prototype National Theatre, prior to the establishment of the Teatre Nacional de Catalunya in 1996. The Romea is a medium-sized, proscenium-arch theatre, which has a long association with the promotion of theatre in Catalan: see *Romea, 125 anys*, ed. Ramon Bacardit et al. (Barcelona: Generalitat de Catalunya, 1989).

at the Sala Gran, he has to think what play would be best suited to that venue, as it is a space that strongly conditions any production. It is a difficult, tiring theatre to play in, partly because of the size of the stage and partly since the acoustics are not good. Banacolocha claimed that it is impossible to mount a small-scale production there, while Òscar Roig explained the difficulty of writing music for the Sala Gran with its problematic acoustics, which makes it difficult to hear properly from some of the seats. In Banacolocha's opinion, Belbel has never made a mistake in his choice of play for the Sala Gran.

Belbel himself is acutely conscious of the importance of the spaces in which plays are performed, and what these imply for the spectator. He has made his awareness clear in a number of interviews. In one of these he puts it simply: 'working in different spaces implies adapting to the environment'.[5] The actor Lluís Soler shares this perception. In our interview in February 2009 he explained how Belbel deals with a 'difficult' space like the Sala Gran, saying that he knows exactly what is needed for the actor's words to reach the audience. When one begins rehearsals in this space one must have the play ready. They had done readings of *The Government Inspector* for two months prior to its premiere in February 2009, so they were fully cognisant of the play's details and subtleties.

Although we have observed a general trend in Belbel's directing, from smaller to larger spaces, it is interesting to note comments made to me by Ronald Brouwer, Deputy Artistic Director of Madrid's Teatro de la Abadía, in which *A la Toscana* was performed in 2008. We discussed the stage space of that theatre, which Brouwer confirmed is much smaller than the Sala Petita of the TNC, where the play received its Barcelona premiere. The set for the play was the most complicated the Abadía has done in its fifteen-year history, and it barely fitted onto the stage. The sheer number of technicians who came from Barcelona was also a challenge for the Abadía. He felt that the proximity of the audience to the sloping stage greatly aided the production. In an interview for the dossier to accompany the TNC production, Belbel confirmed Brouwer's view of the play as a chamber work:

> a chamber work, for four actors, and it was unthinkable to do it in a venue other than the Sala Petita. And we are not only doing it in the

---

[5] 'trabajar en espacios diversos implica adaptarse al medio' (Orozco, *Teatro y política: Barcelona (1980–2000)*, p. 307).

Sala Petita, but we are also doing it on a small stage. We are using a
very small set, because it is, after all, a very small story. And now
it's the director speaking: for me, a small story must be explained in
a small place, and that is why we have made the stage smaller and
turned it into a container, which is really a metaphor for Marc's
brain.[6]

At the risk of over-simplification, the types of theatre in which Belbel
has directed reflect the development of his career from bright young
hopeful in the mid-1980s to part of the Catalan theatrical establishment
by 2010. However, as the following section will demonstrate, his
working fundamentals remain similar in all cases.

**Working fundamentals**

Belbel likes to direct with an established team of practitioners, a
number of whom have been involved with him since his early career.
The actress Laura Conejero, the composer Òscar Roig and the costume
designer Mercè Paloma began their careers with Belbel when they were
all students. This illustrates the director's desire to have in his team
people he knows intimately and who understand each other's working
methods, mixing these with appropriate practitioners from other back-
grounds. The composer Albert Guinovart, another practitioner who
works regularly with Belbel, confirmed in our interview that the
director is keen to be surrounded by people he enjoys working with,
such as stage designer Max Glaenzel, who, together with his wife Estel
Cristià, have realised the set designs for most of Belbel's productions
over the last ten years.

Another regular member of the team, Jordi Banacolocha, discussed
with me the team ethos that characterises Belbel's working methods.

---

6 'obra de cambra, per a quatre actors, i era impensable fer-la en un altre
lloc que no fos la Sala Petita. I no només la fem a la Sala Petita, sinó que
també la fem en un escenari molt reduït. Fem servir un decorat molt petit,
perquè aquesta no deixa de ser una petita història. I ara parla el director: per a
mi, una petita història s'ha d'explicar en un lloc petit, i és per això que encara
hem reduït més l'escenari de la sala i l'hem convertit en un contenidor, que no
deixa de ser una metàfora del cervell de Marc' (Interview with Belbel in
programme notes to *A la Toscana*, pp. 15–23, p. 22).

He said that, during his lengthy acting career, he has seen examples of characters played by minor actors who were given no guidance as to how they should perform apparently menial tasks such as making a cup of coffee. This, he felt, goes back to the Spanish tradition of the dominance of the leading actor or actress, to whom other actors were subservient.[7] Belbel, however, works with all actors, be they leading or minor, with equal intensity. Banacolocha gave as an example *En Pólvora* (2006), in which the actors who were brought from different amateur theatres in Sabadell to play factory workers were treated with great respect and care by the director, as if they were the best-known actors in the world. Some of these were youngsters who may have aspired to become professionals, while others were old-timers who harboured no such ambitions, but all were delighted with the way they were directed by Belbel. For Banacolocha this is very important, as, for him, acting depends very much on teamwork. Here is a clear example of Belbel's 'ensemble' working methodology, and this he has been keen to maintain even in a financially more austere climate.[8]

It is interesting to compare Banacolocha's observation with one by the Andalusian actor Roberto Quintana, who played the role of Pedro Crespo in Belbel's 2000–01 production of *El alcalde de Zalamea*. Quintana speaks approvingly of the atmosphere in which directors and actors worked:

> It's not usual to work with directors who trust actors. What usually happens is that they hide you in costumes, in furniture ... because they don't trust you. When you meet someone who gives you

---

[7] The powerful leading actors and actresses, some of whom ran their own theatre company, has a long tradition in Spain. A prime example would be the husband and wife team of the late nineteenth and early twentieth centuries, Fernando Díaz de Mendoza and María Guerrero.

[8] In some respects, Belbel's establishment of a long-standing and settled team would seem to constitute an exception to Klaic's view that 'many repertory companies, some of them calling themselves National Theatres, in Western and Eastern Europe and in Scandinavia, have been forced to introduce a range of compromises that have diluted the notion of the ensemble' (Dragan Klaic, 'National Theatres Undermined by the Withering of the Nation-State', in *National Theatres in a Changing Europe*, ed. S. E. Wilmer, Studies in International Performance (Basingstoke and New York: Palgrave Macmillan, 2008), pp. 217–27, p. 221).

freedom and confidence, you feel good. Perhaps for this reason we
have been working for two months without a single moment of
discouragement.[9]

Care Santos, who attended a rehearsal of the play in Barcelona, humorously and vividly portrays what appears to be a genuinely democratic
and collaborative atmosphere in the canteen of the theatre during a
coffee break: 'In the TNC canteen, rapists, women who have been
raped, sergeants, nobles, old women, soldiers, peasants, a notary, a
mayor and even a king share their afternoon coffee and laugh
together.'[10]
     Another performer who has occasionally worked with Belbel, Anna
Lizaran, explained to me how Belbel the director is extremely good at
creating a team ethos. This might include taking the cast to the cinema
and discussing the film later, or playing games. In the actress's case
this creates enjoyment, which has a positive effect on her desire to
rehearse. It also illustrates that Belbel is a good psychologist. It was
evident to me that Lizaran very much supports the concept of ensemble
acting, which she feels Belbel achieves. This led us on to a discussion
about the actress's work at the Teatre Lliure, where again the team
ethos was important. This is, of course, made easier by the existence of
an established team who regularly work with him, and the continuity
that affords. Laura Conejero confirmed this view, adding that the
familiarity with Belbel's working methods allows the team to feel more
relaxed and confident, which means that the director can get the best
out of them. The danger of this approach, of course, could be a sense of
repetition, or even the stifling of creativity as practitioners remain in
their comfort zone, although knowing what they are capable of may
allow him to push them further.

     [9] 'No es habitual trabajar con directores que confían en los actores. Lo
normal es que se preocupen en taparte con vestuario, con muebles ... porque
desconfían de ti. Cuando encuentras a alguien que te da libertad y confianza,
te sientes muy bien. Tal vez por eso llevamos dos meses trabajando sin un solo
momento de desaliento' (Care Santos, 'El honor con sangre se limpia', *El
Cultural*, 20 September 2000, pp. 46–47, p. 47).
     [10] 'En la cantina del Nacional, violadores, violadas, sargentos, nobles,
mujerucas, soldados, labradores, algún escribano, un alcalde y hasta un rey
comparten entre risotadas el café de la tarde' (Santos, p. 47).

## Basic preparation methods: the process

Having established the overall structure of Belbel's directing career, his disinclination to alter the text, and the importance he attaches to the building of a reliable team of practitioners, the next step is to analyse in more detail how his vision translates into practice. This will be accomplished by examining firstly the preparation process and then the resulting productions.

Belbel's concept of production is characterised by his stress-free approach, his clarity of purpose and his perfectionism. A number of the practitioners who regularly work with him said that he wants the team to be content and likes to avoid conflict. Benet i Jornet added that, if a problem emerges, Belbel always attempts to solve it amicably. He prefers to resolve directing issues prior to the beginning of rehearsals, but has no objections to the playwright attending these, and is open to his and the actors' suggestions. Both Conejero and Glaenzel thought that Belbel feels more at ease directing another playwright's work than one of his own. She put this down to the distance he is able to establish in the case of the former, while he attributed it to the fact that the critics' main focus of attention is the text, which helps to explain why Belbel tends to be more nervous as an author than as a director.

Anna Lizaran provided an example of another feature of Belbel's quality as a director: his clarity. She spoke to me of Racine's *Andromaque*, which had just been premiered at the TNC's Sala Gran when I interviewed her. She said she did not remember the play very well, and asked Belbel to explain it to her as if he were explaining a story. He was able to do this in such a way that she wanted to see it. For her it was illustrative of his charm, which he uses to convince people to work in a production with him. Conejero confirmed the general opinion among the interviewees that, perhaps because of his own logical mind and orderly personality, he is clear about what he wants from the beginning. While not averse to making changes, he likes to have the foundations of a production firmly in place at the outset. He aims to have a coherent vision of what the characters are like, at the start, although the way the actors put his concepts into practice is, of course, another question. He is less abstract and more rational than other directors, which Conejero said suits her acting style. He wants to have a clear pattern of the work, its rhythms and its moments of intensity.

It is not only Belbel's actors who spoke to me of his having a clear vision, from the outset, of the direction the play he is directing should take. The costume designer Mercè Paloma confirmed this character-istic of his directing style, which she contrasted with that of Belbel's fellow Catalan director Calixto Bieito, who will improvise and make changes right up until the last moment. Curiously, the word she uses to portray working with Bieito, 'una bogeria' ('craziness'), is exactly how Anna Lizaran described Belbel's plays: both descriptions were meant positively. Max Glaenzel confirmed that, as with the rest of his team, Belbel is often quite clear about what he wants from the scenographers. They act as interpreters, which he and Estel Cristià find an attractive way of working, while Belbel is also open to their suggestions. He has the capacity not only to be quite clear about what he needs in terms of the stage design but also to foresee what will actually happen once the play transfers from the rehearsal room to the stage. From my discussion with Òscar Roig I was able to ascertain that Belbel's approach to the music that forms part of his productions parallels that of the other cogs in the wheel that is the play on the stage. Belbel, said the composer, knows from the beginning of the process where the music is to be placed, how long it should last and what function it should have, although he will not specify which instrument is to play a specific piece.

Both Anna Lizaran and Jordi Banacolocha commented on the math-ematical structures of Belbel's plays, citing the example of *Morir*, in which the fact that actors played different roles in each rehearsal was challenging and exciting but also exacting. Each actor had to play three different parts, explained Banacolocha. He compared the experience to trying to work out a jigsaw puzzle. It means that actors cannot be lazy, but have to forget the lifelong habit, or vice, of thinking they know how to portray a character and to separate actor from role. Another diffi-culty arises from the frequently sudden torrent of words they have to utter, which makes the characters difficult to study and portray. Belbel will challenge the actors, as in *Morir*, while Lizaran also felt that Belbel's doubling of the parts in *Forasters* illustrated his mathematical approach to the theatre.[11] Both Paloma and Roig referred to his meticu-

---

[11] The emphasis on the formal aspects of theatre is, of course, a feature of Belbel's own plays, and one that on occasions elicits hostile criticism: see, for example, reactions to *Tàlem*, discussed in Chapter 4.

lousness in ensuring proper effects of lighting, music, entrances and exits. Roig confirmed that the director really enjoys this detailed work, and is a perfectionist: the timing has to be right to a half-second. The composer felt that this type of meticulous attention would be well suited to the cinema, and he is convinced Belbel will end up directing films.

My interviews with Roig, fellow composer Albert Guinovart and Glaenzel shed valuable light on how Belbel develops the design of the plays he directs prior to the production process. Glaenzel explained how *Forasters* and *A la Toscana* are the two plays in which the designers' work has been most synthetic. The latter, he said, contains the kind of minimalism that used to be associated with Joaquim Roy, who was responsible for the sets on many productions during the early part of Belbel's career. Despite this, the set had to reflect the complexities of Marc's troubled mind, and Glaenzel said he was full of admiration for the way in which Belbel was able to convey the struggle between the two realities – the dream and the 'real' world – in a confined space. We also discussed the use of mirrors in this and other productions, and Glaenzel's view is that, in both *A la Toscana* and *Forasters*, the mirror is an integral part of the text, whereas in *The Government Inspector* it was merely decorative. He explained how, in *Forasters*, the creation of the two time frames was complemented by changes of costume, lighting and music, reinforcing the idea of Belbel as an author who also directs.

As for Belbel's directing methodology, Guinovart explained that, when Belbel has given him the text, they discuss the tone the director requires for the production. Since the composer knows Belbel's requirements so well, he is usually quick to detect and able to convey accurately the director's needs. Equally, Belbel has a very sharp musical ear, said Guinovart, is demanding with the music, and knows what he does not like and when an instrument is out of tune. Before rehearsals begin in the theatre proper, he brings Belbel a 'model' of the music. It is then that detailed timing is worked out: for instance, if Belbel decides that the curtain should go up five seconds earlier, or later, Guinovart must add or remove those five seconds, once more confirming the importance he attaches to precise timing. The first week of full rehearsals is normally hectic for the composer, as it is at this point that Belbel decides on changes, such as 'the music needs to be lighter here, or slower in tempo there'.

Although Guinovart chooses the music to suit the tone, it is Belbel who determines what this should be, and also where in the play the music should be located. This confirms what Òscar Roig told me. Guinovart explained that his task is to have the music prepare the spectator's subconscious for the tone of the text. For instance, in the case of *A la Toscana*, Belbel wanted moments of terror,[12] which the composer felt is quite difficult to convey on the stage. In addition, Belbel required a 'modern' type of music to convey Marc's nightmares, whereas the 'real' world had to be evoked differently. The solution was to move between the rather scary, eerie music chosen for the nightmares and a more Romantic style to convey the 'real' world, although the distinction between reality and imagination becomes more difficult to detect as the play progresses. In the earlier *Forasters* the music was to be chosen to distinguish between the two time periods. In his productions of plays from previous centuries Guinovart explained that Belbel likes to include a moment of sparkle and spectacle. For Eduardo de Filippo's 1959 play *Sabato, domenica e lunedì* (performed as *Dissabte, diumenge i dilluns*) Guinovart chose Italianate music, while for Gogol's *The Government Inspector* he went for the style of Russian popular music, in order to harmonise with the realist décor and costumes. For *Les Fausses confidences* he wrote Xavier Cugat-style music to convey a Latin-flavoured Hollywood setting,[13] while for Jordi Galceran's 2006 adaptation of Ben Hecht and Charles MacArthur's 1920s *Front Page* (as *Primera plana*), Guinovart composed music in the style of early Chicago jazz that melded with the production aesthetic created by Belbel.

Belbel may dictate one musical theme for a male character and a different one for the female, while he also requires music for scene changes. Guinovart expressed his awareness that the music is incidental to the plays themselves, for which reason he tends to limit himself to one or two themes rather than choose three or four. He added that he felt it significant that Belbel's productions use original music, in contrast to the majority, which employ classical or other forms of

---

12 This would seem to confirm my view that it is possible to see *Hivern* as a precursor of *A la Toscana*.

13 Xavier Cugat was born in Girona in 1900, but his family emigrated to Cuba when he was only four years old. He is considered to be the man mainly responsible for introducing Latin-style music to the USA.

music on disk. Just as a set is designed for a specific production, so music is especially composed for it. This, he feels, is important for the composer as it allows him the opportunity to be creative.

Finally as far as the preparation of the production is concerned, my interviews (essentially those with the actors) clarified a number of issues about the treatment of the text in rehearsal. Some of them spoke of how Belbel likes to rehearse the play quickly so that the actors can understand the whole before proceeding to a more detailed, scene-by-scene rehearsal, building up the architecture of the play. Banacolocha contrasted this approach with that of some other directors, who tend to leave the rehearsal of the final scene until a week before the premiere. For Benet i Jornet, Belbel's approach makes for a more relaxed rehearsal process. As regards Belbel's style of directing, Lizaran reinforced Banacolocha's point that he directs quickly, wanting the team to get the whole picture before sorting out the minutiae later. He is in a hurry to see the whole play. Lizaran finds that this style is perhaps too rapid for her: she feels incapable of learning a part some three months in advance of rehearsals, but needs real contact with the text first. However, the Belbel method has the advantage, for instance, of influencing the way in which the actor might portray a character in the first act if they know what happens in Act 3.

Lluís Soler, too, confirmed this characteristic of the Belbel methodology. For Soler, another advantage of the methodology is that, although Belbel indicates the trajectory of the character, the actor is able to add details (if Belbel does not like the additions he says so), thereby making the character their own: indeed, according to Soler, the character belongs to both the director and the actor. Belbel provides the frame for the character, to the actor, who can then add his or her own individual details. Soler gave *The Merchant of Venice* as a specific example of how an actor can contribute to a Belbel production. He said that he (Soler) did a lot of background work on the play prior to rehearsals, studying critical literature on Shylock as he was preparing the part. He declared that he enjoys playing characters with a long history like Shylock, as the actor can do their research on them. He travelled to see a production at the Barbican, and has some half a dozen versions of *The Merchant* on DVD. Studying a historical character like this allows the actor to steep himself in him painlessly, and subconsciously to absorb details that may some day prove useful. He discovered that Henry Irving was the first actor to afford Shylock a human dimension. He read that Irving had his character fall as he left the court after his defeat, and tried this out one day himself in a rehearsal. The rehearsal was stopped because they thought that Soler had accidentally fallen, but, when Belbel realised what he had done, he said that he liked the touch and told him to include it in the performance.

Conejero commented on how Belbel sometimes reads a specific part with exaggeration, bordering on parody at times, but this, she claims, allows her to connect with the music or rhythm that lies beneath the dialogue. This seems to evoke the concept of the actor/director rather than the author/director. She drew an interesting, and for me surprising, contrast between the rehearsal process in the theatre and that of the cinema. In reply to my question about the differences (with specific reference to *Carícies*), Conejero said that, for an actor, the working methods are completely different. In a play the rehearsal time means that the character can be much more fully developed and more complex than in the cinema. Just one day of rehearsal for the film meant that that was not possible, but, on the other hand, the cinema method lends a greater freshness and spontaneity to the creative process than the theatre does. The many rehearsals of a play, on the actual stage, give the actor more confidence than the preparation for filming, which would be a reading around a table and not on the actual set. However, she then went on to say that the freshness in the cinema might be lost in subsequent takes, so that what one might have achieved in one take is impossible to recapture in the next. In contrast, in response to my question of whether playing the two parts in the cinema was easier than in the theatre, Lizaran said that it was, as in *Forasters*, the scenes from the 1970s were filmed days before those from the start of the twenty-first century. On the other hand, playing the dual roles on the stage was a pleasure and a challenge, with just half a minute to change costumes.[14]

## The resulting productions

The final phase in our tracing of the stages from conception to performance involves the detailed analysis of a selection of productions. I

[14] Ventura Pons's adaptations of three Belbel plays for the cinema will be considered in Chapter 3.

will explain what the designs of the plays are like, and how they emphasise the text and 'release' the play. The use of space, lighting, costumes and music is analysed, as well as their role in creating an atmosphere. I have written solely on productions I have seen myself, either live in the theatre or on video recording, and they range from the French and Italian eighteenth century, to Catalan theatre ('classical' and contemporary), to contemporary France, and finally to Belbel's own writing. I am aware that there are other choices I could have made, and I have omitted some productions that received critical acclaim, most notably Eduardo de Filippo's *Sabato, domenica e lunedì*, which Belbel directed in the Sala Gran of the TNC in 2004, or plays that have achieved great commercial success, as was the case with Jordi Galceran's *El mètode Grönholm*, which premiered at the TNC's Sala Tallers in 2003 prior to its record-breaking run in Barcelona's Teatre Poliorama from 2004 until 2007.[15] My reasons for not choosing these two specifically are that I have preferred to select a play by Bernard-Marie Koltès to represent a European contemporary as he has been such a key influence on Belbel's own dramatic work, while I have opted for one by Josep M. Benet i Jornet to embody Belbel's direction of contemporary Catalan writing because of the long-term, close ties between the two men.

As might be expected from an author's director like Belbel, his directing also foregrounds the primacy of the text, from whatever period and country its author may emanate. His 1992 production of *La filla del mar* (1900), by Catalonia's most famous playwright Àngel Guimerà, is a case in point. In 1971, Catalan director Ricard Salvat had used Xavier Fàbregas's modernised version of the play. In contrast, Belbel maintained the original Guimerà text, complete with its barba-

---

15 Of Belbel's direction of the latter, Joan-Anton Benach wrote: 'Sergi Belbel has applied his proven skill to the direction of the play and has achieved a sparkling vivacity in the movement of the characters based on a text in which there is no action as such' ('Sergi Belbel has aplicado su probada maestría en la dirección de la obra y ha logrado una centelleante vivacidad en el movimiento de los personajes a partir de un texto en el que no hay acción propiamente dicha') ('El malicioso método Galceran', *La Vanguardia*, 1 May 2003, p. 35, consulted at http://hemeroteca.lavanguardia.es/preview/2003/05/01/pagina-35/34008747/pdf/html?search=metode%20gronholm, accessed 13 August 2009).

risms and anachronisms.[16] At the same time, in the case of both the
Guimerà plays he has directed, *La filla del mar* and *En Pólvora* (2006),
Belbel made those changes and additions he felt were dramatically
necessary, which accounts for the historical gloss in *En Pólvora* and
his controversial depiction of Àgata's suicide in *La filla del mar*: both
are linked with the familiar Belbelian open ending.[17]

Various features of the set for his production of *La filla del mar*, too,
lend a naturalistic quality to the production. Belbel wanted the audience to feel that they were witnessing 'real' people living in a 'real'

[16] As he explained to me at the time, 'Of course, I chose Guimerà's original version, with all the power of its language, which was full of borrowings
and colloquialisms. With all due respect, Xavier Fàbregas's version is influenced by some linguistic (and sociological!) concerns or prejudices of Catalan
culture in the 1970s: the need to preserve the purity of the language etc. I don't
think that such considerations are still valid in the 1990s, when what is
demanded in all the media is a fresh, dynamic, flexible language, which is
precisely what the Guimerà original is!!' ('Vaig triar, evidentment, la versió
original de Guimerà, amb tota la força del seu llenguatge, farcit de
barbarismes i col·loquialismes. La versió de Xavier Fàbregas està, amb tots
els meus respectes, mediatitzada per alguns "condicionaments" o "perjudicis"
lingüístics (i sociològics!) de la cultura catalana dels anys 70: preservar la
puresa de la llengua, etc. No crec que aquestes consideracions siguin encara
vàlides als anys 90, en què es reclama, en tots els mitjans de comunicació, una
llengua fresca, dinàmica i gens encarcarada (que és la de l'original
guimeranià!!') (from a personal interview with Belbel). This approach appears
to contrast with that observed by Orozco in the Teatre Nacional de Catalunya's
approach to staging the classics (admittedly during the pre-Belbel era): 'As
Domènech Reixach (director of the TNC, 1998–2005) admitted, the production of classic texts entailed some level of linguistic "cleansing":
*castellanismos* – a feature of nineteenth and early twentieth-century Catalan –
were removed from the TNC's productions of Rusiñol, Guimerà and Sagarra
to reinforce language standards not rigorously adhered to by the media and
cultural forms such as music and cinema' (Lourdes Orozco, 'National Identity
in the Construction of the Theater Policy of the Generalitat de Catalunya', in
*Catalan Spaces*, ed. P. Louise Johnson, special issue of *Romance Quarterly*,
53:3 (2006), 211–22, p. 216).

[17] I have analysed Belbel's productions of both Guimerà plays elsewhere;
see David George, 'A Young Lad in the Arms of an Old Man – Sergi Belbel
Directs Àngel Guimerà's *La filla del mar* (*The Daughter of the Sea*)', in
*Spanish Theatre 1920–1995: Strategies in Protest and Imagination* (3), Con-
temporary Theatre Review, 7:4 (1998), 45–64; and David George, 'Belbel
Rescues a Forgotten Guimerà', *Catalan Review* (forthcoming).

place. As he said in an interview earlier that year, 'we will mount a very visceral production in order to reflect tragedy in the young world that is depicted there'.[18] To that effect he had several tons of sand imported, and made the characters cook and eat sardines on stage. This attention to realistic detail had its parallel years later in his production of *En Pólvora*, with his use of real explosives, and textile machinery that required the strengthening of the stage of the TNC's Sala Gran. The elaborate set – including the factory and the boilerhouse – reinforces the effect. Belbel's striving to create a realistic environment in the two plays is further evidenced by his choice of period costume, both for the fishing community in *La filla del mar* and for the textile workers of *El Pólvora*.

The parallel between Belbel's approach to writing and directing as far as the importance he gives to the text is concerned is even more apparent in his socially progressive attitude towards the theme of the outsider in both areas. His 2000–01 production of one of Spain's most famous plays, Calderón de la Barca's *El alcalde de Zalamea*, which he was invited to direct as part of the centenary celebrations for the playwright, is a case in point. Critics were clearly not expecting from Belbel a traditional or historicist reading of the play.[19] He strove to bring out the play's human dimension,[20] and did indeed reject the readings of Calderón that typified the Franco era.[21] He sees *El alcalde* as a socially progressive work, particularly because of what he views as the

---

[18] 'farem una posada en escena molt visceral per reflectir la tragèdia en un món jove que s'hi retrata' (Andreu Sotorra, 'Sergi Belbel reprèn per quarta vegada la direcció d'una obra pròpia amb *Carícies*', *Avui*, 24 February 1992, p. 21).

[19] '*El alcalde de Zalamea* will be faithful to the text, but with a reading that is not at all historicist' ('*El alcalde de Zalamea* serà fidel al text, però amb una lectura gens historicista') (Marta Monedero, 'El TNC obrirà la temporada amb un Calderón en castellà', *Avui*, 13 July 2000, p. 30). I suspect that what is meant by historicist here is that Belbel was not expected to provide a conservative reading of Calderón but rather one that would challenge the production history of the plays that typified the Franco era.

[20] 'Beyond the philosophies of honour and kings, Belbel has tried to bring out the human drama' ('Más allá de filosofías de honras y reyes, Belbel ha buscado resaltar el drama humano') (Pablo Ley, 'Un clásico bien montado', *El País (Cataluña)*, 23 September 2000, p. 15).

[21] As the headline of an interview with him by Pedro Manuel Villora prior to the Madrid premiere of *El alcalde* in the *ABC* theatre page of 20 December

King's pragmatic attitude towards the *pueblo*'s desire for justice.[22] He highlights what he regards as the complexity of the characterisation and the presence of a social and political tension, which may be as keenly felt by a modern audience as it was by audiences of Calderón's time.[23]

Belbel's view of the characters as far from black and white creations is evident from press interviews with him. As he said to Gonzalo Pérez de Olaguer, he considers this to be especially true of Crespo and the Captain, who are not so diametrically opposed to each other as one might suspect.[24] In the same interview Belbel even wonders whether Isabel rejects the Captain as firmly as her words suggest:

> 'We know that Isabel tells the Captain "don't touch me" with her mouth', says the director, 'but who knows what she tells him with her eyes', he argues. This possible attraction felt by Isabel for the Captain, which is absent from the usual readings of the plays over three centuries, will be one of the keys of Belbel's production.[25]

---

2000 put it: 'No veo por ningún lado al Calderón de la Barca reaccionario' ('I don't see the reactionary Calderón anywhere'; p. 77).

[22] See 'No veo por ningún lado al Calderón de la Barca reaccionario'.

[23] My information comes from Belbel's article in the programme notes to the production.

[24] 'Neither is Crespo so good as has always been claimed, nor is the Captain, his daughter's rapist, so perverse. We have looked for the black areas of the former and the white ones of the latter: they both have them' ('Ni Crespo és tan bo com sempre s'ha dit, ni el capità, violador de la seva filla, tan pervers. Hem buscat les zones fosques del primer i les blanques del segon; tots dos en tenen') (Interview with Gonzalo Pérez de Olaguer, *El Periódico* (Catalan- language edition), 16 September 2000, p. 47). As J. B. Hall puts it, '[The Captain] is not an incarnation of evil from the outset, and critics who view him as totally negative and perverse miss the complexity of his characterisation. ... Crespo and Álvaro at least have this much in common: their experiences show the limitations of human intelligence and foresight which are adequate to predict and prevent disaster. It is typical of Calderón's sense of life as frequently complex and paradoxical that he should make this point by linking characters who appear to be diametrically opposed' ('Madness and Sanity in Calderón's *El alcalde de Zalamea*', *Iberromania*, 43 (1996), 52–67, p. 64).

[25] 'Sabemos que Isabel le dice al capitán "no me toques" con la boca', dice el director, 'pero ¿quién sabe qué le dice con la mirada?', argumenta. Esta posible atracción de Isabel por el capitán, ausente en las visiones habituales de la obra durante más de tres siglos, será uno de los ejes del montaje de Belbel.'

The primacy of the text, then, is one feature of both Belbel's playwriting and his directing. Another is his interest in the racial outsider, which is evident in two of his productions: *La filla del mar* and Shakespeare's *The Merchant of Venice* (1994). I have written elsewhere about the outsider/racism issue in *La filla del mar*.[26] In an interview Belbel himself made the connection between this play and the situation in contemporary Catalonia: '[The racism exhibited by the village inhabitants towards the Arab girl] is very similar to what has happened in Catalonia with emigrants from other areas of Spain: we welcome them as if we were doing them a favour, whereas deep down we are rejecting them because they are different.'[27] As was observed in Chapter 1, a similar situation occurs in *Forasters*, in which, in the 1970s sequences, a North African family is rejected by their traditional Catalan middle-class neighbours, just as their Andalusian predecessors had been in the 1960s. Here is another illustration of how Belbel may be viewed as a social progressive, while not being a political writer or director in a party-political sense.[28]

A feature of Belbel's production of *The Merchant of Venice*, too, was his highlighting of the rejection of a racial outsider, in this case, of course, Shylock. At various points in his *Merchant* Belbel ensures that his audience reflects on the question of racial stereotypes that Shakespeare questions in this complex play.[29] For example, in Act 1 Scene 3,

[26] David George, 'A Young Lad in the Arms of an Old Man', pp. 56–58.

[27] 'No deja de ser un caso muy parecido a lo que en Catalunya ha pasado con los emigrantes de otras zonas: los acogemos como si les estuviéramos haciendo un favor y, en el fondo, los rechazamos porque son diferentes' (*El Observador*, 8 October 1992, p. 55).

[28] This would be a very different conclusion from that drawn by Manuel Molins, quoted in Chapter 1, p. 50.

[29] Nick Potter affirms that 'there is more to Shylock than the pantomime Jew', and highlights some of the ambiguities in his character that actors over the ages have brought out ('*The Merchant of Venice*', in *Shakespeare: The Play of History*, ed. Graham Holderness, Nick Potter and John Turner (Basingstoke and London: Macmillan, 1988), pp. 160–79, p. 174). In the words of the American director Peter Sellars (who directed a much-praised version of the play in Chicago in 1994), 'I think Shakespeare is trying to break apart any of that kind of mono-cultural thinking of "all the Blacks think this way, all the Asians are like that, and Chicanos always do this to Guatemalans". Those types of generalisations are totally destroyed by the structure of the play itself' (Interview with Peter Sellars, in *In Contact with the Gods? Directors*

Shylock emphasises immediately his sense of resentment at how he is treated by (Christian) society; they call me dog, he says, and now they want money – he isolates and emphasises the word 'gos' ('dog') to Antonio. Similar emphasis is placed on the word 'jueu' ('Jew'), addressed to Shylock and repeated often. The ending also highlights not the happy resolution for the Christians but the fact that the Jew has not been satisfied, and the state has connived to ensure that the letter of the law has not been obeyed. It is achieved by the slowing down of the music, with Shylock mechanically playing a triangle. The lights are dimmed to almost complete darkness with a spot on Shylock, ensuring that it is the isolation of this outsider that remains in the audience's mind.

Another type of outsider that is strongly present both in Belbel's plays and in his productions is the individual whose sexuality differs from the social norm. The questioning of sexuality and passion is another key feature of both Guimerà plays highlighted by Belbel in his productions. There are similarities between Guimerà's portrayal of the destructive effects of female jealousy that bubbles beneath the surface in *La filla del mar* and Lorca's in *La casa de Bernarda Alba*.[30] One is reminded of Benet i Jornet's view that Guimerà's plays are marked by 'a deviant eroticism that on occasions is worked out through fierce acts of sadism'.[31] Belbel is also of the opinion that the Guimerà play is about a 'debate between physical love and deep love, about whether love must first of all pass through a stage of physical attraction'.[32] As was observed in Chapter 1, the link between physical attractiveness and love is a central concern of Belbel's own *Sóc Lletja*.[33]

---

*Talk Theatre*, ed. Maria M. Delgado and Paul Heritage (Manchester: Manchester University Press, 1996), pp. 220–38, p. 227).

[30] See George, 'A Young Lad in the Arms of an Old Man', p. 53.

[31] 'un erotismo que se desvía y se resuelve a veces en sadismos feroces' (Josep M. Benet i Jornet, 'Guimerà sin naftalina', *El Correo Catalán*, 30 June 1974, p. 14).

[32] 'debate sobre el amor físico y el amor profundo, sobre si el amor pasa o no por un primer atractivo físico' ('Una tragèdia de Guimerà abre el Romea', *El Periódico*, 27 October 1992, p. 55).

[33] However, as I explained in an earlier article, Belbel warns against seeing any real connection between *La filla del mar* and his own works, preferring instead to equate the situation of Àgata with his own position as the son of Andalusian immigrants in Catalonia: see George, 'A Young Lad in the Arms of an Old Man', p. 57. See also Chapter 1, p. 47.

Love in its different guises is one of the main themes of *En Pólvora*, one of Guimerà's lesser-known plays.[34] Taneta's mixed feelings for Francesc and Marcó cause her great suffering and provide much of the passionate drama Belbel admires in its author. He observes how, during the rehearsal, the actors became passionately attached to the play, with the result that 'the spectators will see a succession of very young actors really making an effort and doing it really well'.[35] As in his production of *The Merchant of Venice*, it is precisely the visceral passion of the play that Belbel was at pains to bring out. However, it is not just heterosexual love that Belbel sees in *En Pólvora*, and his production supports his view that Toni's love for Marcó is more sexual than brotherly.[36] The presence of homoerotic desire in this play is as delicately suggested as it was in Belbel's production of *Desig*.[37] At the same time, love in *La filla del mar* is hardly orthodox, and more of the type that traditional society would condemn. This applies in particular to the Don Juan figure of the play, Pere Màrtir, but also to that between him and his fellow outsider, Àgata.

His highlighting of the racial or sexual outsider is by no means the only – or even the principal – feature of Belbel's directing. A detailed analysis of some of his major productions will illustrate some of the others.

### *Marivaux:* Les Fausses confidences

His 2006 production of this play, staged a few months before he took over as Artistic Director of the TNC, proved popular with audiences, attracting 34,546 spectators during its two-month run, but provoking a mixed critical reaction. As is well known, Marivaux was heavily influenced by the *commedia dell'arte*, and worked with the Theâtre Italienne in productions of his own plays. However, by the time of *Les Fausses confidences* (1737), *commedia* figures had become blended

---

[34] See George, 'Belbel Rescues a Forgotten Guimerà' (forthcoming).

[35] 'els espectadors hi veuran un seguit d'actors molt joves esforçant-se al màxim i fent-ho realment bé' (Anon., 'Entrevista a Sergi Belbel', in *Àngel Guimerà, "En Pólvora", versió i direcció de Sergi Belbel* (Barcelona: Teatre Nacional de Catalunya, 2006), 20–21, p. 23).

[36] See George, 'Belbel Rescues a Forgotten Guimerà' (forthcoming).

[37] See below, pp. 84–85. This is in contrast to the more overt homo-eroticism in some of Belbel's own plays, such as *Forasters* and, more especially, *Carícies*.

with non-*commedia* characters to a much greater extent than in Marivaux's earlier Italianate plays. He was now more interested in the psychological than in the physical and purely comic aspects of his characters, and in the interplay between them. Masks and disguises are not used in a literal sense as in the *commedia* but rather are psychological.[38] The only comic servant from the *commedia* to survive is Arlequin, and here he plays the role of the stupid servant.[39]

The world portrayed by Marivaux is uncertain and duplicitous. Nothing is as it seems and appearances are deceptive. The play is set in contemporary Paris, at the time of the financial crash caused by John Law, in which Marivaux himself was ruined. It accurately portrays a society in flux, as the old values of the aristocracy and the bourgeoisie could no longer be relied upon. The play deals with moral issues, in particular the cunning servant Dubois's use of duplicitous means to secure Amarinte for Dorante. However, as Connon points out, Dorante is not a fortune hunter, but is genuinely in love, while Amarinte is no young innocent, but a widow and therefore presumably well versed in matters of the heart.

For some critics Belbel's production accentuated the comic, spectacular aspects of the play at the expense of the subtlety of the language. In some ways, with his emphasis on the comic, he was following Jean-Louis Barrault in his 1952 production. Barrault – who played the role of Dubois – reintroduced a strong *commedia* element to the play. As Connon says, 'Arlequin is there to remind us that, despite all of the emotion and moral questioning, *Les Fausses confidences* is ultimately a comedy', while Ragué opines: 'his aim is to entertain'.[40] Belbel was also criticised for his vulgarisation of some of the language of the play,[41] adding to what some critics saw as a loss of subtlety. It will be

---

[38] Detailed information on this play is found in Derek Connon, 'Marivaux's *Les Fausses confidences*', Exeter Modern Languages Tapes, no. F317, 1987. I am most grateful to Professor Connon, a colleague at Swansea University, for providing me with a copy of the tape.

[39] This was his original role in the *commedia dell'arte*: it was only subsequently that he became the clever, scheming character who has passed into history.

[40] 'su objetivo es el de distraer, el de divertir' (María-José Ragué, 'La espectacularidad del TNC', *El Mundo*, 25 November 2005, p. 70).

[41] Belbel was responsible for the translation and the adaptation.

useful, therefore, to consider what he was aiming to do with the production, and how he went about achieving it.

He thought long and hard about which of the TNC spaces would be better suited to his production. He felt that, if he used the Sala Petita, the version would be less spectacular, and more intimate. He opted for the Sala Gran, which meant a very different sort of spectacle would ensue:

> If you want to do a work subtly, delicately, then don't choose the Sala Gran because it won't allow you to. The physical conditions of this theatre won't allow it. If you're doing a Chekhov, you either do it rather like an opera or you put it on in another space because it won't go well with that architecture. It's a space for great comedies, for great classical works, for great tragedies but not for certain types of subtle drama.[42]

The length of the spectacle matched the size of the stage. It lasted for around three and a half hours, with two long intervals. Several critics felt that the evening – and the intervals in particular – were far too long, although Marcos Ordóñez, arguably Spain's most demanding and knowledgeable theatre critic, felt that the time flew by![43] Belbel himself points out that Marivaux's own premiere of the play lasted nine hours: 'it's fantastic that, when Marivaux himself premiered *Les Fausses confidences*, due to its resounding success, and the laughter of the audience, the production lasted nine hours'.[44]

Belbel set the action not in mid-eighteenth-century France but in 1940s Hollywood. His original intention had been to put on the play in

---

[42] 'Si vols fer una obra amb matisos, amb una delicadesa, no vagis a la Sala Gran perquè no t'ho permet. Les condicions físiques d'aquesta sala no t'ho permeten. Si tu fas un Txèjov, o ho fas amb un aire operístic, o millor que el posis en un [*sic*] altra sala perquè no s'hi adiu allò amb aquesta arquitectura. És un espai per a grans comèdies, per a grans obres de teatre clàssic, per a grans tragèdies, però no per subtilitats de segons quin tipus de dramatúrgia' (Albert Miret, 'Sergi Belbel parla sobre *Les falses confidències*', http://www. teatral.net/asp/traientpunta/cos.asp?idtraient=41, p. 1, accessed 3 December 2008). This is a fascinating interview for anyone who wishes to understand Belbel's purpose and methods in this and other plays, as well as his view on public and private theatres.

[43] 'La novela de un joven pobre', *El País*, Babelia section, 7 January 2006, p. 14.

[44] 'és fantàstic que quan Marivaux va estrenar *Les falses confidències* ell

the Sala Petita, which, as we saw above, would have implied a very different kind of production from the one that eventually emerged. However, as he explains to J. Antón, the idea of setting it in Hollywood provided him with the key to making it a large-scale spectacle and playing it in the Sala Gran: 'this key was the iconographical parallel with the great Hollywood comedies of the 1940s'.[45] In the same interview Belbel reveals that he and the actors began by viewing fourteen screwball comedies, which, with their emphasis on duplicity, amorality and game play, presented clear parallels with Marivaux:

> We immersed ourselves in Cukor, Howard Hawks, Preston Sturges … Those films have a 'delinquent' style, a freedom against the moral code of the day, implicit sexual bombs. All of that was a key to our playing Marivaux as we wanted, and to revealing all the richness and power of the world of the female protagonist.[46]

If Cukor, Hawks and Sturges were the directors of reference, then, according to Antón, Katharine Hepburn, Barbara Stanwyck and Marilyn Monroe were the iconic actresses, while the sumptuous costumes supported the atmosphere that Belbel was trying to create. As if to reinforce the Hollywood link, Laura Conejero's Amarinte wore several elegant costumes in the course of the play, including a trouser suit, a long mauve dress and a long dress with furs. Míriam Iscla's Dubois was clad in a waistcoat, dress coat, and striped trousers – with 'his' hair parted on the left and greased to one side.

The set was every bit as elegant as the costume (see Figure 2), and received praise from most critics. Ragué was particularly fulsome:

mateix, el propi autor, de l'èxit esclatant que va tenir, de les riallades de la gent, la funció es va estirar nou hores' (Miret, p. 2).

45 'esta clave fue el paralelismo iconográfico con las grandes comedias de Hollywood de los años cuarenta' (J. Antón, 'Belbel monta Marivaux al estilo de las comedias clásicas de Hollywood', *El País*, 15 November 2005, p. 44). The 'golden age' of Hollywood was also clearly in Belbel's admiring mind in his 2001 production for the Centro Dramático Nacional of Jardiel Poncela's *Madre (el drama padre)* at Madrid's Teatro La Latina.

46 'Nos empapamos de Cukor, de Howard Hawks, de Preston Sturges … Esas películas tienen un estilo gamberro, una libertad contra el código moral imperante, unas bombas sexuales implícitas. Todo eso era una clave para interpretar Marivaux como queríamos, y mostrando toda la riqueza y poderío del mundo de la protagonista.'

2. Laura Conejero and Eduard Farelo in *Les falses confidències*, Teatre Nacional de Catalunya, 2005–06.

It's a luxurious and elegant set, which highlights and gives movement to the action with its beautiful choreography and splendid
costumes, with a real American cinema feel. It's a luxurious and
brilliant production with actors who move with agility over the huge
stage.[47]

Belbel used the full width of the large stage in the Sala Gran, with an
ingenious set devised by Max Glaenzel and Estel Cristià.[48] Apparently

[47] 'Es una escenografía lujosa y elegante que realza y da movimiento a la
acción en su bella coreografía y su espléndido vestuario, todo con un *look* de
cine americano. Es una lujosa y brillante puesta en escena con unos actores
que se mueven con agilidad por el vasto escenario' (María-José Ragué, 'La
espectacularidad del TNC').

[48] With the skilful collaboration of stage designers Max Glaenzel and
Estel Cristià, Belbel has generally been successful in using this space, which is

there had been resentment in some circles about the perceived cost of the set. Belbel addresses the issue and puts the record straight in the Miret interview in *Teatralnet*, revealing that the set was recycled from the one used in his production of Rossini's opera *Il viaggio a Reims* at the Teatre Liceo in 2003 (p. 4). It was appropriate to the elegance, subterfuge and simmering sexuality of the production. It consisted of three sections, and gradually moved from left to right over the course of the play (at a rate of 3mm per second!). He says that this is a cinematic technique:

> It's a technique I like a lot, applying winks to the cinema in the theatre, because we have a very cinematographic culture, and because I think that we have to tear down frontiers and use elements from the cinema in the theatre just as cinema people have fed off the theatre throughout the twentieth century.[49]

It also suggests, perhaps, that everything shifts and is unstable in the elegantly duplicitous world of the play. The action begins at the front of the house, stage right, as a car arrives at the mansion, with the ultra-green grass and wide driveway providing an early indication of the social class of the protagonists. It then centres mainly on the inside of the mansion, around a stairway, table, chair, and decanter at the foot of the stairs, with the outside steps and green grass still visible. It finally moves to the garden on the left side of the building, the garden being an appropriate setting for the romantic happy ending.[50]

not easy to fill; see, for example, the comments below on his production of *En Pólvora*. However, in my opinion, his 2009 production of Gogol's *The Government Inspector* was less successful in this respect. The stage was filled by a very large set, but this in some ways appeared redundant, as most of the action took place in a relatively reduced area at the front of the stage. One wonders whether Belbel's much greater familiarity with the idiom of the Italian and, in particular, the French eighteenth-century plays has influenced his ability to stage them more successfully than a Russian play, whose language he does not know.

49 'És una tècnica que a mi m'agrada moltíssim, aplicar picades d'ullet del cinema en el teatre, perquè tenim una cultura molt cinematogràfica, i perquè jo crec que les fronteres cal tombar-les i cal aprofitar coses del cinema pel teatre igual que la gent del cinema s'alimenta del teatre, al llarg del segle XX' (Miret, p. 4).

50 The idea of the set that slowly moves was Belbel's, I was informed by

There were a number of places or objects that served as means of concealment. In the opening scene, Arlequí, the stupid and lazy servant, conceals for future use a bottle of whisky in a plant pot, which is placed at the entrance to the house, only for Dubois, the clever servant, to drink it. This is a neat way of highlighting how Arlequin has been supplanted in his role by a more sophisticated, socially aware character. Laura Conejero made use of a screen to indicate her feelings towards the lovestruck Dorante. She took off one dress, just showing some thigh to Dorante, before donning her sexy dress, and then telling him she intended to marry the Count. Her teasing is all part of the game, of course, but costume, subterfuge (with the aid of a suitable screen) and splendid acting combined to produce an elegantly sensual scene.[51] Its barely concealed sexual desire is an example of the director's interpretation of the 38-year-old widow Amarinte's overwhelming sexual needs: 'she needs love and sex. Her body tells her it is now or never'.[52] Furthermore, for Belbel the play is about a woman who asserts her sexual freedom, which he compares with a contemporary homosexual man coming out, another instance, perhaps, of the playwright/director's concern with sexual difference. As was noted above, what he saw as a rebellion against a restrictive moral code was one of the principal reasons for his setting the play in 1940s Hollywood.

Conejero was part of an acting team that drew high praise from most critics. Perhaps the most interesting piece of casting was that of T de Teatre actress Míriam Iscla in the role of Dubois.[53] According to

the set designer Max Glaenzel, who called the set a 'great cake' ('un gran pastís'). He agreed with my comments that the realism of both *Les Fausses confidences* and *Forasters* was more apparent than real, and undermined by, for example, the shifting of the stage in both plays, which lent an element of stylisation to the productions.

[51] Begoña Barrena highlights Belbel's use of appropriate props: 'a column for Dubois to hide behind or for Marton, in the service of Amarinte, to flirt with Dorante; a screen for Amarinte to change dresses' ('una columna para que Dubois se esconda o Marton, al servicio de Amarinte, coquetee con Dorante; un biombo para que Amarinte se cambie de vestido') ('Entre Hollywood y la Italia del XVI', *El País*, 25 November 2005, p. 41).

[52] 'necesita amor y sexo. El cuerpo le dice que es ahora o nunca' (Antón interview).

[53] T de Teatre is an all-female group of Catalan actresses who perform mainly rapid-fire, ironic, bittersweet comedies, including two part-written by Belbel, *Homes!* (1994) and *Criatures* (1998).

Santiago Fondevila, this was because, in Belbel's view, 'the astuteness, intelligence and ability to manipulate shown by Dubois belong more to the female sex than to the male'.[54] It is only at the end of the play that she reveals her true gender. For Belbel, this character 'is the Revolution fifty years before it happened'.[55] One is reminded of a similar historical gloss, looking towards a more revolutionary future, in his creation of the character of Vailet in *En Pólvora*, just as the feminisation of Dubois seems to anticipate Belbel's conversion of Minguet to Mingueta in that play.[56] Dubois is a consummate actor, a controlling servant and puppet master, turning emotions on and off, facilitating the love of his master, in a similar manner to that of Crispín, Jacinto Benavente's comic servant in his 1907 version of the *commedia dell'arte, Los intereses creados*.[57]

Another familiar feature of Belbel's productions that is repeated in *Les Fausses confidences* is the presence of music, composed by Albert Guinovart. The jazzy 1940s music at the start sets the tone and mood. When Amarante and Dorante first meet each other, their love at first sight is evoked with a stylised gaze, backed up with Glenn Miller-style big band music. The dancing and singing of 'Què és l'amor?' ('What is Love?') that accompanies the champagne reinforces the sense of a happy ending but, as ever, Belbel provides a final surprise, as the orchestra plays a riff from the *Marseillaise* while Dubois marches towards the French Revolution. Some critics see this as merely accentuating several anachronisms, but Belbel has explained that he was reinforcing his historical gloss: 'Dubois's final march means: "issue resolved, I'm off to sort out other things", ending at the barricades holding aloft the flag of the Revolution.'[58]

---

54 'la astucia, inteligencia y capacidad de manipulación que demuestra Dubois son más propias del sexo femenino que del masculino' ('Viuda rica, hombre pobre' ('Rich Widow, Poor Man'), *La Vanguardia*, 15 November 2005, p. 39).

55 'és la Revolució cinquanta anys abans de produir-se' (Miret, p. 3).

56 See George, 'Belbel Rescues a Forgotten Guimerà' (forthcoming).

57 For an analysis of this play, within the tradition of the *commedia dell'- arte*, see David George, *The History of the* Commedia dell'arte *in Modern Hispanic Literature with Special Attention to the Work of García Lorca* (Lewiston/Queenston/Lampeter: The Edwin Mellen Press, 1995), pp. 59–64.

58 'La marxa final de Dubois vol dir: "assumpte resolt, vaig a resoldre altres temes" per acabar a la barricada enarborant la bandera de la Revolució'

## Two Goldoni plays

Belbel's other excursions into the eighteenth century are the two Goldoni plays he has staged to date: *La locandiera* (as *L'hostelera*), which premiered at Barcelona's Grec Summer Festival in 1995, and the *Trilogia della Villeggiatura* (presented as *L'estiueig*, 1999). Like *Les Fausses confidences*, *L'estiueig* was staged at the TNC's Sala Gran, and it shared a number of features with the later production. This time, Belbel used period costumes, designed to emphasise elegance. In broad terms, both plays are social comedies. Belbel's *Trilogia* is performed as an elegant, stylised comedy, and some scenes are played with slightly exaggerated irony. His view is that 'Goldoni's portrait of the bourgeoisie becomes particularly caustic and critical in one of his most complex plays.'[59] The age-old theme of love versus economic interest is played out through the central character Jacinta and her finally unsuccessful attempt to marry the man she loves.

Two of the actors play similar roles to the ones they were to perform in the Marivaux play, reinforcing a sense of familiarity (or repetition). Jordi Banacolocha plays the not very bright father, Laura Conejero the clever, vibrant, scheming daughter, Jacinta, who is used to getting her way. However, unlike her Portia in *The Merchant of Venice* and Amarante in *Les Fausses confidences*, this time she is unlucky. Her unhappy marriage to the man her father wants her to marry contrasts with the happy outcome for the two servants. As duty wins out over love, Belbel highlights the contrast between the two couples through the static situation onstage of the unhappy couple set against the joyous

---

(Miret, p. 3). In response to Miret's question: 'You are telling me about the French Revolution in a 1930s film, with a 1940s Cadillac and a 1950s Biscuter' ('M'estàs parlant de la Revolució francesa en una pel·licula dels anys 30, amb un Cadillac dels anys 40 i un Biscuter dels 50'), Belbel replies: 'We were conscious of all these anachronisms from the outset [...] It's not the first time that mixing anachronisms and symbols has been done in the theatre; we did it deliberately and wholeheartedly, and fully aware of what we were doing' ('Tots aquests anacronismes ja els sabíem d'entrada. [...] És una cosa que en teatre no és la primera vegada que es fa això de barrejar anacronismes i símbols, que fem totalment a consciència i jugant-hi a fons i amb coneixement de causa'; p. 3).

[59] 'el retrat que Goldoni fa de la burgesia es torna especialment àcid i crític en una de les seves obres més complexes' (Sergi Belbel, Programme note to the production).

jumping of the servants. Physical movement across the whole stage is a consistent feature of Belbel's directing style and is particularly well illustrated in his production of Guimerà's *En Pólvora*.[60]

The trilogy's first and third parts featured a two-storey building, with stairs to balcony. There were flexible spaces a quarter and halfway up the stairs, so that the characters could move around in some exchanges: this was also a feature of *En Pólvora*. In the second part of the trilogy, rocks and grass are used to represent the countryside in a non-naturalistic way, and to provide a contrast with the elegant city environment of Part One,[61] while the presence of a space under the rocks at the front of the stage for characters to meet and talk is another instance of Belbel's creative use of space.

Contrasting light and darkness are employed too, although much more sparingly than in his earlier production of *The Merchant of Venice*. As in most Belbel productions, music plays a role in his *Trilogia*. An orchestra is present throughout, playing music, composed by Albert Guinovart, which enhances the neo-classical feel of the production.[62] The design of the buildings and the sense of balance in a bitchy, hypocritical conversation between Jacinta and Victoria on what they will wear for the trip further emphasise Belbel's approach to directing at the Sala Gran, as do the dresses worn by the two ladies (Jacinta peach, Victoria mauve), who are seated on period chairs.

In short, Belbel's versions of the French and Italian eighteenth century are essentially traditional, despite the historical glosses. The scenery and the costumes are elegant, lavish even, and music reinforces a sense of slightly decadent splendour. They are excellent examples of twenty-first-century Belbel: gone is the minimalism of the earlier

---

60 See George, 'Belbel Rescues a Forgotten Guimerà' (forthcoming).

61 The contrast, of course, is more apparent than real, as the upper classes transport their possessions and their lifestyle to the countryside.

62 In his review of the production, Pablo Ley considers the orchestra a waste of money, 'Un reloj mal montado' ('A Badly Assembled/Staged Clock', *El País*, 15 November 1999, p. 51, consulted at http://www.lexisnexis.com: 80/uk/nexis/results/docview/docview.do?docLinkInd=true&risb=21_T432702 0767&format=GNBFI&sort=BOOLEAN&startDocNo=1&resultsUrlKey=29 _T4327020770&cisb=22_T4327020769&treeMax=true$treeWidth=0&csi=1 66103&docNo=9, accessed 8 August 2008).

period as plays have been designed to fit the Sala Gran, which is the space most associated with recent Belbel productions.

### *Benet i Jornet:* Desig

Clearly, Belbel has had to confront rather different problems when directing plays by his own contemporaries, but he applies the pragmatism one has come to associate with him in order to meet the challenge.[63] *Desig* is one of four plays by Benet i Jornet that Belbel has directed to date, and their close friendship is well known, as is the mutual influence they have exercised on each other's work. Indeed, *Desig* is dedicated to Belbel and to his predecessor as Artistic Director of the Teatre Nacional de Catalunya, Domènec Reixac. It contains a number of themes which Belbel takes up in his own plays, including the difficulty of communication between human beings, mid-life crisis, love and sexuality, and identity. The lack of understanding between the Husband and She is clear in the first scene (as it is in many Belbel plays, such as *Caricies* and *A la Toscana*). It also contains the same kind of 'dialogue of the deaf' to which reference was made in Chapter 1,[64] but without the absurdist humour that one finds in *Minim.mal Show* and *Després de la pluja*, for instance. In contrast to *A la Toscana*, in *Desig* it is a female character (She, in this case) who suffers from the crisis. She claims not to have a problem with being forty, but seems to lack energy and purpose, and finds her married life boring. Unlike some of Belbel's own plays, in particular *Caricies*, the couple are not violent or aggressive towards each other, either linguistically or in their actions. At one point she declares that she would like her husband to shout at her,[65] but there is no obvious cause of their problems, and only gradually is the audience brought to realise that her crisis is linked with her sexuality, specifically her closet lesbianism. It is not until the end of the play that she 'comes out', and finds the tranquillity she was lacking, in her tender embrace with the Woman.

[63] For his pragmatic approach to his role as Artistic Director of the Teatre Nacional de Catalunya (TNC), see Chapter 5.

[64] See Chapter 1, p. 13.

[65] Josep Maria Benet i Jornet, *Desig*, 2nd edn (Valencia: Tres i Quatre, 2000), p. 57; Josep Maria Benet i Jornet, *Desire*, trans. Sharon G. Feldman, in *Modern Catalan Plays*, ed. John London and David George (London: Methuen, 2000), pp. 105–74, p. 120).

The intimate, suggestive nature of the play is reflected in the simple, uncluttered stage. There is minimal scenery,[66] a feature that is evident from the first scene, which is set in a sparsely furnished room in the couple's house. The mysterious road on which the seemingly chance meetings between She and the Man take place is set against a geometrical hill. It is an empty and unreal landscape, reminiscent of Belbel's own *En companyia d'abisme* (1988), while this landscape of the mind underlines the fact that *Desig* is very far from the realist or naturalist tradition. This idiom seems to make a surprise appearance in the scene that follows She's monologue, as the café in which the Woman is sitting when She and the Man arrive is naturalistically evoked, and, on the face of it, the scene is no more than an overheard conversation by an interested bystander. The appearance of naturalism in this and other scenes in the play – most notably those between the Man and She – is deceptive. It is, however, appropriate in the sense that it reinforces the fact that their relationship lacks imagination, and that the true sexuality (the desire of the title) of She is hidden in her subconscious until the prompting of the Man and the Woman brings it to the surface. The seemingly naturalistic scenes (set in the family home or the café) suggest that her ordinary, everyday existence (including her married life) is no more than a mask for her true self. The play seems to question the nature of one's authentic identity, and to suggest that we are really no more than masks.

Through the use of lighting, music, fine acting and superb pacing (with particularly suggestive pauses), Belbel's production beautifully builds up to the audience's realisation of the existence of She's true sexuality.[67] Lighting is used carefully and to powerful effect in the four monologues interspersed throughout the play. When each character speaks their specific monologue, their faces are only gradually illuminated. As Josep Maria Pou (the Man) begins to speak his, there is a

---

[66] This may be an occasion when viewing the production on a video recording may have given me a somewhat erroneous picture. When I discussed the production with Benet i Jornet he insisted that it was, in fact, quite spectacular, in no way a chamber work, but one in which the use of spaces was rather complex.

[67] See, for example, Enric Gallén, '*Desig*', consulted at http://www. pencatala.cat/ctdl/autors_catalans/josep_m_benet_i_jornet/obra/desig.php, accessed 25 March 2009.

very faint light on his face (this is the first we see of him) – with just his forehead, nose and cheeks illuminated; the music continues playing, all reflecting the strangeness and mystery of the words, with references to cold and clouds, and to old age. Gradually, the whole face and shoulders are lit as the urgency of words is mixed with a sense of mystery. Then, as the monologue nears its close, the light is once more just focused on the face, as it becomes smaller, fading into the background.

The lighting is used sparingly and suggestively throughout the rest of the play too. As in the monologues, the road scenes are only partially lit. The light is focused on the centre of the stage, shining from above the hill, which is in darkness, and there is a bluish hue over the road. The sense of darkness punctuated by shafts of light seems to convey the essence of this mysterious play in which the dark secrets of She are only gradually illuminated, while her love also recalls the *amor oscuro*, or dark love, with which readers of García Lorca's poetry would be so familiar, as well as reinforcing once more Belbel's concern with deviant sexuality. Lighting is one of the devices used by the director to suggest what one might call the landscapes of the mind, while its subtle variations offer the audience signs that this is a play whose every detail is suggestive and a clue to the unfolding, understated drama.

Sound, too, played an important part in Belbel's production. The fade to complete darkness between scenes is accompanied by the playing of somewhat eerie music, while She's anguished monologue is preceded by slightly mournful string music. The presence of slow, soft music in a number of scenes enhances the delicacy of the play, especially in the final scene, in which the two women simply hold hands and touch each other.

Another sound that punctuates the play is that of a telephone ringing. It may be that Belbel owes something to this feature in his two latest plays, *Mòbil* and *A la Toscana*, in which the mobile phone becomes a frustrating barrier to communication between human beings and serves to highlight a lack of interaction in families and between couples. In *Desig*, She receives several mystery phone calls that one assumes are from the Woman, although doubt is maintained as to whether these are real or simply the product of her imagination and her suppressed subconscious struggling to make itself felt. A particularly poignant phone call occurs in Scene 4. In the previous scene, the Husband had revealed his own feelings of frustration in his monologue, in which he curses the day he met his wife (p. 150; p. 122). He presents himself as a patient man; but waiting, as in Lorca's *Así que pasen cinco años* (*When Five Years Pass*), and, of course, in *Waiting for Godot*, also brings tension and suffering. This scene fades (with no dimming of the light on this occasion) into the next, which teases the audience into anticipating reconciliation between man and wife. However, the element of frustration that characterises the play is provided when, just as they are about to make love, the telephone rings. Once more there is no one at the other end, but, following the resulting row between them, She rushes off declaring that 'this time I'll get there' (*Desire*, p. 162).[68] This is the clearest indication that the telephone is no more than a symbol of her true sexuality striving to express itself when, under the influence of drink, she was attempting to reassert her heterosexual – but false – relationship with her husband.

If the staging is a key to the audience's understanding of the play, then the quality of the acting is no less so. The understated yet intense performances that highlighted the suppressed emotion that character-ises the play are especially evident in the four monologues. The wife's is preceded by passionate and insistent string music, which links this scene with the preceding one in which She rushes off following the interrupted lovemaking with her husband and their subsequent row. She is torn between maintaining her relationship with her husband – she is not satisfied with the relationship for reasons that we gradually discover, but does not hate him – and heeding her inner voices, which are externalised by the presence of the Woman and the Man.

As I have suggested, it could be argued that the Man and the Woman are external expressions of the wife's internal anguish, and the under-stated performance idiom of Josep Maria Pou and Imma Colomer is central to the evocation of the two characters. Nowhere are these more evident than in the café scene between them and the wife (Scene 3). The Woman is trying to remember the only time she fell in love; she makes a paper butterfly and places it on the glass, to the clear unease of She. The latter does not like the frank discussion of sexuality and of how the Woman masturbated when her love was not returned, which seems to anticipate the difficulty of accepting one's sexuality in Belbel's own *Carícies* and *Forasters*. When She tells the Woman about

---

68 'aquesta vegada hi arribaré' (*Desig*, p. 152).

how she loves her husband, the latter is upset, and declares that she is still in love with the same person – which makes She very uncomfortable. The Woman describes how she and the person made love, but giving no indication of the gender of the person in question. She is clearly tortured by the description – the Woman looks at her, but, significantly, She does not return her gaze, saying simply that she has not understood her story, and leaves.

This whole scene is played slowly and gently, and with beautifully understated emotion; it is an excellent example of how a sensitive director is able to enrich and clarify a play that does not lend itself to rapid comprehension. Belbel's production demonstrates how he respects plays (be they classics or contemporary works), and highlights their characteristics, subtly bringing out their meaning. The acting, lighting, stage design and music enhance the overall quality, and blend together into a finely tuned whole. At the same time, one may point to a further link between his own plays and some of those he has directed. As in the two Guimerà plays and his own *Carícies*, *Sóc Lletja* and *Forasters*, Belbel gives prominence to alternative sexualities, which is intimately linked to the outsider theme.

### *Bernard-Marie Koltès,* Quai Ouest
The outsider is also prominent in this complex and atmospheric play, which Belbel translated and directed in a 2002 production (as *Moll Oest*) at Barcelona's Teatre Romea.[69] Set in a desolate abandoned port on an unnamed river in an unnamed city, the production conveys the menace and the uncertainty of this world, while, in Delgado's words,

> Belbel's taut, brilliant translation captures both the colloquial excesses and poetic registers of the French text. And the haunting production, evolving against a mutating skyline which echoes the moods of the play, renders a landscape where nothing is sacred and everything can be bought and sold if the price is right.[70]

The use of sound (seagulls, distant fog horns, barking dogs and strains

---

[69] I was able to view a video of a performance of both this play and *El temps de Planck* at the premises of Focus, S.A. in Barcelona.

[70] Maria M. Delgado, 'In Barcelona', *Plays International*, September 2002, pp. 26–29, p. 28.

of Arabic song) reinforces the haunting atmosphere, as does the mysterious steam that occasionally rises from the stage.

The use of space in this production was of necessity very different
from Belbel's recent ones in the TNC's Sala Gran. Rather than attempt
to fill a huge stage, his *Quai Ouest* often burst out of the Romea stage.
Characters moved in and out of the audience, they would sit at the edge
of the stage, facing them or speaking to other characters who had
moved to the stalls, or climb up the scaffolding (at the side of the stalls)
that reinforced the effect of the industrial wasteland. In this production
Belbel appears to be 'speaking' to the audience. The suggestion of
water behind the steps at the back of the stage indicated the river on
which the quay is situated and into which the body of Maurice Koch is
thrown towards the end of the play.[71] In Marcos Ordóñez's view, the
Romea is quite the wrong space for this production:

> *Quai Ouest* cries out for any space other than an Italian-style theatre,
> and in the Romea, even though they have covered the stalls with a
> false roof that is full of holes and rusty, having the characters move
> about among the seats distracts us time and again.[72]

My own feeling is that the movement and a sense of characters trying
to burst out of a space in which they were trapped convincingly
conveyed the constant feeling that they did not wish to be where they
were, and wanted to break out and move off to they knew not where. In
contrast to the rather static nature of Belbel's 1991 production of
*Carícies* at the same theatre,[73] the movement in his *Quai Ouest* not

---

[71] In Delgado's view, the river serves both to suggest that the characters
are trapped and to evoke a world beyond the desolate setting: 'the water which
runs at the back of the stage is both an escape, a symbol of the void beyond
and a fence which hems the characters in' ('In Barcelona', p. 28).

[72] '*Moll Oest* pide a gritos cualquier espacio menos el de un teatro a la
italiana, y en el Romea, por mucho que hayan recubierto la platea con un falso
techo agujereado y roñoso, los paseos de los actores entre las filas del patio de
butacas nos 'sacan de situación' una y otra vez' ('Koltès, siempre hacia el
oeste', *El País*, Babelia section, 3 August 2002, viewed at http://www.elpais.
com/articulo/arte/Koltes/siempre/Oeste/elpbabart/20020803elpbabart_9/Tes,
accessed 3 March 2009). Despite his criticism of what he considered the
inappropriate nature of the space, Ordóñez's view of the production is highly
favourable.

[73] This element was greater in comparison with the more fluid action of

only resulted in an entirely appropriate sense of restlessness but was also testimony to his growing subtlety as a director.

In addition to their movement around and on and off the stage, the physical gestures of the actors are significant in this production. As in Belbel's own *En companyia d'abisme*, the relationship between a given pair of characters in *Quai Ouest* is one of dominance and subservience, as one might expect from a play in which, in typical Koltès fashion, human relationships are conceived as a commercial transaction. The terms of the transaction often vary in the course of an individual scene, with the dominant character taking the place of the subservient one, and vice versa.[74] Pleading, kneeling, lying stretched on the stage supported by an elbow, one character leaning over another, are all positions taken at various points in the play by actors who convert this into a highly physical production. At one point Lluís Soler's injured Maurice Koch is kicked off the stage by Julieta Serrano's Cécile, only to be affectionately picked up by his secretary, Laura Conejero's Monique. Hunching, sitting and slow movement increase later in the play, as the older characters become physically exhausted. Indeed, some of the later scenes resemble a kind of visual frieze. The physicality and physical positioning demanded of the actors of this Belbel production recalls that of some of Belbel's own plays: *En companyia d'abisme* once more comes to mind.

One character, of course, functions only through his presence and his limited physical actions. This is socially the lowest-class character in the play, the Arab/African Abad. In Delgado's words, 'Babou Cham renders an enigmatic Abad who observes the action from the back steps, a shadow haunting the men in Cécile's life.'[75] He does not speak, but Ordóñez perceptively writes of 'the aura of menace latent in the silent Abad (Babou Cham), which terrorises the other characters each time he holds his incongruous Kalashnikov in his hand'.[76] This

Ventura Pons's 1997 cinema adaptation of *Carícies*: for further details see Chapter 3, pp. 97–98.

[74] This is exactly the situation in Federico García Lorca's *El público* (*The Public*) (1930).

[75] 'In Barcelona', p. 28.

[76] 'el aura de amenaza latente del silencioso Abad (Babou Cham), que aterroriza a la parroquia cada vez que empuña su incongruente Kaláshnikov' ('Koltès, siempre hacia el oeste').

simmering menace explodes when, with the final action of the play, Abad shoots the preening Charles dead. He speaks no words, but his final action is devastating. This is a further demonstration of how Belbel, so adept at using the verbal tirade in some of his own plays, is also capable – when the time and place require it – of replacing words with actions and gestures.

### Sergi Belbel, *A la Toscana*

If *Quai Ouest* is one example of Belbel's multifaceted activity as a theatre practitioner, the final production to be considered in this chapter, Belbel's own *A la Toscana*, forces us to confront once more the issue of how close the connections are between the writing and the directing processes for this particular author/director. Bombí-Vilaseca, however, suggests that there are significant differences between the two professions:

> In truth the playwright and the director are very different from each other, even though they belong in the same theatrical bag, since directing demands rhythms that have nothing to do with those of the writer, who is alone and is much closer to the world of literature.[77]

Belbel has directed most of his own plays, at least within Catalonia and the rest of Spain. Following the failure of *Mòbil*,[78] he was particularly keen to direct his next (and at the time of writing his latest) play, *A la Toscana*. I attended the Madrid production – at the Teatro de la Abadía – and admit to being rather sceptical before seeing it, wondering whether what seemed to me an interesting but perhaps over-complicated piece could actually work on the stage. What in my view was a successful production was due in no small measure to the quality of the acting (with the same Catalan cast as in the Catalonia production),[79] Belbel's directing, including the use of music and sound

[77] 'La veritat és que la faceta d'autor dramàtic i la de director són, tot i que estan dins el mateix sac teatral, molt diferents, perquè la direcció demana uns ritmes que no tenen res a veure amb els de l'autor, que està sol i té molt més a veure amb l'àmbit literari' (Francesc Bombí-Vilaseca, 'L'escriptura surt quan trobes que la forma va lligada amb el contingut', *Avui* (Cultura), 25 November 2004, pp. x–xi, p. xi).

[78] For further discussion of the failure of this play – and its success in Germany and Denmark – see Chapter 4, pp. 140–49.

[79] There was one change of name in the Spanish-language production, with Jaume being transformed into Santi.

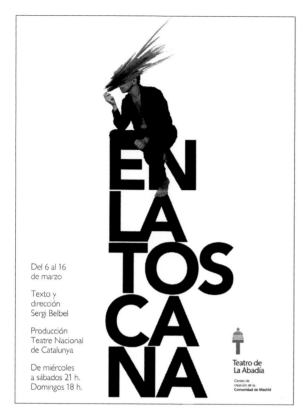

Del 6 al 16
de marzo

Texto y
dirección
Sergi Belbel

Producción
Teatre Nacional
de Catalunya

De miércoles
a sábados 21 h.
Domingos 18 h.

Teatro de
La Abadía

Centro de
creación de la
Comunidad de Madrid

3. Cover design for
the programme for
the production of A
la Toscana, Teatro de
la Abadía, Madrid,
2008.

effects, and the stage design by Max Glaenzel and Estel Cristià. This included the use of a mirror at the back of the stage, which reinforced the theme of narcissistic self-contemplation and added to the audience's identification with Marc, as we too saw ourselves reflected in the mirror. As was observed in Chapter 1, the mirror is a frequent image in Belbel's theatre, often suggesting self-reflection and contemplation, which seemed to be its primary purpose in the Madrid production. The closeness of the audience to the stage of the Abadía was another factor in the sense of identification between audience and actors.[80]

Almost a year after being a spectator at the Abadía, I was able to view the Teatre Nacional de Catalunya production on a video recording, and would add the following observations. The set was essentially

[80] For the imaginative design of the cover of the Abadía production, see Figure 3.

black, white and grey, which heightened the aseptic nature of the
action, suggesting, perhaps, the psychiatrist's studio. On occasions, a
prison seemed to be evoked, as in Scene 8, in which Marc, having just
strangled Joana, desperately felt his way along the wall of the room as
he tried to find her mobile phone, which was ringing. It also allowed
for the occasional splash of colour – in particular red – to be especially
noticeable.[81] One such example occured in the bar scene between Marc
and Jaume in Scene 3. The bare walls, the floor, chair, table and the
clothes of the two men were in black, white and grey, with the only
colour the red of the wine in their glasses. Red was again used effectively in Scene 21, in which Marta and Jaume made love and which
contained the typically Belbelian use of the sudden shock. It began in
darkness, we heard the sounds of their lovemaking, then we saw a
couple covered by a blanket, Marc was revealed to the audience, and
then Marta. She was wearing a red dress and red boots, which
suggested the passion that is entirely appropriate to the scene.

As well as the sparing use of colour, music played a prominent role
in Belbel's productions of *A la Toscana*, in particular in heightening the
contrasts between the relatively calm and tender scenes and those that
are tense or aggressive. The rather gentle music that linked the scenes
early in the play contrasted sharply with the menacing string music that
accompanied Marc's saying that he had been shot, at the end of Scene
2. As Marc's mind became progressively more disturbed, the music
that linked the scenes became stranger and more frightening. After the
rescue in the Third World War scene, Joana's embrace of Marc was
accompanied by soft piano music, followed by lively orchestral music
as the four characters joyfully embraced each other. This faded to
gentle piano music once more, which marked the transition to the next
scene, in which Marc was about to leave home, and in which Joana told
him not to bother to look for her should he return. The mood of this
scene was once more underlined by the tone of the music, which this
time was a melancholy piece for piano and wind instruments, reflecting
perfectly Marc's sadness at the separation.

In both the Barcelona and the Madrid productions, only one of the

---

[81] This device of a bright colour (red, green) punctuating the dominant
black and white was famously used in Federico García Lorca's *La casa de
Bernarda Alba* (1936).

two alternative endings was used, namely the first one, in which Joana does not recognise Marc's voice on the answerphone. The splendour of the Tuscany scene was reflected into a mirror door, with Marc's reflection superimposed on it. He then opened the door, and looked out onto the landscape. This whole visual image allowed the audience to ponder the nature of objective and subjective realities.

## Concluding remarks

One can confidently state that Belbel's work as a director does not fall into the category of directors' theatre as defined by Bradby and Williams, when they write that 'it is a distinguishing feature of directors' theatre that here the director claims the authorial function even though he has not written the original play. Where he is working with a classic text, he will rearrange, cut and rewrite to fit his production concept.'[82] Belbel respects – reveres even – his source text in a very different fashion from the way in which other Catalan directors, in particular Calixto Bieito and Àlex Rigola, respect theirs, and is at pains to re-create settings, dress and atmosphere one can readily associate with the original. To date he has not adopted the radical deconstructive approach so conspicuously favoured by Bieito.[83] Having said that, he will provide historical glosses where appropriate – as, for example, in *Les Fausses confidences* and *En Pólvora* – and he does on occasions favour the open endings, refusing closure, that characterise his own plays. A number of similarities between Belbel the writer and Belbel the director have emerged, in particular his presentation of the racial and sexual outsider. A Belbel production is marked by a creative use of space, while pace and movement over the whole of the stage generally characterise his directing at the TNC's Sala Gran. Over the years he has

---

[82] David Bradby and David Williams, *Directors' Theatre*, Macmillan Modern Dramatists (Basingstoke: Macmillan, 1988), p. 1.

[83] See Maria M. Delgado, 'Journeys of Cultural Transference: Calixto Bieito's Multilingual Shakespeares', *Modern Language Review*, 101:1 (2006), 106–50. See also Maria M. Delgado, 'Staging Excess In and Across the Stages of Europe', in *Contemporary European Theatre Directors*, ed. Maria M. Delgado and Dan Rebellato (Abingdon: Routledge, 2010), pp. 277–97. Bieito enjoys an international reputation as a director, whereas Belbel's is essentially as a writer.

assembled a team that is used to working with him, including actors, designers and composers. My interviews with them have revealed that his approach is to direct as far as possible without conflict, he is extremely methodical, and is careful that the detail of individual scenes does not obscure the vision of the whole play. Despite his traditional approach to directing and his respect for the texts he has directed, Belbel puts his own distinctive mark on them both as director and, in several of them, in his translations. His later productions have mainly been on the large stage of the TNC's Sala Gran, but, despite a general trend away from minimalism and towards maximalism, his production of *A la Toscana* reveals that he is still capable of working more simply and in a smaller space.

# 3

# From Stage to Screen:
# Ventura Pons's Adaptations of the Plays

Belbel has written for the small screen, in particular the TV soap *Secrets de família* (*Family Secrets*), which he co-authored with the novelist Maria Mercè Roca. He has also been tempted to write for the cinema. His first incursion (which remains something of a mystery) ended with his withdrawing from the project during the filming. His second was a collaborative venture with Antonio Chavarrías entitled *Dictado* (*Dictation*), which had to be put on hold when Belbel became Director of the TNC. His third – and apparently most important – venture into the cinema is entitled *Eva*, an ambitious science fiction project that has still to be filmed.[1] Belbel is an avid film spectator, and, as was observed in Chapter 2, had his cast of *Les Fausses confidences* view fourteen Hollywood films in preparation for his production of the play. However, what he said in a 1998 interview about theatre being 'a living thing, where no two performances are the same' seems to suggest that his priorities lie on the stage rather than on the screen.[2] The following extract from a joint interview between Belbel and film-maker Ventura Pons, on the occasion of the premiere of the latter's version of *Forasters*, underlines the point that Belbel's plays are perceived to have a cinematic quality about them, while at the

---

[1] My information on these three ventures comes from Cristina Savall, 'Belbel firma una superproducción cinematográfica' ('Belbel Signs a Cinematographic Super-Production)', *El Periódico de Catalunya*, 29 September 2008, viewed at http://www.elperiodico.com/default.asp?idpublicacio_PK= 46&idioma=CAS&idnoticia_PK=45481&idseccio_PK=1013, accessed 13 October 2008.

[2] 'un fet viu, que no té mai dues funcions idèntiques' (Andreu Sotorra, 'Belbel a la Tarantino', *Avui* DDD, 17 April 1998, viewed at http://www.andreusotorra.com/teatre/entrevista3.html, accessed 20 October 2008).

same time he stresses that he is essentially a playwright not a film scriptwriter:

[V.P.] Sergi Belbel's plays are very cinematographic, playing with narrative discontinuity, and in some cases with narrative deconstruction. I've done this in many films, I've broken conventional narrative rules.

**Do you agree, Sergi Belbel, that your theatre is cinematographic?**

S.B. Many people tell me that. In truth, I watch more cinema than I do theatre, and its influence is very tangible in structures, in games, in breaking the plot–link–ending formula. I do it because I like to, I enjoy playing with that, and the theatre has a very important ludic element that offers challenges to the spectator. That said, I write theatre not film scripts.[3]

Whereas the previous two chapters have been concerned with Belbel's work as a theatrical writer and director, the current one concentrates on how his plays have been adapted to the screen. One such co-production between Galician and Catalan Television brought *Després de la pluja*, as *Después de la lluvia*, to the screen in 2007. This version, directed by Mallorcan director Agustí Villaronga, kept close to the original text, although some minor changes were introduced. For instance, towards the end of the film both the Head of Administration and the Female Managing Director lose their jobs. In his case, it is for sexual corruption because of rumours of his liaison with the lift attendant. As a result, he commits suicide by jumping out of his office

---

3 '[V.P.] Les propostes teatrals de Sergi Belbel són molt cinematogràfiques, amb un joc de la discontinuïtat narrativa, i en alguns casos de la desconstrucció narrativa. Jo ho he fet amb moltes pel·lícules, he trencat amb les normes convencionals del relat.
¿Està d'acord Sergi Belbel que el seu teatre és cinematogràfic?
S.B. M'ho diu molta gent. De fet, veig més cinema que teatre, i la seva influència és molt palpable en estructures, en jocs, en trencar la fórmula argument-nus-desenllaç. Ho faig perquè m'agrada, disfruto jugant amb això, i el teatre té un component lúdic molt important que planteja reptes a l'espectador. Ara bé, escric teatre, no guions de cinema' (Interview with Bernat Salvà in *Avui*, 24 November 2008, consulted at http://www.avui.cat/article/cultura_comunicacio/47155/ventura/pons/sergi/belbel/excel·lim/tot/nomes/falta/la/ gent/ ho/sapiga.html, accessed 5 December 2008).

window, a (male) victim of sexual persecution and the ruthless business world. The rumours about his relationship with the lift attendant
are present in the original play, but there they are one element of the
black, biting comedy. In the television adaptation this particular
element has been converted into tragedy.

Although the adaptation brought *Després de la pluja* – Belbel's most
successful play – to the potentially wide audience of television, by far
the most important figure in the 'stage to screen' adaptations of his
plays is internationally renowned Catalan film director Ventura Pons. It
is no coincidence that Pons began his career in the theatre, and between
the late 1960s and the early 1980s he directed a number of plays,
mainly in Catalan, including *Twelfth Night*, plays by the Catalans Joan
Oliver and Jordi Teixidor, a Catalan adaptation of José Zorrilla's 1844
classic *Don Juan Tenorio* and works by such contemporary foreign
playwrights as Christopher Hampton, and Joe Orton and Richard
O'Brien's *The Rocky Horror Show*. Pons's strong grounding in the
theatre has powerfully influenced his cinema output, and he has stated
that his work with actors has shaped what he does as a film director.[4]

Pons has won numerous prizes for his films, many of which have
been shown in film festivals all over the world. His first film was
*Ocaña, retrat intermitent* (*Ocaña, an Intermittent Portrait*) (1978), a
portrait of the Andalusian painter José Pérez Ocaña, who was a
colourful presence in Barcelona's Rambles and Plaça Reial in the late
1970s. Pons set up his own company, Els Films de la Rambla, in 1985,
since when he has directed such films as *La rossa del bar* (*Blonde in
the Bar*) (1985) and *Què t'hi jugues, Mari Pili?* (*What's Your Bet, Mari
Pili?*) (1990), *Food of Love* (2002), *Amor idiota* (*Idiot Love*) (2005)
and *Animals ferits* (*Wounded Animals*) (2005). It is with his seven
adaptations of works by contemporary Catalan playwrights that Pons
has chosen to pursue a particular Catalan cinema in the 1990s and into
the twenty-first century: two films based on plays by Benet i Jornet –
*Actrius* (*Actresses*) (1996) and *Amic/amat* (*Beloved/Friend*) (1999);
Lluïsa Cunillé's *Barcelona, mapa d'ombres* (*Barcelona, Map of
Shadows*), presented as *Barcelona (un mapa)* (Barcelona: a Map)
(2007); and three Belbel plays, *Carícies* (1998), *Morir (un moment*

---

4  Maria M. Delgado, *Ventura Pons Retrospective*. Publicity leaflet for the
Institute of Contemporary Arts (London), 1999, p. 1.

*abans de morir)*, as *Morir (o no)* (2000) and *Forasters* (2008). Even prior to his adaptations of plays for the screen, Pons's work was very character and situation driven. He loves the language of artifice, and it is not entirely surprising that he should turn once more to the stage for inspiration in the early to mid-1990s. If Belbel is a quintessentially theatrical author who is also a great cinema fan, then Pons is someone who cut his teeth in the theatre, and who has an eye for plays that will transfer successfully to the big screen. Pons explains what attracted him to Belbel's plays, and why he felt they would make good films. In an article, he has explained that, normally, his first interest is in the story, but with Belbel it is his narrative approach that most attracted him. *Carícies*, he explains, allowed him to establish a temporal dislocation whose ending returned to the beginning, in which the ending was already prefigured. In *Morir (o no)* he was able to set up binary opposites, starting from the life-in-Part-One to death-in-Part-Two dichotomy. In *Forasters*, the temporal shifts permitted density, volume and narrative agility. He sums up the importance of Belbel's plays to him thus: 'I think that for many spectators in the world there is a before and after of my first versions of Belbel.'[5]

Belbel and Pons are listed as co-authors of *Carícies* because it is closer to the play than are the other two adaptations, although Belbel did not actually collaborate on it.[6] However, the films are very much the work of Pons, who is in sole charge of the adaptations. Having said that, he does involve Belbel in some way. For instance, in April 2008 I was able to participate in a meeting between the actors and Belbel organised by Pons prior to the shooting of *Forasters*. The aim of the meeting was so that the actors could listen to and question Belbel on how and why he came to write the play.

I have analysed elsewhere Pons's adaptation of *Carícies*,[7] and here

---

5 'Crec que per a molts espectadors del món hi ha un abans i un després de les meves primeres versions de Belbel' (unpublished commentary by Pons that he kindly made available to me).

6 This was confirmed to me in an email correspondence with Ventura Pons (23 November 2008).

7 David George, 'From Stage to Screen: Sergi Belbel and Ventura Pons', *Anales de la Literatura Española Contemporánea*, 27:2 (2002), 89–102. See also Sally Faulkner, *Literary Adaptations in Spanish Cinema*, Colección Támesis, Serie A: Monografías, 202 (London: Tamesis, 2004); Phyllis Zatlin, 'From Stage to Screen: The Adaptations of Ventura Pons', in *Catalan Theatre,*

refer to those features that find echoes in his two other adaptations of Belbel's plays, in particular *Forasters*. I concentrate on this adaptation, his latest, for three reasons. Firstly, as his most recent film at the time of writing, it has received the least critical attention of the three. Secondly, I have published on the play, in which I have a particular interest,[8] and thirdly, I was fortunate enough to be present at part of its shooting, in May 2008.

## *Caricies*

In contrast to *Forasters*, the film script of *Caricies* is almost identical to the play. Such changes as there are, are minor, such as the word for an old people's home, 'asil', becoming the more modern 'residència'. The principal changes involve the setting of the action firmly in Barcelona.[9] In *Caricies* the visual images of the city enhance its fast and aggressive nature, as the speeded-up traffic and metro sequences that link all but the penultimate and final scenes underscore the hostile nature of the relationships between the various pairs of characters. The Barcelona locations also provide a social context for the action, and range from a park where teenagers drink alcohol, to Barcelona's main railway station, to the interior of an old people's home.[10] In *Forasters*, as will be observed, the social contextualising is much more important than the portrayal of a violent city. As in *Forasters*, in *Caricies* Pons

*1975–2006: Politics, Identity, Performance*, ed. Maria M. Delgado, David George and Lourdes Orozco, special issue of *Contemporary Theatre Review*, 17:3 (2007), 434–45, pp. 440–41.

[8] David George, 'Beyond the Local: Sergi Belbel and *Forasters*', *Contemporary Theatre Review*, 17:3 (2007), 398–410.

[9] As Sally Faulkner writes of Pons's adaptation of *Caricies*, 'While in a literary text a space may remain unnamed, this is far more difficult in cinema as the filmed image, unlike the written word, bears the mechanical imprint of place in the very essence of its form' (*Literary Adaptations in Spanish Cinema*, p. 73). It is interesting to compare Pons's Barcelona with that of Woody Allen in his 2008 film, *Vicky, Cristina, Barcelona*. Pons's is much harsher, and more 'authentic', than Allen's superficially glimpsed city.

[10] Anton Pujol perceptively analyses the significance of the wide social panorama of Barcelona captured by the camera in this film, in 'Ventura Pons y la crónica de un territorio llamado Barcelona', *Arizona Journal of Hispanic Cultural Studies*, 13 (December 2009), 61–81 (pp. 65–67).

conveys a modern urban environment, although, in the later film, this is contrasted with the less hectic period of the late 1960s/early 1970s. In *Carícies* he uses some obvious visual images of the urban setting, such as graffiti on the walls, rubbish containers, and the contrast between the affluent and the poor – a feature of any society – that is effectively conveyed through the juxtaposition of the tramp scavenging in the rubbish cart and the bank that lies next to it.

As in *Forasters*, the movement between the identifiable Barcelona locations lends *Carícies* a fluidity that was not present in the play. For example, Belbel's stage directions in Scene 4 of the play make it clear that the whole of the dialogue between the Old Woman and the Old Man (the tramp) takes place in the street beside the rubbish container, whereas, in the film, they move between the street and the bank lobby. Another similarity between the two films is that the camera constantly shifts between internal locations (flats, the old people's home), the stairwell to flats (which, as I have shown, lends an extra structural unity to the film[11]) and the street. This movement contrasts with the more static situation of the stage setting.

### Morir (o no)

Although this adaptation is closer in some respects to the Belbel original, there are more textual changes than in *Carícies*, and in this sense the adaptation is closer to that of *Forasters*. This is especially true of his reduction of long speeches, which produces similar effects to those we shall examine in more detail in *Forasters*. The effects will be illustrated through the following examples. Generally, as in *Forasters*, the film is tighter linguistically than the play, as in a conversation between the film director and his wife in the first scene: 'DIRECTOR: Someone might think it a reactionary story./ WIFE: What are you talking about?/ DIRECTOR: No, but at bottom it is.'[12] The word 'ho' in the Director's second speech replaces a repeated 'una història reaccionària' in the

---

11  See George, 'From Stage to Screen: Sergi Belbel and Ventura Pons'.

12  'DIRECTOR: A algú pot semblar-li una història reaccionària./ DONA: Què dius, ara?/ DIRECTOR: No, però en el fons ho és.' I cite from an unpublished copy of the dialogues for the film, which the director kindly made available to me. The text does not contain directions or page numbers.

play, thus avoiding the repetition of the phrase.[13] Although this is a small, perhaps trivial, example, taken together with other similar ones, it does result in more concentrated dialogue.

Other verbal cuts remove some thematic concerns or character traits that are evident in the play. As was observed in Chapter 1, Belbel is interested in time, particularly in the mathematical nanosecond set against infinity. The nanosecond concept is also present in the first scene of *Morir (un moment abans de morir)*, as the Guonista (Scriptwriter) (not Director as in the film) refers to time stopping in the split second before the motorcyclist's possible death, during which he is offered the choice of a long, comfortable but boring life or a 'heroic', violent death in the accident.[14] Belbel's fascination with time is encapsulated in the 'moment' of the title. Pons removes this and replaces it with 'o no', which encourages the viewer to concentrate on the question of the alternative outcomes in the second part of both play and film rather than on the temporal aspects. Pons shortens all the Scriptwriter's long speeches in this scene, leaving out the following specific sentence about time: 'But in the last tenth of a second before the crash, everything stops.'[15]

Likewise, the hospital patient's description to the nurse in Scene 4 of the play, of how he fell down the stairs, is shortened in the film. The reference to his imagining his students laughing at him as he fell is retained, but the time element in his words 'as I was falling down the stairs, do you know what went through my mind? I had time to think that when I reached the bottom of the stairs I would be dead'[16] – which carry echoes of the halting of time a split second before the motorcyclist's death in Scene 1 – is, like those, omitted. Something similar happens with his description of how his character has changed since the fall (pp. 62–63). The psychological dimension inherent here, and

---

[13] Sergi Belbel, *Morir (un moment abans de morir)*, Teatre 3 i 4 (Valencia: Eliseu Climent, 1995), p. 15.

[14] The Argentinian writer Jorge Luis Borges's short story 'El sur' ('The South', 1944) comes to mind in this context.

[15] 'Però tot just a l'última dècima de segon abans de la topada, tot s'atura' (p. 17).

[16] 'mentre queia per les escales, sap què vaig pensar? Vaig tenir temps per pensar que quan arribés al replà estaria mort' (p. 59).

also, of course, in the fact that the director's wife is a psychiatrist, is far less evident in the film than in the play.

As in Koltès's plays, characters define themselves through language in Belbel's work. Several in *Morir (un moment abans de morir)* are obsessive, rambling individuals. Long speeches are an essential trait of their personalities, and Pons's reduction of their speeches lessens the impact of this trait. A case in point is the mother, whose incessant bombardment of her spoilt young daughter with her inane, hectoring conversation partly contributes to the latter's eventually bolting down her chicken, which leads to her choking. The fact that her ramblings are greatly reduced in the film lessens both the obsessive effect and the sharp and typically Belbelian contrasts between verbal diarrhoea and short, clipped monologues in the form of dialogues.[17] Cinematic time, of course, works differently from theatre time. It is more concentrated and less discursive, and the idiom requires the language to be different. What might work in the theatre would probably seem excessively prolix in the cinema, which, at least in Pons's adaptations of Belbel, relies much more on visual language than do the plays.

Four other characters who ramble far less in the film than in the play are the nurse, the motorcyclist's mother (Senyora) (Lady), the police-woman and the film director's wife. The nurse seems to be a compulsive talker, the mother a pill-popping nervous wreck, the policewoman someone whose nerves are constantly on edge, especially after she has collided with the motorcyclist, and the director's wife a moralising psychiatrist. Belbel's female characters are often tormented and cruel, while Pons looks more sympathetically at women. The fact that they speak less than they do in the plays reduces the neurotic element of their characters. An example of the type of speech that Pons cuts is the following confused rant by the policewoman:

> I always think of things like that when I'm driving. When I'm driving alone. If we don't talk, it's like I was driving alone. You did say you didn't mind if I spoke, didn't you? When I drive alone at night, I think of strange things I never think of. That the only things that exist are me and the car, and the rest ... is like a film: everything has existed previously, not now; that's why everything I see through

---

[17] Pons compensates for the staccato rhythm of Belbel's dialogues by employing stuttering visuals and shrill music.

this screen doesn't exist, but it did exist once. Nothing exists or everything has ceased to exist, it doesn't matter. I don't know if you get my meaning. I'm expressing myself so badly. I don't think you can understand me.[18]

The speech emphasises her extreme nervousness, which is, of course, entirely unsuitable for an officer of the law who is driving a high-speed patrol car. But more than this it indicates a rather disturbed mind and a febrile imagination. Furthermore, the image of the cinema screen suggests the unreality of her experience, and enhances doubt over whether what happened is real or imagined.

Like all of his adaptations of Belbel plays, *Morir (o no)* is situated in Barcelona.[19] In Anton Pujol's words, 'in contrast to the anonymous and invisible modern city of the plays, Pons sets the action firmly in Barcelona; not only in order to open the theatrical action but also as a map he draws to track characters enclosed within the Barcelonan transformation of space'. In comparison with *Carícies*, writes Pujol, 'in *Morir (o no)*, [...] Pons creates a city that is even more out of its territory, with more intense flight lines, although he indicates unambiguously that we are dealing with Barcelona'.[20] The scene between the mother and her daughter who chokes on a chicken bone takes place in a flat in the middle-class Eixample area, while the motorcyclist's mother lives in a house in the lively, previously Catalan working-class area of Gràcia. Pons is precise too about street names. When

---

[18] 'Sempre penso coses d'aquestes quan condueixo. Quan condueixo sola. Si callem, és com si conduís tota sola. Oi que m'has dit que no et molesta que parli? Quan condueixo sola de nit, penso coses estranyes que no penso mai. Que només existim jo i el cotxe, i la resta ... és com una pel·lícula: tot ha existit abans, no ara; per això tot el que veig a través d'aquesta pantalla no existeix, però algun cop sí que va existir. Res no existeix o tot ha deixat d'existir, és igual. No sé si m'entens. M'expresso tan malament. No crec que puguis entendre'm' (p. 81).

[19] The original play is set in 'different spaces of a city' ('diferents espais d'una ciutat') (p. 7).

[20] 'a diferencia de la anónima e invisible ciudad moderna de los textos teatrales, Pons ubica claramente la acción en Barcelona; no sólo para abrir la acción teatral sino como mapa que delinea para rastrear a los personajes encerrados dentro de la transformación espacial barcelonesa'; 'en *Morir (o no)*, [...] Pons crea una ciudad aún más desterritorializada, con líneas de fuga más intensas, aunque indica que se trata, sin ningún tipo de ambigüedad, de Barcelona' (Pujol, pp. 65–66, p. 68).

the policeman and policewoman in the patrol car are assigned urgently to deal with a possible murder, in the play they are told to go to the vaguely named Gran Avinguda (Grand Avenue) 735, while in the film they are sent to a real Barcelona street, Bosch i Gimpera 735, which is situated in the wealthy Pedralbes district. This setting is a completely appropriate dwelling place for the possibly corrupt businessman who, in Part 1 of both play and film, is murdered by a hit man, and who turns the tables on him in Part 2.

Another area in which *Morir (o no)* differs from *Morir (un moment abans de morir)* is the ending. In the play the scriptwriter collapses on the floor and is not breathing. Whereas at the end of the first part of the play Belbel makes it clear that he dies, at the end of the second part we are left with his wife's ambiguous attitude to what has happened: '*The Wife looks at him ... terrified?... surprised?... expressionless?*'[21] In the film, however, she calls an ambulance, and, as they travel together to hospital, she urges him to fight to live: 'Fight, my love, fight! You must live. Living is the most important thing. (*Offscreen.*) Live, live, live, live, live, live ...'[22] The contrast between the two endings is in keeping with and sums up one of the essential differences between play and film: the former is more philosophical, its characters suffer from great angst, and the life–death contrast is less clear-cut, whereas the latter is more direct, specific, optimistic and affirmative.[23]

### Forasters

In this too, his latest adaptation of Belbel, Pons makes more concrete what is less specific in the play. As is usual for him, Belbel gives his characters generic names, but, in contrast to his adaptations of *Carícies* and *Morir*, Pons assigns most of them common proper names.[24] Thus,

---

[21] '*La Dona se'l mira ... aterrida?... sorpesa? ... Inexpressiva?...* (p. 162).

[22] '*Lluita amor meu, lluita! Has de viure. Viure és el més important. (Off.) Viu, viu, viu, viu, viu, viu ...*'

[23] I cannot entirely agree with Pujol's view that, in the second part, all the characters are saved, 'with the exception of the scriptwriter whose fate is, ironically, ambiguous' ('a excepción del guionista cuyo desenlace es, irónicamente, ambiguo') (p. 68). Despite an element of ambiguity that remains, the ending of the film seems to me to be less open-ended than that of the play.

[24] Anton Pujol's view, expressed in email correspondence with me, is that,

Mare (Mother) becomes Emma, Filla (Daughter) becomes Anna, Pare (Father) Francesc, Fill (Son) Josep, Avi (Grandfather) Avi Joan, Nét (Grandson) Marc, and Néta (Granddaughter) Rosa. Most of the upstairs neighbours too are named in the film: the older lad and Anna's future husband is Salva, while in the second time period the elder North African son is Ahmed and the orphan boy Alí. The Maid – and Francesc's wife – is called Patrícia. While Belbel's character is unnamed, is from an unspecified country and simply speaks with an accent, Pons's is specifically from Santo Domingo, and has Indian features.[25] As in the play, the Andalusian wife is simply referred to as Veïna (Neighbour), and we never learn her proper name. On the other hand, the Man, who is the grown-up Boy from the earlier period, does have a proper name, Manuel.[26] However, by the end of the film, he has been Catalanised, saying to the young neighbour Alí 'my name is Manel'.[27]

As in *Morir (o no)*, Pons has cut a number of the dialogues from the play, and often economises on words, with cuts that are sometimes small, but which generally serve to sharpen the dialogues, something one might expect from a film adaptation of a play, and also to fit with the rhythm imposed through cinematic editing. The point will be illustrated by comparing the discussion of the removal of the 'for sale' sign from the flat balcony in the Prologue (of the play) with Sequence 4 of the film. Pons takes advantage of his shooting this scene in the street outside the flat, and substitutes a simple hand gesture for a line of dialogue:

in *Morir (o no)* and *Caricies*, the characters do not move from very specific confines/scenes and they relate only to one or two characters, whom they can address directly. In *Forasters* and *Barcelona (un mapa)*, on the other hand, there is interaction among the characters, thus requiring a name.

[25] In the original film script Patrícia was from Bolivia: this was changed to a Caribbean location as the actress Marieta Sánchez, who played the part, is Cuban.

[26] The film is set in the late 1960s or early 1970s.

[27] 'em dic Manel'. This detail was added during the actual filming. When I questioned Pons about the significance of this change he did not attach any special importance to it: 'My name is Manel, I just did it like that, it's more colloquial I think' ('Em dic Manel, ho vaig fer dir així, és més col·loquial, em sembla') (email correspondence with me, 23 November 2008). However, in a Catalonia where the question of Catalan and Castilian is a sensitive issue, the change does inevitably carry political overtones.

**PLAY**

'HOME: El rètol que diu "en venda" que hi ha penjat al balcó ja no cal, oi? (*Pausa.*) Doncs ja el pot treure.'[28] (twenty-one words), translated as:

'MAN: By the way ... that "For Sale" sign on the balcony ... you won't be needing it anymore, will you?'[29]

**FILM**

'*L'Home s'atansa al balcó i assenyala el rètol que diu "en venda" penjat a la barana.*

HOME: Ja no cal oi? Doncs ja es pot treure.' (p. 32, nine words), translated as:

'*The Man leans over the balcony and points to a sign hanging from the rail that reads "For Sale".*

MAN: It's no longer needed, is it? So it can be taken down.'[30]

---

[28] Sergi Belbel, *Forasters*, Col·lecció TNC (Barcelona: Proa, 2004), p. 32.

[29] Sergi Belbel, *Strangers*, trans. Sharon Feldman, in *Barcelona Plays*, trans. Marion Peter Holt and Sharon Feldman (New York: Martin E. Segal Theater Center, 2008), pp. 107–231, p. 112.

[30] I have included the Catalan originals in the main body of the text rather than in the footnotes on this occasion in order better to illustrate the point about the reduction of the number of words in the film. The references to the film script are to a version updated in December 2007, including page numbers, which Ventura Pons kindly sent me. There is no published version of the script. In the course of the chapter I refer to some of the changes between the script I read and the film itself. Pons has explained one of them in an email to me: 'I have also changed the ending, it's not the Berber boy who comes down to the empty flat, as in the play, but that boy's uncle, who has had a brief fling with Josep's daughter (they have it off in the bathroom). The ending was forced on me because I was scared about the boy-actor who played the Moroccan. That's why I made the change which, when you consider it, did not turn out too badly since I was afraid of so much repetition' ('També hi ha el final canviat, no és el nen berber el que baixa al pis buit, com a l'obra, sinó l'oncle d'aquest nen que ha tingut una història curta amb la filla d'en Josep (s'ho monten al bany del pis). Aquest final va venir imposat pel terror que em feia el nen-actor que interpretava al magrebí i em vaig inventar el canvi que, ben mirat, no queda tan malament ja que tanta repetició em feia por') (email correspondence with Pons, 23 November 2008). It should be noted that changes are carried out through the various drafts of the script and during the actual shooting.

Similarly, the Mother's words in the following dialogue with her daughter in the play

'DAUGHTER: What did you want to tell me?
MOTHER: Help me sit up a bit.' (p. 114)[31]

are replaced in the film by an action: '*Anna helps Emma sit up in bed*.'[32] Further examples are the following:

**PLAY**
'DAUGHTER: You want your medicine?
MOTHER: These pills don't do anything for me anymore.' (p. 117)[33]
**FILM**
'EMMA: They don't do anything for me anymore.'[34]

The play's audience learns that the Mother's father hailed from a family of farmers, before moving to the city and marrying a rich girl, whose angry parents disinherited her, leaving the Mother's father to work hard to replace the luxuries his wife had lost as a result of the disinheritance. The absence of these admittedly minor details from the film means that one possible reason for the Mother's harsh character is omitted, while the fact that her family were immigrants in the city, just like her family's neighbours, is absent from the film. Pons's family belongs to a lower stratum of the middle class than Belbel's, corresponding to what in Catalan is known as the *menestralia*.[35] Having said this, Emma does talk to Josep about her past, albeit more briefly than in

---

31 'FILLA: Què em vols dir?/ MARE: Ajuda'm a incorporar-me una mica' (p. 36).

32 '*L'Anna ajuda l'Emma a asseure's al llit*' (p. 5).

33 'FILLA: Vols la medecina? / MARE: Aquestes pastilles ja no em fan res' (p. 38).

34 'EMMA: Ja no em fan res' (p. 8).

35 In early May 2008 I was present at the shooting of some of the scenes, which took place in the Poble Nou location used by Pons. The Producer, Maite Fontanet, explained to me how the pictures on the wall of the set for the lounge were chosen to give colour, while the sense of a lower middle-class family that has seen better times was conveyed by the patched-up broken glass on the door, a stain on the wallpaper where a piece of furniture had been removed, and a mark from a leak in a water pipe on the wall.

the play, when she explains how she spent on her husband the inheritance her father had worked so hard to build up.

It is the longer speeches from the play that are subjected to the greatest number of cuts. Sometimes these have the effect of limiting the bile and sense of a rotting society that are present, particularly in Emma's diatribes. For instance, her bitter riposte to her son in Part 1, Scene 3 is full of the sense of her own rottenness:

> SON: Mom, you're not dying, don't be such a pain.
> MOTHER: Here, the only pains are your father, your sister and you, who don't stop with all your foolishness. I'm already dead. Inside I'm completely dead. Decayed. It's just a matter of the decay extending everywhere. It's horrible to see your body fail you this way when your mind still functions. (p. 125)[36]

In the film the three sentences 'Inside I'm completely dead. Decayed. It's just a matter of the decay extending everywhere' ('Per dintre estic absolutament morta. Podrida. Només falta que la podridura s'estengui del tot') are reduced to a single word, 'decayed' ('podrida'; p. 17). Another of her outbursts that is reduced in the film is her reaction to her father-in-law's (Grandfather's) taking her morphine. The film retains her words that if her husband does not take him to the old people's home she will kill him off by injecting ten or twelve doses of morphine into his neck, but cuts the part of her invective that describes how his wife killed herself because she could not put up with him any longer, as well as a typically Belbelian reference to bodily functions that indirectly underscores her own physically repugnant degeneration (*Strangers*, pp. 137–38, *Forasters*, p. 59, film, p. 30). Similarly, if one compares Josep's reduced diatribe to his father with the Son's original, some of the bile is lost (*Strangers*, pp. 164–65; *Forasters*, pp. 84–85; film, p. 52). A certain amount of abuse is also removed from the scene between Daughter/Anna and Neighbour/Salva in Part 2, Scene 3 (play)/Sequence 131 (film), including her insulting his family and his

---

[36] 'FILL: Mare, no t'estàs morint, no siguis pesada./ MARE: Aquí els únics pesats sou el teu pare, la teva germana i tu, que no pareu de dir bajanades. Jo ja estic morta. Per dintre estic absolutament morta. Podrida. Només falta que la podridura s'estengui del tot. És horrible veure com et falla el cos d'aquesta manera i que el cap encara et funcioni' (p. 48).

accusing her of being like a convent girl who gets good marks just to please Mummy and Daddy.

It is the Mother's speeches that are mostly subjected to cuts. When she complains to the elder Andalusian boy about the noise they make, Belbel makes it clear that she is addressing him from her own perceived sense of superiority, as she emphasises that they live in a quiet neighbourhood. She claims to understand that, when they speak loudly, they are not necessarily having a row, but says that they need to respect the customs of the host community (*Strangers*, p. 155; *Forasters*, pp. 75–76; film, p. 48). The film certainly retains the sense of her clear, dogmatic views, but some details are lost, particularly the cutting irony in the sentence: 'We are peaceful people, sensible and quiet, and we can't stand when people from the outside cause upheaval in our lives and destroy our peace and tranquility by taking advantage of our generosity and good will' (p. 155).[37] Similarly the Son's speech attacking the Andalusians in Part 2, Scene 3/Sequence 107 is shortened, and some of his more racist comments are lost. For instance, the following does not appear in the film: 'A bunch of pigs, illiterate people, involved in corrupt businesses, you can only imagine where they got the money to be able to rent an apartment in this neighborhood' (p. 199).[38] The play emphasises, perhaps to a greater degree than the film, the racist attitudes not only of the Son/Josep but also of his mother, father and grandfather. None the less, there is greater specificity to Father's/Francesc's anti-foreigner insults in one of the film's twenty-first-century sequences, in which his reference to the neighbours as 'estrangers de merda' in the play (p. 46) ('fucking foreigners', p. 124) becomes 'moros de merda' ('fucking Arabs') in the film. This detail was changed between the December 2007 script and the actual film.[39]

---

[37] 'Nosaltres som gent pacífica, sensata i silenciosa, i no podem tolerar que vinguin de fora de casa nostra a esvalotar-nos i a destrossar la nostra pau i la nostra harmonia aprofitant-se de la nostra generositat i la nostra bona fe' (p. 76).

[38] 'Una colla de grollers, analfabets, mala gent, ficats en negocis bruts, que vés a saber d'on han tret els diners per poder-se pagar el lloguer d'un pis en aquest barri' (p. 121).

[39] Pons has commented that the racist dialogue in *Forasters* is 'muy actual' ('very contemporary') (http://actualidad.terra.es/cultura/articulo/ventura-pons-forasters–2885065.htm, accessed 16 December 2008).

Other details are omitted from the film. In a conversation between the Daughter and the Man, she tells her former brother-in-law about her ex-husband's children, who, she says, are unfortunately also hers. The eldest has drug problems, she says, the second son is an alcoholic, like his father (and grandfather, one might add), while the third joined the army as it was the only institution that would have him. None of this conversation is included in the film, and neither is the Man's rebuttal of her accusation that he has come to see her because his brother has sent him.

Sometimes, the reason for a particular cut has simply to do with the details of the plot. During the conversation between Josep and Anna in Sequence 84, Pons has to omit the latter's describing how, after he ran out of the house the night their mother was dying, he roamed the streets and slept on a railway station bench. As we shall see later, what happened in the film version was very different, and constitutes one of the major changes – in this case an addition – made by the director.

If Pons makes conversations more concentrated by frequently cutting sections, particularly from the longer dialogues, he also switches between scenes more frequently than Belbel. As was observed, the switching between the time frames speeds up as the play nears its conclusion. However, the nature of the medium allows Pons to accentuate this, moving not only chronologically but also between the two rooms, the two flats, the stairway, the street outside the flat and other recognisable Barcelona locations. This lends the film an even greater fluidity than the play and, taken together with the reduced dialogues, adds sharpness and speed, accelerating the action.[40] The different chromatic palettes that Pons uses throughout the film – and that Glaenzel/Cristià also employed in the theatre – are very telling and afford him versatility in the chronological leaps.

Pons's shifts between the bedroom and the living room occur at natural breaks in the dialogue, for example during the alternating

---

[40] Jordi Batlle Caminal writes approvingly of the film's fluidity and precision: 'Pons shoots fluently, with a measured *tempo* for the powerful scenes: the parallel death throes of Lizaran's two characters (mother and daughter) are carried out with an admirable precision and impact' ('Pons rueda con fluidez y un tempo medidísimo para las escenas fuertes: la paralela agonía de los dos personajes de Lizaran (madre e hija) es de una exactitud y un impacto admirables'), see http://www.fotogramas.es/Peliculas/Forasteros/Critica, accessed 16 December 2008.

discussions between Josep and Francesc (bedroom) and Anna and the Man (living room) (pp. 49ff.). In the play (Scene 8, pp. 157ff. *Strangers*, pp. 78ff. *Forasters*) the dialogue between the Daughter and the Man is uninterrupted and precedes that between the Father and the Son. Further changes in the order had been introduced by the time of the actual shooting of the film.

The greatest number of changes occurs right at the end of what is Part 1 of the play and at the beginning of Part 2. Street scenes alternate with interior ones, as in the Granddaughter/Rosa's conversation with the Grandson/Marc, in which she accuses him of neglecting his mother, he attacks her liberalism for accepting her father's living with his gay partner, and she counter accuses him of hypocrisy and lack of maturity. Their conversation (reduced from the equivalent in the play, of course) begins in a tobacconist's when she sees him as she is passing by in the street, and concludes in the lounge of the flat. A particularly significant instance of an added outside scene occurs when Patrícia accompanies Anna in an ambulance that brings her home after a chemotherapy session at the Hospital del Mar – another well-known Barcelona land-mark. The suffering Anna vomits, but refuses help (*'she is stronger than anyone'*) (*'és més forta que ningú'*) (p. 75). However, the changes made in these sequences simplify rather than complicate what happens in the play. There are fewer switches between the two chronological periods, and the Eliot-like complexity is less evident in the film than in the play.

On the other hand, in the film there is more alternation and greater variety between the twentieth and the twenty-first centuries during the scenes leading up to and including the deaths of the Mother/Emma and the Daughter/Anna. Whereas Belbel specifies the fact that the conver-sations apply to both time periods, Pons varies things, with some conversations duplicated whereas others are spoken only in the twenti-eth- century sequences. Of course, it must be remembered that in all of the exchanges Belbel uses the same actors for both periods, whereas Pons just has Anna Lizaran duplicating roles. For this reason it is much easier for Belbel than for Pons to pull off the doppelganger.

As one would expect, Pons makes more of the visual element than Belbel does, which is particularly true of the exterior scenes he added. He sets the film firmly not only in Barcelona but in the Poble Nou district in the east of the city. This is a traditional working- and lower middle-class area, with a history in the early twentieth century of heavy industry and left-wing militancy. The film opens with the Man leaving one of the terminal buildings at Barcelona Airport, and getting into a taxi for the journey to the flat. The camera follows the taxi on its journey through the recognisable cityscape, accompanied by gentle string music, thus initiating right from the outset the motif of travel and the journey. Unlike the traffic scenes in *Caricies*, this journey is not speeded-up,[41] but, as in the earlier film, it does serve to locate the action firmly in the city that is the backdrop to all Pons's films. Later in the film (Sequence 75) we observe Manuel alighting from a tram in the Diagonal, another instantly recognisable Barcelona location.

These street or road scenes serve to heighten the specificity of the location. This is further stressed in one of the dialogues, between Daughter/Anna and Man. Whereas in the play he informs her that 'I don't live here [in this city]' (p. 159),[42] in the film he says 'I don't live in Barcelona'.[43] When she asks him if he has seen his elder brother (her ex-husband), in the play he replies: 'I went to give a lecture at another university very close to where he's living' (p. 159),[44] while in the film he says: 'I went to give a lecture in Granada'.[45] Apart from the specificity issue, one may also note that Pons's character uses six words, while Belbel's needs fourteen to express the same idea. It could be argued that the specific detail of the university has been missed, although the viewer already knows by this point that the Man is a university teacher. Also, Pons is more specific, less suggestive about the person who is the object of their discussion:

**PLAY**
'DAUGHTER: (*Silence. Referring to somebody else.*) You've seen him, haven't you?' (p. 159)[46]

---

[41] Pujol refers to the varied speed of the camera work in *Caricies* in the following terms: 'The camera searches out its victims on this unstructured, mobile map that Pons speeds up and slows down, focusses and diffuses, creating a disordered, decentralised effect' ('La cámara busca a sus víctimas en este mapa, inestructurado, móvil que Pons acelera y ralentiza, enfoca y difumina creando un efecto desorganizador, descentralizante') (Pujol, p. 66).

[42] 'no visc en aquesta ciutat' (p. 80).

[43] 'no visc a Barcelona' (p. 54).

[44] 'Vaig anar a fer una conferència a una universitat molt a prop d'on viu ara' (p. 80).

[45] 'vaig fer una conferència a Granada' (p. 54).

[46] 'FILLA: (*Silenci. Referint-se a una altra persona ...*): L'has vist, oi?' (p. 80).

**FILM**
'ANNA: (*Referring to her ex-husband*) You've seen Salva, haven't you?'[47]

The use of the street and stairwell locations allows characters to be seen in a slightly broader set of contexts in the film than in the play. For example, Pons adds a link between Belbel's Scenes 9 and 10 by showing Patrícia leaving a supermarket with her bags, crossing the street, entering the house, meeting Alí, who is sitting on a stair, speaking to him and entering the flat with him. In the next sequence (90) she takes a sandwich to the boy, who is now sitting in the dining room, which is how Scene 10 begins in the play. With this simple device Pons has emphasised a sense of everyday life, the coming and going in public places of transit, while the shot of the supermarket, an almost non-existent institution in 1960s or early 1970s Spain, suggests how society has evolved in the thirty-year period covered in the film.

Pons uses exterior scenes in a particularly effective way to highlight Josep's sexuality. It is, of course, clear from the play that he lives with his male partner, a situation that is accepted quite happily by his daughter. However, the audience does not really become fully aware of this situation until quite late on in the play. In the film, on the other hand, the camera observes Josep and his daughter Rosa being dropped off by a smart 50-year-old man. Josep tells him that there is no need for him to collect him later, the two men kiss on the lips, and Rosa kisses her father's partner on the cheek. The sequence highlights the complete normality of such a situation in the early twenty-first century, which contrasts with the social attitudes displayed by Anna and particularly Emma in the earlier period.

Indeed, the play is generally less specific, more suggestive perhaps, than the film. For example, Pons did not include the stage direction from the play that evokes the strange sensation felt by the Father when he sees his own father's suitcase that the Son has taken out of the cupboard so that his belongings may be moved to the room at the end of the corridor to which he has now been dispatched so as to accommodate his dying daughter in the main bedroom: '*His eyes seem to evoke a distant image*' (p. 167),[48] presumably of when his father was to be sent

---

[47] 'ANNA: (*Referint-se al seu ex-marit*) I al Salva, l'has vist, oi?' (p. 54).
[48] '*Els seus ulls semblen evocar una imatge llunyana*' (p. 87).

to the old people's home.[49] In his obituary on Paul Newman, Philip French writes: 'Alistair Cooke, a very shrewd film critic, once wrote of "stage acting as a form of sculpture and film acting as a performance with the face only – the best film actors do best with the eyes only." '[50] In the case of Pons's *Forasters* the actor Joan Pera was able to combine the two, and, more specifically than a 'distant image', his facial expression evoked the sense of fear he felt, at this point, that he was about to share the fate he had inflicted on his own father. Pons has explained to me that Pera's ability to express facial emotions influenced him to add the sequences in which his character Francesc reacted facially to the conversation between Josep and Patrícia when she reveals to his son that she and his father are married (Sequences 46–52).[51] His facial reaction is one of displeasure when Patrícia tells Josep she will return to her Santo Domingo family when her husband dies (p. 33), but he shows more satisfaction when she tells him that she has looked after him for years and that he loves her (p. 34). When she finally informs Josep that she and his father are married, he gives a sly smile of satisfaction, closes his eyes and snores (p. 35).

Pera's face seems to combine two apparently contradictory features, namely the benign and the wicked. Pons's reading is that, in the earlier period, Pera's Father was a rather timorous figure, under the thumb of his dominant matriarchal wife. However, as an old man in the early twenty-first century, free from the memory of his wife, he enjoys life until his daughter returns and reawakens all his past memories. His relationship with the maid contributes in no small measure to his acquiring a new lease of life, something, Pons says, that is not an uncommon occurrence in Catalan life.[52] Likewise, during the conversation between Father and Maid in the long Scene 8, Belbel explains in a

---

[49] I discussed how this might be conveyed with Jordi Banacolocha, the actor who played the stage part of the father in the 1960s and his son from the early twenty-first century. He did not remember the stage direction, perhaps suggesting that Belbel felt it impossible actually to convey to a theatre audience, many of whom would be seated a long way from the stage. He felt that this would be much easier to achieve in the cinema than in the theatre.

[50] Quoted in Philip French, 'An Actor of True Genius and a Man of Great Decency', *Observer*, 29 September 2008, pp. 2–3, p. 2.

[51] Conversation during the shooting of the film in Barcelona in May 2008.

[52] Pons confirmed this to me in email correspondence (23 November 2008). He explained that he worked extensively with Pera in the theatre during

stage direction how, on the Father's seeing his sister fold a bed sheet, the image of their mother passed through his mind (*Strangers*, p. 169; *Forasters*, p. 89). This is dealt with more directly in the film, with Josep actually saying 'La ma...re' ('Mo...ther'; p. 58). Curiously, one might have expected the reverse of the situation, given cinema's ability to use a flashback and his usual love for flashbacks, but Pons chooses not to do that here nor when the distant image passes through the Father's mind as he sees his father's suitcase.

Pons does retain Belbel's suggestive stage direction from the final scene of Part 1 of the play, with reference to Father/Francesc: '*He gets up with difficulty and goes to the bedroom, slowly, startled, taken by the memories. An unreal atmosphere imbues the scene*' (p. 183).[53] He also retains another evocative direction from the same scene, which is intended to produce a kind of Dorian Gray effect in reverse and again refers to Father/Francesc, who '*old, upon crossing the threshold, has magically become younger*' (p. 183).[54] The switch is justified as the Father, as an old man, dwells guiltily on his broken promise to his dying wife not to re-marry, and, as he enters the bedroom, morphs into his younger version entering the same bedroom to attend to the remembered wife and to make his promise to her. This is immediately followed, in both play and film, by the young orphan boy (Alí in the film) morphing into the young Andalusian boy.

One very small but intriguing example of greater specificity in the film concerns the old book that Mother/Emma reads and gives to the young neighbour (in the film but not in the play, nor indeed in the December 2007 film script), and which he as the adult Man gives to Daughter/Anna. In the film script, as in the play, it is described simply as 'an old hard-covered book' (p. 162).[55] However, the film includes a close-up shot of the book, which reveals that it is the *Complete Works* of the Mallorcan writer Llorenç Villalonga, which the Mother opens at the

his early career, and had waited for thirty years to find a role that he felt suited him.

[53] '*S'aixeca amb dificultats i va a l'habitació, a poc a poc, atemorit, presa dels records. Una atmòsfera irreal tenyeix l'espai*' (p. 103). The quotation comes from p. 71 of the film script.

[54] '*vell, en creuar la porta, ha rejovenit màgicament*' (p. 104). This quotation is also from p. 71 of the film script.

[55] '*un llibre antic, de tapes dures*' (p. 83). The quotation comes from p. 71 of the film script.

first page of perhaps his most famous novel, *Bearn, o la sala de les nines*, which was first published in Spanish in 1956 and in Catalan in 1961. In email correspondence, I asked Ventura Pons if his reason for choosing this particular novel for the Mother to read was due to the fact that two of its key themes are the passing of time and the decadence of (in the case of *Bearn*) a well-to-do family. In his response he explains that the reality was more prosaic and had more to do with practical reasons:

> I asked Belbel which book he used in the theatre. And he answered, 'a book. A red one'. 'But which one?' I insisted. 'A big one'. Of course, in the theatre you don't have to be specific, but in the cinema you do. Rummaging through my library I came across the first volume of Villalonga's *Complete Works*, which suited me well. It was a big enough book for the daughter to threaten her mother with, and it was written by a Majorcan novelist, which suited my purpose, namely to emphasise the unity of the Catalan language. She reads *Bearn* since to have her read *Death of a Lady*, which is in the same volume, would have been pushing it too far. When you [i.e. me, in my email question to Pons] talk about 'the decadence of a family ... time passing ...', I did think of that, but, when all is said and done, I have to be honest.[56]

It is interesting that Pons chooses Villalonga – a writer from one of the so-called Catalan lands outside Catalonia proper – thus emphasising what is currently the polemical issue of the unity of the Catalan language.[57] At the same time, the fact that he resists the temptation to

[56] 'Li vaig preguntar a en Belbel quin llibre feia servir al teatre. I em va contestar, un llibre. Vermell. Però quin?, vaig insistir. Un de gran. Clar, en teatre no has de concretar però en cine, sí. Remanant a la meva biblioteca vaig trobar el primer volum de l'edició completa de les obres de Villalonga que m'anava molt bé. Era un llibre prou gros per a que la filla pugui amanaçar a sa mare i, a més, era d'un autor mallorquí que m'anava bé per subratllar la unitat de la llengua catalana. Llegeix *Bearn* ja que fer-li llegir *Mort de dama* que és al mateix llibre hauria sigut apretar massa. En el què tu dius de "La decadència d'una família ... El pas del temps ..." hi vaig pensar, però després a misses dites, t'he de ser franc' (email correspondence with me, 23 November 2008).
[57] The issue of linguistic unity is especially polemical in the Valencia region.

have the Mother open the *Complete Works* at the first page of the novel *The Death of a Lady* reveals his awareness of the need to avoid what would have been a tritely obvious visual effect.

This visual detail, unsupported by dialogue, is obviously much easier to achieve in a film close-up than in a 450-seat theatre. Pons uses the visual element particularly well to highlight the characteristics of, and the similarities and differences between, the two generations of immigrant neighbours. On several occasions the camera moves unobtrusively from one immigrant family to the other as it straddles the two time frames, emphasising the links between them. An example is found in his fading from Sequence 85 to 86. The former consists of the following directions: *'The music the Moroccans from upstairs play is louder than ever. The camera reaches the balcony and pans out over the city. It links with ...'*,[58] which then seamlessly moves to 86: *'The same vision of the city but in the 1960s. The camera repeats the same movement but in reverse order, revealing now the Andalusian family.'*[59] The fact that we have already observed and listened to members of the earlier neighbours puts Emma's reference to them as 'gentussa' ('scum') into context. The Andalusian father's violent assault on his wife, which is overheard in the play, is witnessed by the film's audience, in Sequence 118. This detail not only enhances our sense of him as a violent wife-beater but emphasises Emma's bravery in standing up to him, and also the confusion of his dazed reaction to the dying woman's action. It is another example of how the film uses action rather than words to reinforce a situation. On the issue of authenticity, Pons has changed a detail in the scene in which the injured Neighbour appears in the flat and is helped by Emma and her family. The Neighbour – who we know from the play understands and speaks Catalan imperfectly – now lapses into Andalusian dialect, which is entirely appropriate given the stress she is under at this moment.

In the twenty-first-century sequences in the upstairs flat, the North African neighbours are almost invariably playing autochthonous music.

---

[58] *'La música que fan els magrebins de dalt és més forta que mai. La càmera arriba fins al balcó per veure la ciutat. Encadena amb ...'* (p. 60).

[59] *'La mateixa visió de la ciutat però als anys seixanta. La càmera repeteix el mateix moviment però a l'inrevés per a descobrir ara a la família andalusa'* (p. 60).

Indeed, the film ends with their music being played louder and louder. They also speak Berber rather than Arabic, whereas, in the play, the stage direction merely indicates that they speak their own language (*Strangers*, p. 149; *Forasters*, p. 70). As we have seen, the film is more precise than the play about the origins and identity of the Maid/Patrícia. The film heightens the sense of the otherness of the immigrants as well as providing a rather fuller and perhaps more sympathetic glimpse of their culture, particularly that of the North Africans. This is reinforced by two further details. The Granddaughter's assumption that the neighbours' flat is illegally sublet is absent from the film (*Strangers*, p. 146; *Forasters*, p. 68), although this detail probably tells us more about the prejudices of the Catalan family than it does about the neighbours, and is reinforced later in both play and film as the Granddaughter/Rosa assumes that Orphan/Alí was yelling because he was being beaten by the Young Man/Ahmed and not because he was having a tantrum. As with the wife beating of the previous generation, we actually witness Ahmed's attempt to restrain Alí during his tantrum in the film, thus making the contrast clearer and also pointing up Rosa's prejudice in assuming the worst. Whereas the constraints of the stage mean that the audience sees the two generations of immigrants only within the confines of the Catalan family's flat, the film also shows them in other spaces, including their own flat, the stairway and the street.

I have mentioned that Pons heightens the otherness of the play, but he also develops another of its features that, at first sight, seems to contradict the above, but that, through a sense of perspective, complements it. This is the vision of the Catalan family as other as seen through the eyes of the immigrants. In short, although the switching between the two rooms and two periods is highly effective in the play, by the very nature of the film medium Pons has more variations at his disposal than Belbel–Glaenzel/Cristià. The switching between bedroom and lounge is even more apparent in the film, while the use of exterior spaces and the stairway allows the director to view the Catalan family and more particularly the neighbours in the wider social context of a working- and lower middle-class area.

Although sexuality is an important theme in the play, in the film it is more prevalent and more directly evoked. Sometimes this is through a saucy comment or action, particularly from Francesc to Patrícia, as when, in Sequence 116, he calls from his bed: 'Patricia, come back woman, the tablet's working!!!'[60] The passionate encounter between Granddaughter and Young Man becomes an explicit – if briefly glimpsed – sexual encounter between Rosa and Ahmed. The direction specifies the 'beauty of the nakedness of the two bodies',[61] a detail that is absent from the play.

Where Pons really does accentuate the sexuality is during the completely new scenes he added following the Son/Josep's running out of the house as his mother lies dying in her bed. The camera follows him down the stairs – where he passes Salva – and out into the street. Later we view him running soaked to the skin in the storm that is raging, and pushing open the gate of the Cementeri de l'Est in Poble Nou. He sits disconsolately on a step inside the cemetery, and a series of cars passes by, the male drivers soliciting for sex. Finally, Josep gets into one of the cars (with a Madrid number plate!), and we witness a sexual encounter between him and his casual pick-up, in which Josep is the passive partner. It is as if he were carrying out his mother's order to him to fulfil his sexual needs with a complete stranger and not with his sister's boyfriend. It is also his way of expressing his frustration and releasing his pent-up emotions that have built up as he listens to his mother's insults and watches her approach death. An interesting visual parallel is drawn between the expression of homoerotic desire here and its heterosexual equivalent more than thirty years later, as Pons follows the lovemaking scene between Rosa and Ahmed with a shot of the cemetery in the rain.[62]

He follows up the cemetery scenes with another added sequence set during the following morning (p. 167). Josep is dropped at home by the man with whom he has had sex in the car, only to see Anna leaving the flat with Salva, suitcase in hand, and backed by the same sad string music Pons used in the previous scene, in which Anna and her father are crying over the death of Emma. One may also note the contrast between the sordid, furtive nature of his earlier sexual encounter and his early twentieth-century relationship with his established partner, which is accepted as quite normal by his own daughter. The car

---

[60] 'Patrícia, torna, dona, que la pastilla ja ha fet efecte!!!' (p. 86).

[61] 'bellesa de la nuesa dels dos cossos' (p. 103).

[62] Pons confirmed this to me when I viewed the shooting of the film in May 2008. He emphasised to me that Josep's desperate search for sex is an illustration of how sex and death are inextricably linked.

sequences involving the young Josep are in stark contrast to his being dropped off in his partner's car in Sequence 42.[63]

## Concluding remarks

In conclusion, the film version of *Forasters* encapsulates several features of Pons's adaptations of Belbel plays. Sexuality – especially homoeroticism – is even more to the fore in the films than in the plays, especially in *Forasters*. This sexual 'otherness' reinforces the racial 'otherness', and is visually more accentuated in the film than in the play. There is a greater specificity and variety of location in the films, together with a sense of the urban world that is Barcelona. Whereas the Catalan capital may be the setting for the plays, they could take place in any urban centre, the films explore specifically Barcelonan landscapes. Allied to this feature, their dialogue is more natural and less stylised than that of the plays, and Pons indulges in a progressively greater concentration of this aspect in the three films. Taken together, the dialogue and the depiction of Barcelona lend the films a greater specificity and social realism than the plays, reinforced by Pons's lessening what might be termed the latter's philosophical element.

[63] Pons himself has emphasised the difference between the two periods, and, indirectly, the optimism of *Forasters*: 'I am clearer and clearer that there is a very great difference between the two periods, between 1968 and today, in the film. People may think that some things are exaggerated, but, symbolically, it is a depiction of the moral misery of the period, the end of the dictatorship, of a way of repression and self-repression' ('cada vegada tinc més clar que hi ha una diferència molt gran entre els dos temps, entre l'any 68 i l'actualitat, al film. La gent pot trobar exagerades algunes coses, però és, simbòlicament, una representació de la misèria moral de l'època, del final de la dictadura, d'una manera d'oprimir i d'oprimir-se un mateix') (Interview with Bernat Salvà in *Avui*, 24 November 2008, consulted at http://www.avui. cat/article/cultura_comunicacio/47155/ventura/pons/sergi/belbe/execel·lim/tot/ nomes/falta/la/gent/ho/sapiga.html, accessed 5 December 2008).

4

# Belbel and the Critics:
# the Reception of the Plays in Barcelona,
# Madrid and Beyond

Having analysed thematic and stylistic features of Belbel's plays in Chapter 1, I now turn to an examination of the reception of a selection of them, both inside and outside Catalonia. Whereas Chapter 1 was concerned mainly with the plays as literary texts, the present one concentrates on how they have been received in live performance. It draws mainly, but not exclusively, on press reviews, and attempts to judge the extent to which such factors as quality of writing and of production, stage space and national or local taste may have influenced the reception.

In an article written in the TNC's programme notes to *A la Toscana*, Enric Gallén comments on how Belbel's reputation has spread far and wide beyond Catalonia. In his view the international projection of Belbel has been responsible for Catalan drama's moving from being unknown internationally to becoming 'a focus of attention for agents and professionals in Western theatre'.[1] According to Gallén, Belbel has opened the way for the work of other Catalan dramatists to be published and performed in Europe. Indeed, a number of his plays have been performed abroad prior to their Catalan premiere. For instance, *Morir (un moment abans de morir)* was staged in Finland and Germany before its Romea production, *Sóc Lletja* received its premiere in Denmark and Norway, and *Mòbil* and *A la Toscana* premiered in Denmark.[2] The reception ranges from the highly enthusiastic to the

---

[1] 'un focus d'atenció per als agents i professionals del teatre occidental' (Enric Gallén, 'Belbel: el nou contemporani', from the programme note to the play, p. 12).

[2] Pep Tugues, 'Sergi Belbel i *El temps de Plank* [*sic*]', http://www.teatral.net/entrevista/belbel-plank.html, accessed 20 October 2008. In the

damning, the contrast being especially marked in the case of *Mòbil*. There is not always uniformity in the reception of any single play, and, as our analysis of *Mòbil* in particular will demonstrate, this can vary quite wildly from location to location. Drawing on plays from the early 1990s to 2008, this chapter will set out the particulars of the reception and attempt, where appropriate, to offer some explanation for it. The plays chosen have been staged in a number of locations, in Catalonia, Madrid, and cities outside Spain. I have concentrated on premieres of plays at individual centres and not on any later productions.

## *Caricies*

Prior to *Mòbil* this was probably the Belbel play that received the most negative reaction in his native Catalonia. F. Burguet Ardiaca in the *Diari de Barcelona* writes disapprovingly of the references to male and female genitalia, and considers the comic element to be 'superfluous' ('supèrflua'), while the playwright is viewed as more of an experimenter than a surgeon. In general Burguet approves of the acting, and of Joaquim Roy's impeccable set – glacial, with its massive geometry – which, he feels, perfectly conveys the 'pent-up brutality that lies behind the words'.[3] Veteran critic Joan de Sagarra is rather less impressed with the stage design. He accepts that the urban space Roy creates is 'correct and harsh',[4] but feels that it lacks magic. He also criticises the use of the Romea theatre space:

> The use of the Romea stalls as an extension of the urban space, where certain characters emerge and disappear, doesn't really work either. In a smaller theatre, without the Italian-style stage, it could work; in the Romea it can't, especially with that spotlight pursuing the characters over the heads of the spectators.[5]

same interview Belbel describes the pressure he feels when foreign companies and directors ask him for new plays.

   [3] 'sorda brutalitat que coven les paraules' (F. Burguet Ardiaca, 'Una caricia pot ferir la sensibilitat dels rosegaaltars' ('A Caress May Wound the Feelings of the Pious'), *Diari de Barcelona*, 1 March 1992, p. 37).

   [4] 'correcto y duro' (Joan de Sagarra, 'Mal rollo' ('Bad Vibes'), *El País*, 1 March 1992, p. 39).

   [5] 'Tampoco la utilización de la platea del Romea como prolongación de ese espacio urbano, por donde aparecen o desaparecen determinados

Sagarra also disapproves of the music, which does nothing to create the atmosphere that he judges necessary.

However, it is the text that provokes Sagarra's harshest criticism. Although he argues that the dialogues are well constructed, he also describes them as empty, while the crude sexual content of some of them, which may even be dangerous on the stage, serves to highlight the insignificance of some of the text. From a literary point of view, says Sagarra, some of the dialogue is 'resoundingly poor and ingenuous'.[6] However, he does finish his review on a positive – if rather patronising – note, saying that it is a sincere text, important for Belbel's development, and that he is convinced that 'one day, in the not too distant future, Belbel will surprise us'.[7]

The Spanish translation of the play was performed in Madrid in 1994. It was directed by Guillermo Heras and was the final production by the Centro Nacional de Nuevas Tendencias Escénicas (CNNTE) prior to its merger with the Centro Dramático Nacional (CDN). According to Enrique Centeno, in celebration of the swansong of the CNNTE the Sala Olimpia was packed with an enthusiastic audience, who followed the production very attentively and applauded each of the eleven scenes.[8] Centeno considers *Carícies* to be Belbel's best play to date, says that Heras's production was inspired by Mark Rothko's abstract expressionism, and sees the lighting technician's role as vital. Unsurprisingly perhaps, Alberto de la Hera, writing in the conservative daily *Ya*, is far less enthusiastic, playing on the 'New Tendencies'

---

personajes, es demasiado feliz. En un teatro más chico, sin la escena a la italiana, podría funcionar; en el Romea, no, y menos con ese foco que persigue a los personajes por encima de las cabezas de los espectadores.' *Carícies* was the first production at the Romea following its modernisation. This criticism of the Romea space seems to anticipate Marcos Ordóñez's in his review of Belbel's production of Koltès's *Quai Ouest*. For details, see Chapter 2, p. 86.

   6  'de una pobreza y de una ingenuidad apabullantes'.

   7  'llegará un día, no lejano, en que Belbel nos ha de sorprender'. For further information on reviews of the Barcelona production of *Carícies*, see Esther Perarnau, '*Carícies*, de Sergi Belbel', in *Veinte años de teatro y democracia en España (1975–1995)*, ed. Manuel Aznar Soler, Cop d'Idées (Barcelona: CITEC, 1996), pp. 177–81, p. 178.

   8  Enrique Centeno, 'Caricias como zarpazos' ('Caresses like Blows'), *Diario 16*, 27 May 1994, p. 34.

('Nuevas Tendencias') of the theatre group: 'But when one attends a performance of *Carícies* one knows that the play disappears up its own exhaust and that we are not dealing with new trends in the theatre. Quite simply, we are nowhere.'[9]

Haro Tecglen rejected the production from a moral standpoint. The opening two sentences of his review make his position abundantly clear: 'It's a steep curve; after a brave and decisive entrance, the play reaches great heights of repugnance. It's horrible.'[10] The adjectives he uses to describe Scene 7, in which the man complains of the odour from his mistress's vagina, are indicative of his position: 'crude, obscene, pornographic, scatalogical and repulsive'.[11] He seems to be drawn into assuming that the occasionally coarse language and the brutality of some of the actions mean that the play is naturalist in style, although he perceptively uses the idea of theatre of cruelty to categorise it. The laughter that the play provoked was, for the reviewer, a means of distancing for the audience, a kind of gesture to demonstrate that they were not too alarmed by what was on stage. Like Centeno, Haro points to the prolonged applause the production received, although his feeling of disgust at what he and they supposedly witnessed is far removed from Centeno's enthusiastic approval.

The review in the conservative daily *ABC* was just as concerned with the Viennese literary antecedents of the play as with *Carícies* itself and the production. Belbel, whose Christian name the reviewer Castilianises to 'Sergio', is accused of using pornographic language.[12] The reviewer feels that the play is scandalous but not profound, while its structure is an imperfect copy of Schnitzler's *La Ronde*.[13]

---

[9] 'Pero cuando se asiste a una representación de *Caricias* se sabe que la obra se agota en sí misma y que no estamos ante nuevas tendencias escénicas. No estamos, simplemente' (Alberto de la Hera, 'No es nuevo' ('It's Not New'), *Ya*, 4 June 1994, p. 32).

[10] 'Es una gradación rápida, después de una entrada valiente y decidida, la obra va alcanzando grandes cimas de repugnancia. Es odiosa' (Eduardo Haro Tecglen, 'Da bastante asco' ('It's Quite Disgusting'), *El País*, 28 May 1994, p. 31). The title, too, of course, is symptomatic of Haro's attitude.

[11] 'soez, obsceno, pornográfico, escatalógico y repulsivo'.

[12] Lorenzo López Sancho, '*Caricias*, la muestra y el modelo en la Olimpia' ('*Carícies*, the Sample and the Model in the Olimpia'), *ABC*, 4 June 1994, p. 98. He calls the playwright 'Belber' at one point in his review.

[13] López Sancho does not elaborate on the point.

The Madrid press certainly had a field day in their condemnation of *Carícies*. As was to be expected, this was particularly true of the conservative newspapers, although, as Haro Tecglen's *El País* review illustrates, at least one of the more liberal dailies joined in the chorus of criticism. The titles of two reviews of the play are indicative of the general mood of moral revulsion the play seems to have provoked among the critics. Haro Tecglen's 'Da bastante asco' is paralleled by Santiago Trancón's 'Provocadores de la nada' ('Agitators of Nothing') in *El Mundo*.[14] The title of Trancón's review is indicative of the content of what is the most damning of all the Madrid reviews. Much more than Haro's, this review makes the fundamental mistake of categorising *Carícies* as a naturalist play. For Trancón,

> neither sadomasochism nor naturalism (which here doesn't even get as far as Zola) have ever provided a work of art for the stage [...] Fill the stage with all human miseries and you won't have produced one iota of art. Besides, if we want reality we have telly-junk.[15]

Here, of course, is a trenchantly personal view of realism and naturalism in the theatre, which the reviewer seems to equate with the grittier kind of television soap. He also seems to conflate the two terms, thus exhibiting a certain vagueness about their historical significance. More importantly, he demonstrates a fundamental misunderstanding of *Carícies*'s essentially non-naturalistic format, which is nowhere more evident than in its language. Trancón is especially critical of this aspect of the play, of course: indeed, he writes that *Carícies* 'demolishes theatre and language' ('demoledora del teatro y del lenguaje)'. Finally, he accuses the director of wasting public money by putting on this play.

In a 2004 interview, Belbel himself reveals his sensitivity to criticism, specifically a propos of *Carícies*. The mauling the play received from the critics in Madrid and Barcelona almost made him give up

---

[14] In *El Mundo*, 9 June 1994, viewed at http://www.elmundo.es/papel/hemeroteca/1994/06/09/cultura/718602.html, accessed 6 March 2008.

[15] 'ni el sadomasoquismo ni el naturalismo (que aquí no llega ni a Zola) jamás han dado una obra de arte para la escena [...] Llene usted el escenario de todas las miserias humanas y no habrá producido por ello un átomo de arte. Además, para "reality", ya tenemos la tele-basura.'

writing.[16] However, some of the Madrid reviews were more favourable, and certainly more balanced and penetrating, than Haro's or
Trancón's. Lest we are tempted to fall into the trap of assuming that
conservative newspapers were bound to review the play negatively,
Luis Antonio de Villena's *El Mundo* piece is much more intelligent
than that of his fellow *El Mundo* reviewer cited above. Villena perceptively notes the Beckett-like silences in the play (Beckett is clearly a
much more obvious point of comparison for the early Belbel than is
Zola). He sees the play as 'radically modern' ('radicalmente moderna')
in its destruction of topics that mask reality. He perceptively recognises Belbel's importance within the 'return to the text' syndrome of
the period, of which he enthusiastically approves:

> On occasions theatre has tried hard not to speak, but to do panto-
> mime and contortions. I have always believed that text-based theatre
> was the future. Sergi Belbel agrees with me. *Caricies* is a masterly
> work because it speaks, suggests and is silent. Because its characters
> try to understand each other even though they might not manage it.[17]

Unlike Haro and Trancón, Villena is able to look beyond and measure
the meaning of the play's shocking elements, locating the moral
element that underpins it.

Some ten years after its Madrid premiere, *Caricies* was performed in
Sydney by the Vicious Fish Theatre Company, directed by Scott
Gooding. The Australian writer Alison Croggon writes an interesting
appreciation of the play and the production on her blog. Despite a
certain haziness in her chronology (among the new Catalan playwrights whose work she claims was facilitated by the international
presence of such performance groups as Comediants, she includes

16 Francesc Bombí-Vilaseca, 'L'escriptura surt quan trobes que la forma va
lligada amb el contingut', *Avui* (Cultura), 25 November 2004, pp. x–xi, p. x.
17 'A veces el teatro se ha esforzado en no hablar, sino en hacer pantomima
y contorsiones. Yo siempre he creído que el teatro de palabra (de texto) era dueño
del futuro. Sergi Belbel me acompaña en la creencia. *Caricias* es una obra
magistral porque dice, sugiere y calla. Porque los personajes buscan entenderse
aunque no lo consigan' (Luis Antonio de Villena, 'Teatro de texto y realidad'
('Text-based Theatre and Reality'), *El Mundo*, 27 May 1994, viewed at
http://www.elmundo.es/papel/hemeroteca/1994/05/27/opinion/716496.html,
accessed [accessed 6 March 2009]).

Sanches [*sic*] Sinisterra, Benet i Jornet, Rodolf Sirera and Àngel Guimerà!), she makes some comments on the play itself, and conveys a sense of what it looked like onstage. She finds the form 'elegantly satisfying', but also feels that it reinforces the disturbing element of the play ('the disconnections as disconcerting as the connections').[18] She sees it as 'a work of considerable complexity that operates at a number of emotional and metaphorical registers'. She uses a comparison between Belbel and Australian dramatist Daniel Keene to make perceptive observations on *Caricies*: 'From this play at least, it seems that Belbel is stylistically less spare than Keene, more given to sonorities of repetition; but they share an ability to generate cruel humour while retaining a compassionate vision, and an unsentimental preoccupation with an urban geography of despair and alienation.' The designer Kathryn Sproul, we learn, used second-hand furniture, while Belbel's having just the relevant pair of characters onstage at any one time is replaced by choreographer Alison Halit's employing 'the actors not immediately involved in scenes to inhabit the space and amplify the action, creating the movement of a city around these isolated dialogues'. In other words, the Sydney production seems, in this sense, more akin to Ventura Pons's film adaptation than to Belbel's Romea or Heras's Olimpia productions.

As will become even more evident from my discussion of *Mòbil*, from the one review I have been able to consult, *Caricies* was received far more positively in Germany than in either Madrid or Barcelona.[19] The reviewer of its German premiere (as *Liebkosungen*) at the Münchner Kammerspiele in Munich in 1995 detects parallels with Botho Strauss, Fassbinder and Almodóvar.[20] His characterisation of the play as cool and sexually hot contrasts sharply with the moralising standpoint of Haro and Trancón, while he also appreciates that it

18 Alison Croggon, 'Caresses', http://theatrenotes.blogspot.com/2004/08/caresses.html, accessed 19 December 2008.

19 While recognising that one cannot draw general conclusions from just one review, I draw attention to it because of the qualities it highlights. I am most grateful to my colleague at Swansea University, Dr Katharina Hall, for her summaries of this and other reviews of Belbel plays.

20 Peter von Becker, 'Geile Welt, heute Welt' ('Cool World, Today's World'), *Theatre Heute*, June 1995, p. 4.

conveys a feel for ordinary speech that can be sensed in the translation.[21] The dialogue, he writes, is short and sharp, while Belbel is a shrewd observer of human conduct who knows what makes people tick. Possible explanations for the more positive reception of this – and other – Belbel plays will be considered in the conclusion to this chapter.

## Després de la pluja

If the reception of *Carícies* sent Belbel to the edge of despair, *Després de la pluja* has probably been his most popular and widely staged play to date. Despite its popularity with audiences worldwide, its approval ratings were, as usual with Belbel, not particularly high in the English-speaking world. In London, it was performed on the small stage of the Gate Theatre, which describes itself as 'London's international theatre'.[22] For Liese Spencer, 'the acting is fine, particularly from Steven Elder as a slightly psychopathic computer programmer'.[23] Steven Elder seems to win most of the English critics' plaudits, whereas in the original Catalan, the Spanish and the Portuguese versions of the play, it is the Blonde Secretary who earns the most praise. Laura Conejero, who played the part in the Catalan original, Amparo Larrañaga in the Madrid and Murcia performances and Inês Câmara Pestana (in the Portuguese version in Lisbon) all received rave reviews. The *El Periódico* reviewer is the most fulsome in his praise: 'Laura Conejero's portrayal of an extroverted and crazy character is extraordinary.'[24] The review of the Mannheim National Theatre production, too, comments on the presence of this character: 'She is in her naivety the most stable individual among the women, never

[21] All the translations into German of Belbel's plays have been done by Klaus Laabs. I am extremely grateful to him for agreeing to meet me in Berlin in May 2009 to discuss the reception of Belbel's plays in Germany and for providing me with copies of reviews of selected plays.

[22] See the theatre's website at http://www.gatetheatre.co.uk/about-the-gate.aspx.

[23] *What's On*, 10 April 1996.

[24] 'el trabajo de Laura Conejero, en un personaje extrovertido y loco, es extraordinario' ('Un brillante Belbel' ('A Brilliant Belbel'), *El Periódico*, 26 November 1993, p. 2).

threatened by falling, and at the end is professionally in the ascendance.'[25]

As far as the staging is concerned, Liese Spencer considers that 'the set is strikingly effective', while the costuming wins the approval of Kate Bassett of *The Times* ('superbly costumed by Johanna Coe like chic yet ridiculous cartoons').[26] The sets varied slightly from production to production. In the Catalan original the throwing of cigarettes and the looking and the leaping over the edge of the balcony happened at the back of the stage. The audience did not therefore see the 'ground', which allowed their imagination to work as to the height of the rooftop, thereby intensifying the sense of vertigo. At the Gate Theatre in London, however, the drop to ground level was clearly visible at the front of the stage, which correspondingly lessened the vertigo effect. Comparing the sets for the Catalan and the Castilian versions, Belbel says 'the Castilian was perhaps a little more "precious", less sober, since it showed the sky and how it developed towards the "storm"'.[27]

Despite the general critical approval of the play, this was not universal. Neither Belbel nor the critics were entirely satisfied with the original ending, a view most clearly spelt out by Joan-Anton Benach. This critic was unhappy with the final scene because it lengthens the play excessively and upsets the rhythm:

> *Després de la pluja* is maybe too long. And, in my opinion, we could do without the happy ending, although I do understand that it might be a question of principle. Sergi Belbel wanted to insert an optimistic note into the depiction of a miserable human world, destroyed by a

[25] Heike Marx, 'Into the Abyss, Into One's Death', translation of 'Vom dach die Tiefe, vom Leben in den Tod', *Die Rheinpfalz*, 3 March 1997. Selected reviews of Belbel's work in German have been translated by students on the MA in Translation with Language Technology (MATLT) at Swansea University. This review was translated by Chloë Driscoll and Josephine McCrossan. I have not included the original text of reviews in German, nor have I been able to locate their page numbers.

[26] *The Times*, 4 April 1996, p. 36.

[27] 'potser era una mica més "preciosista" la castellana, menys sòbria, perquè hi mostrava el cel i la seva evolució cap a la "tempesta" ' (email correspondence with me).

period of crisis. The pleasant final scene is flat and contrasts with the lively, restless style of the whole story.[28]

For Kate Bassett, 'ultimately, perhaps, this play builds to nothing: but en route it is very funny and strangely intriguing'. Liese Spencer of *What's On* is more critical about the ending. While generally positive about the play ('Belbel's characters weave an engrossing and often funny tale of office angst and office dissatisfaction'), Spencer sees the resolution as entirely unsatisfactory, out of keeping with the rest of the play and a failure to realise the potential of the dramatic situation:

> A final apocalyptic storm accompanies the play's disappointingly neat resolution, as the cast of eccentrics, misfits and enthusiastic conformists pair off in couples that seem to have no reference to the previous action. The apparent randomness of these pairings undermines the emotional logic of what has gone before, sealing the feeling of disappointment and wasted potential that has been creeping throughout the second half of the play.[29]

While generally favourable, the London reviews display more reservations than those written in Spain, Portugal or Germany. There is a sense with some of them that the play is not particularly original.[30] Lyn Gardner, for instance, feels that 'it might have been written almost any time in the last 30 years'.[31] Adrian Turpin's view that 'it's not a bad

---

[28] 'Es posible que *Después de la lluvia* se prolongue excesivamente. Y sobra, desde mi punto de vista, el "happy end", aunque comprendo que esta [*sic*] pueda constituir una cuestión "de principio". Sergi Belbel ha querido poner una nota optimista en medio de un cuadro humano perdido, destrozado por los tiempos de crisis. La apacible escena final resulta apagada y contrasta con el estilo vivaz y agitado de toda la historia' ('Dramaturgia de las neurosis urbanas' ('A Play about Urban Neuroses'), *La Vanguardia*, 30 October 1993, p. 36).

[29] The 'happy ending' was removed by Belbel in his own Spanish translation, which was performed in Murcia and Madrid in early 1996.

[30] In John London's words, 'English critics, while enjoying the cranky comic edginess, accorded no great originality to Belbel's play' ('Contemporary Catalan Drama in English: Some Aspirations and Limitations', in *Catalan Theatre, 1975–2006: Politics, Identity, Performance*, ed. Maria M. Delgado, David George and Lourdes Orozco, special issue of *Contemporary Theatre Review*, 17:3 (2007), 453–62, p. 454).

[31] *Guardian*, G2, 4 April 1996, p. 9.

play'[32] is less enthusiastic than that suggested by the title of another *El Periódico* review, 'A Brilliant Belbel' ('Un brillante Belbel'),[33] while for Turpin (the most critical of the English reviewers) it displays a lack of freshness: 'sadly, not all Belbel's imagery is so fresh. From King Lear to TS Eliot, I for one have had enough symbolic storms to last a life. Two year's drought? It's the least we should demand.' Such weariness is nowhere to be seen among the Catalan and Spanish reviewers.

I have managed to see just one positive view of the Australian production, in which Helen Thomson writes approvingly of the acting and of Scott Gooding's direction, resulting in 'an arresting work with an unmistakable European flavour'.[34] A fuller – and much more negative – review is Alison Croggon's in her *Theatre Notes*. She is unusual among critics in finding *Carícies* a much better play than *Després de la pluja*. For her, '*Caresses* was a drama rooted in a gritty urban vernacular, and revealed a complex, poetic playwright with an intriguing formal imagination.'[35] *Després de la pluja*, however, she found a 'structurally predictable' and baffling play, but she finds it much harder to work out why she was 'so bored, puzzled and frustrated'. She objects to the play's sexual politics, finding in it 'a troubling subtext of misogyny', while recognising that 'it could be commenting on misogyny, rather than being itself misogynistic. It is impossible to tell,' a point that was not appreciated by London reviewer Lyn Gardner, who found the play's sexual politics 'prehistoric'.

Croggon tries to find the explanation for her perplexity in the translation (done by John London, Xavier Rodríguez Rosell and myself!), writing of the 'possible shortcomings of the English text', but, in my subjective view, is quite wrong to assume that the fact that there were three translators meant that 'perhaps there were too many cooks muddling the broth'.[36] She also criticises Scott Gooding's 'deadeningly

---

[32] *The Independent*, Section 2, 1 April 1996, p. 27.

[33] *El Periódico*, 26 November 1993, p. 2.

[34] 'Floodgates Open After Bleak Look at Corporate Nightmare', *The Age*, 1 March 2005, p. 11.

[35] Alison Croggon, 'After the Rain', http://theatrenotes.blogspot.com/2005/02/after-rain.html, accessed 21 December 2008.

[36] The translation began as a project completed by an Erasmus exchange student at Swansea, Xavier Rodríguez Rosell, from the Universitat Autònoma de Barcelona, and assessed by me. John London and I then edited the

literal' direction. She is scathing about the design, but provides a detailed description of it:

> Kathryn Sproul's set – a rooftop set forestage, surrounded by metal railings – forces the actors to clamber on and off stage via a ladder, which makes entrances and exits cumbersome, time-consuming and mind-numbingly predictable. A row of watercoolers set behind the raised roof do nothing more than suggest what we already know, that off-stage there are offices. Dominating the back of the theatre is a huge screen, which remains strangely unexploited for almost the entire evening (even some projected clouds would have been welcome). To emphasise the static staging, the lighting states remain monotonous for the whole show, shifting maybe twice to indicate that a particular scene is a dream rather than 'reality'.

Neither is the costuming immune from Croggon's censure:

> These problems are compounded by a lack of attention to detail. For example: perhaps to emphasise the corporate tyranny, the performers are costumed in uniforms that are in no way supported by the script, which means that a long speech by the Blonde Secretary about how she never wears black shoes is somewhat undermined by the fact that she is, in fact, wearing black shoes. And so on.

Croggon's conclusion is that the main problem may be with the 'very naive' production of a 'potentially interesting' play.

If the English-language productions of the play received a generally unenthusiastic or negative press, its reception in Germany was rather more positive. Like a number of other Belbel plays, *Després de la pluja* was staged (as *Nach den Regen*) in several German cities, including Hamburg, Mannheim and Osnabrück. *Der Tages Spiegel*'s review of the Hamburg production was lukewarm, opining that it was a nice play to watch, but not terribly serious.[37] Reviewers in both Mannheim and Osnabrück mention what for them is the play's exaggeration and the grotesque in the productions. The latter felt that the dialogue was over-

---

translation for publication: it was published as Sergi Belbel, *After the Rain* (published with *Sugar Dollies*, by Klaus Chatten) (London: Methuen, 1996), pp. 85–178.

[37] Review of *Nach den Regen, Der Tages Spiegel*, 15 November 1995.

shadowed by these elements, and added that the play received polite but unenthusiastic applause.[38] The Mannheim reviewer referred to the timeliness of the production in that city given the recent German ban on smoking in the workplace.[39] As well as the element of the grotesque, the reviewer pointed to what for him is the play's realism, and also to a quiet, understated absurdity. He commented on the sense of constraint and bleakness underlying the surface comedy. The director brought out this comic element, he said, through body language and gestures. The tempo of the dialogues was quick fire, a positive feature for the reviewer. This production seems to have convinced the audience, to judge from the prolonged applause it received. For one reviewer, a more recent German production – in Cottbus – turned Bob Dylan's 'A Hard Rain's a-Gonna Fall' on its head.[40] It was apocalyptic, said the reviewer, but also pleasurable. The ending brings hope, although it is not clear whether the characters will find happiness.

The mixed reception of *Després de la pluja* abroad is confirmed by contrasting its apparently poor reception in Holland with the positive vibes it generated in Germany. I have not seen Dutch reviews, but its Dutch translator, Ronald Brouwer, said to me in an interview I conducted with him that the play was not well received in Holland, either in Amsterdam or on tour, despite the fact that the company that put it on was well known.[41] The Dutch production, he said, was very different from the Spanish one, employing a smaller format, and bringing out, as with its Mannheim and Osnabrück counterparts, elements of the grotesque, in a style that Brouwer described as 'expressionist'. I pointed out to Brouwer that Belbel has never really set the critical world alight in the UK, but he said that both *Caricies* and *Després* had been successful in Belgium. The main criticism was directed at the text, in contrast to a newspaper review of the Mannheim

---

[38] 'Unausgesetztes Lust-Stöhnen' ('Incessant Moans of Pleasure'), *Oldenburgische Volkszeitung*, 1 October 1996.

[39] Von Heinz Schönfeldt, 'Viel Qualm auf dem Dach' ('Smoke on the Roof'), *Mannheimer Morgen*, 3 March 1997.

[40] Von Gottfried Blumenstein, 'Hochform, wohin das Auge auch blickt' ('Top Quality, Wherever the Eye Looks'), *Lausitzer Rundschau*, 10 December 2001.

[41] The interview was conducted in February 2009 at Madrid's Teatro de la Abadía, of which Brouwer is Deputy Director.

production, in which it was felt that 'the young Spanish author displays extraordinary dramatic creativity, proving that he is worthy of the awards he has received' (Heike Marx, 'Into the Abyss, Into One's Death'). According to Marx, the production seemed to highlight the sense of menace beneath the comedy:

> The author plays with fictitious, real and near-falls with a sovereignty that can be seen on the stage. The scenic framework, created by the stage designer Annette Murschetz, simulates reality and at the same time alienates it by using strange angles and the sort of lighting that makes the symbolism of this place permanently and visibly present. The crusted, enclosed life of the office block, that people think they can hear bubbling underground, is existence; the roof the retreat of those who deviate from the required norm. The menacing abyss is death.

As was later to be the case with *Mòbil*, for German reviewers the play is less one-dimensional than for critics from other countries, even possessing a philosophical dimension. As Marx puts it in his concluding paragraph, 'these eight people find themselves becoming four couples. How this is threaded, propelled and brought to an end is so psychologically gripping and existentially so exemplary that it required neither the verbal ardour that was only sporadically present nor the metaphysical rain. It is a parable about life and as such is pitilessly comedic and insanely tragic.' Such a powerful appreciation is totally different from the views of some of the English-language and Dutch critics.

### *Tàlem*

Like *Carícies* and *Després de la pluja*, this play elicited mixed reviews, as our analysis of its reception in Barcelona, Madrid, London, Vienna and Bolzano/Bozen will illustrate. A full, detailed, and generally favourable review of the Barcelona premiere is Joan Casas's in *Diari de Barcelona*. He sets the play in the context of Belbel's (as yet brief) dramatic output, and sees both familiar and new elements in it. He makes especial mention of Belbel's team: 'Belbel's symbiosis with his team (set designer, costume designer and musician) looks now to be perfect.'[42] He is impressed by the actors, particularly Anna Güell, and

---

42 'la simbiosi de Sergi Belbel amb el seu equip (escenògraf, figurinista i

feels that the Centre Dramàtic de la Generalitat de Catalunya's policy of funding is certainly justified from the evidence of this production. He does have one small quibble, and that is with the quality of the play's language, referring to 'this impoverished, compressed, reiterative, syncopated variant of Catalan that Sergi Belbel has invented'.[43] Rather than seeing this as part of the pleasure, the repetition can be wearisome, he says, and lead one to lose concentration.

Núria Sàbat, on the other hand, finds much to admire in the dialogue: 'Once more the dialogue reflects the special attention that the young dramatist pays to language as a means of communication; the power of the word but also its fragility and its complexity, the value of contextualisation and the ambiguity of meaning.'[44] She writes approvingly of Belbel's ability as an actors' director, and on his care in leaving all the ends tied up despite the apparent disorder of the play. Sàbat also comments on the 'formalist' label that was often attached to Belbel, and, in contrast to some of the London critics (see below), she feels that Belbel has never demonstrated the 'formalist coldness' ('frialdad formalista') that he has sometimes been accused of.

Xavier Pérez too appreciates Belbel's technical skill in constructing this play, and 'the surprising way that scenes are linked, which are at first fragmentary, until the audience is able to grasp the whole story, the discovery of the theatrical machinery half-way through the play'.[45] Here is another critic who, in contrast to his London counterparts, finds the play 'fresh, stimulating, entertaining' ('fresc, estimulant, divertit'), applauds the musicality of the words, admires Belbel's

músic) sembla ja perfecta' (Joan Casas, 'Els perills de l'amanerament' ('The Dangers of Affectation'), Mirador, Diari de Barcelona, 23 April 1990, p. 3).

43 'aquesta variant empobrida, comprimida, reiterativa i sincopada del català que Sergi Belbel s'ha inventat'.

44 'El diálogo refleja nuevamente la especial atención que el joven dramaturgo otorga al lenguaje como medio de comunicación; el poder de la palabra pero también su fragilidad y su complejidad, el valor de la contextualización y la ambigüedad del sentido' (Núria Sàbat, 'Tàlem, el poder de la sugestión' ('Tàlem, the Power of Suggestion'), El Periódico, 23 April 1990, p. 45).

45 'la sorprenent manera de lligar les escenes, a l'inici fragmentàries, fins que el públic pot captar la totalitat de la història, la descoberta de la tramoia teatral just a la meitat de l'obra' (Xavier Pérez, 'Un prolífic investigador' ('A Prolific Researcher'), Avui, 26 April 1990, p. 36).

ability to combine theatrical investigation with the power to make his audiences laugh, and his capacity for working with actors who believe in 'a director-actor and abandon themselves to the pleasure of an entertainment that was shared with their audience'.[46]

Javier Villán, on the other hand, writing on the production at Madrid's Sala Olimpia, is more in accord with the British critics when he finds the play sterile and lacking in substance. He finds that intelligence and brilliance are not sufficient, and that a play needs more content to be worthwhile. As he himself admits, he favours old-fashioned values that no longer seem to be in vogue, opining that

> vacuousness cannot be an absolute value nor inanity be confused with stylisation or suggestion. These may be the signs of times in which the imposter is called progress and modernity. The inevitable agitation of a resistance culture has given way to the asepsis of a broken and sterile postmodernism, as a culture of submission.[47]

Like Haro and Trancón, Villán finds it difficult to empathise with the idiom of Belbel's early plays, and, like them, tends to fall into the trap of using labels (be it postmodernism or naturalism) to attempt to categorise what he dislikes.

María-José Ragué also criticises the play for its lack of substance and interest. She contrasts this deficiency with Belbel's technical skill, particularly as a director. She appreciates his ability to bring the best out of the actors, who she considers gave superb performances. She also approves of Joaquim Roy's stage design, and feels that the music works well as a linkage between the scenes. She accepts that Belbel understands how comedy works, but declares that she is not interested in the story and prefers Cukor and Billy Wilder. She brings up the old chestnut of minimalism in her final sentence, which is ironic in tone:

---

[46] 'un director-actor i es lliuren al plaer d'un divertiment compartit amb el seu públic'.

[47] 'la vacuidad no puede ser un valor absoluto ni lo inane confundirse con estilización o sugerencia. Quizás sean estos los signos de unos tiempos en los que la impostura recibe el nombre de progreso y modernidad. A la crispación inevitable de una cultura de resistencia ha sucedido la asepsia de una posmodernidad deshuesada y estéril, como cultura de sumisión' (Javier Villán, 'Virtuosismo y frustración' ('Virtuosity and Frustration'), *El Mundo*, 12 January 1991, p. 38).

'A passionate game from Sergi Belbel, based on a banal, almost non-existent, certainly minimalist story.'[48]

Of the play's reception in its first London production, directed by Hans-Peter Kellner (as *Fourplay*) at the Lyric Studio in Hammersmith in 1999, John London writes: 'a postmodern bedroom farce ended up being perceived as empty and cold. [...] Veteran critic Michael Billington was not impressed: he noted "the absence of any social context" and compared Belbel unfavourably with Patrick Marber, Tom Stoppard, Harold Pinter, Alan Ayckbourn and Ray Cooney.'[49] John London rejects Belbel's view that his lack of success in the English-speaking world when compared with his reception in other countries is due to his lacking an agent to promote his work, and offers other possible reasons. In the case of Hans-Peter Kellner's *Fourplay*, London suggests that 'Simon Beresford's exaggeratedly techno setting may not have helped, with its green neon light sweeping across the stage after every scene' (p. 455),[50] while 'the way he has been presented and an Anglo-Saxon appetite for a limited, defined style and precise locations may constitute the actual reasons for this disparity' (p. 456).

Interestingly, Kellner's 1997 production of *Tàlem* (as *Spielwiese*) at the Konzerthaus in his native Vienna was a great success, at least according to the one press review of the production I have been able to consult. Such words as 'skilfully' and 'pacy' were used to describe Kellner's direction, while the acting was felt 'to bring this modern work its deserved success'. The review concludes with a glowing appreciation of Belbel: 'The 33-year-old Belbel is considered a cult

---

[48] 'Un juego apasionante de Sergi Belbel a partir de una historia banal, casi inexistente, seguramente minimalista' (María-José Ragué, '*Tàlem*: una comedia de Sergi Belbel' ('*Tàlem*, a Play by Sergi Belbel'), *El Mundo*, 27 April 1990, p. 38). Belbel himself was sceptical about the minimalist epithet. In an interview coinciding with the Barcelona premiere of *Tàlem*, he responds to the question of how minimalist the play is by saying that 'I would say that it is maximalist' ('yo diría que es maximalista') (Interview with Ana Rosa Cánovas, *La Vanguardia*, 20 April 1990, p. 56).

[49] 'Contemporary Catalan Drama in English: Some Aspirations and Limitations', p. 455.

[50] A rather spectacular lighting effect that was to be repeated in Lluís Pasqual's 2007 production of *Mòbil*.

author in his homeland of Catalonia. Will Vienna now follow?'[51] It is always difficult to decide why there should be such a difference between the reception in two cities. It could simply be a question of cultural taste, as suggested by John London. On the other hand, it could be due to a different type of staging, despite the fact that the director was the same in both productions. Jarolin writes of 'the simple stage design by Thomas Oláh', which suggests a contrast with the setting for the Lyric Studio.[52]

As far as the second London production of the play is concerned – Green for Go's double bill at the Tristan Bates Theatre featuring *Fourplay* and Caryl Churchill's *Three More Sleepless Nights*, in April 2008 – I have been able to find just two reviews. *Time Out*'s Andrew Haydon was unimpressed. He found that the structure 'leaves the audience knowing almost immediately how it ends, but having no idea what *it* is or why it ended thus. The play makes precious little sense at all until about half way through, and isn't helped by interminable blackouts between every short scene.'[53] He also finds the actors' performances 'muted', which, combined with the 'echoey acoustics' of this 'difficult space', meant that the production lacked pace.

Molly Flatt is more positive about the play and the production than her *Time Out* counterpart. While considering that neither of the two plays is a masterpiece, she feels that the 'canny juxtaposition of these unlikely bedfellows lends them spark and satisfaction'.[54] She thinks highly of the acting, while, in a sense, Churchill's 'snapshots have effectively prepared the audience for Belbel's piecemeal tableaux'. In both plays, she writes, 'the central image and metaphor of the bed is a potent one, and the concomitant themes of secret lust, public shame, hostility and hope situate the two sets of characters in compassionate and resonant dialogue'.

---

51 Peter Jarolin, 'A Verbal Mirror of Desire', translation of 'Ein verbaler Spiegel der Lust', *Kurier*, 27 September 1997. Translated by L. R. Corper.

52 The role of the director in German-speaking countries may well be crucial in this aspect: for further details see the concluding remarks to this chapter.

53 Review of the double bill in *Time Out*, 10–16 April 2008, p. 150.

54 Molly Flatt, 'Theatre of the Underdog', http://www.guardian.co.uk/stage/theatreblog/2008/apr/16/theatreoftheunderdog, accessed 22 December 2008.

*Tàlem* also received a German-language revival in 2008, this time in the North Italian Tyrolean town of Bolzano/Bozen, by the United Stages of Bolzano (Vereinigte Bühnen Bozen, or VBB), as *Spielwiese, zwei im Quadrat*, under the direction of one of the actresses from the 1997 Vienna production, Nina C. Gabriel. To judge from an interview with her it is clear that she both understands the play and has interesting ideas on how to direct it. She says that it is 'written like a [musical] score and requires a clear choreography', while she also feels that it 'works like a puzzle'.[55]

The production seems to have been a roaring success. One reviewer referred to the 'satisfaction of the audience, who applauded many scenes during the play's premiere evening',[56] while another reviewer writes:

> Playing with the expectations of the audience and misleading them with pleasure: this is what the German adaptation of the piece *Fourplay* by the Catalan author Sergi Belbel manages to do effortlessly. And the audience at the studio of Bolzano City Theatre audibly enjoyed this.[57]

The reviewers seem to have had very few problems with a text that had received such a lukewarm reception in London. One reviewer called it 'a wonderful night at the theatre'.[58] There was appreciation of the play's 'mathematical principles', and 'the mathematically calculated scenes',[59] while Helfer wrote approvingly of 'its precisely arranged sequence of extracts [...] a crafty piece of dramaturgy that works with

55 Kathrin Gschleier, 'Expectations and Insights', translation of 'Erwartungen und Erkenntnisse', *Dolomiten*, 6 March 2008. Translated by Mathew John Francis Dwyer.

56 Margit Oberhammer, 'Keen Sense of Rhythm', translation of 'Sicheres Gefühl für den Rhythmus', *Dolomiten*, 13 March 2008. Translated by L. R. Corper.

57 Anon., 'Yawn of the Sexes', translation of 'Gähnen der Geschlechter', *Tribüne*, 20 March 2008. Translated by L. R. Corper.

58 Klaus Hartig, 'Everything is Just as it Was', translation of 'Alles ist, wie es ist', *Tageszeitung*, 14 March 2008. Translated by Chloë Driscoll.

59 Anon., 'Modern Remix of Love Game', translation of 'Liebesspielwiese im modernen Remix', *Zett*, 16 March 2008. Translated by L. R. Corper.

mathematical configurations'.[60] The *Tribüne* reviewer's take on Belbel is that 'the internationally known author is a linguistic mathematician, he sees through people, he knows what goes on in their heads' ('Yawn of the Sexes'). The puzzle aspect was appreciated in Bolzano, in contrast to London, as was its wit and its successful blending of comedy and tragedy ('Yawn of the Sexes').

The precision of the text of which Helfer approved is also present for some of the critics in Gabriel's direction. For the *Tribüne* critic, she 'has staged an infernal dance, rhythmically and precisely', while for Helfer the staging 'runs like clockwork, sometimes even like a display of fireworks' (*MiMa* review). Oberhammer's view is that 'Nina Gabriel has staged the play with high precision and a keen sense of rhythm', and, in a description that echoes Helfer's 'fireworks', 'did not shy away from explosively infiltrating the frigid, stylised wannabe-perfect designed stage with kitsch lighting and a barrage of music and was nevertheless able to keep the play from slipping into chaos' ('Keen Sense of Rhythm'). The actual music that forms part of the play (in the original Catalan too, of course) is commented on, with Hartig mentioning that Gabriel replaces the Sinatra 'My Way' of the original with 'Michael Jackson's pulsating pop' ('Everything is Just as it Was'). As the title suggests, the musical concept is also in the mind of the *Zett* reviewer, for whom the scenes 'are like a modern DJ remix of a famous hit, focusing on an old theme: relationships and their crises' ('Modern Remix of Love Game').

The Bolzano production had been eagerly anticipated in the city. Indeed, the *Dolomiten* preview of the production quotes VBB president Thomas Seeber on how 'for a long time we wanted to stage a play by Sergi Belbel because his plays have an interesting modern dramaturgy – a challenge for our audience'. However, the perceptiveness of the Bolzano reviews suggests a sensitive appreciation of the play, and it may be simply a question of taste that explains enthusiasm for a genre that provokes indifference elsewhere. The reviews convey a real sense of what the play actually looked and sounded like on stage. The apparently simple, almost clinical stage design received some attention, with Helfer referring to its 'clarity'. For the *Zett* reviewer, 'the yuppie style

---

60 Christine Helfer, review of the play in *MiMa*, 13 March 2008. Translated by L. R. Corper.

of the stage design (by Andreas Lungenschmid) using harsh light and stylish grey-violet is the typification of what these "children of their time" represent' ('Modern Remix of Love Game'), while the *Tribüne* reviewer writes of Lungenschmid's 'simple stage design. A cabinet of horrors with bricked up windows' ('Yawn of the Sexes'). Oberhammer's description of the set as 'frigid, stylised wannabe-perfect', quoted above, reinforces the point, and, in a way, seems to anticipate Max Glaenzel and Estel Cristià's set for *A la Toscana*.[61]

The swift switching between scenes leads this same reviewer to compare the play with 'a running film, and credits included', adding: 'During the first act the characters are shown top-half only high up on the stage, the curtains hiding a part of them, in the second act they are shown full-bodied' ('Yawn of the Sexes'). Here is a clear example of the attention to detail I have mentioned. Helfer refers to the 'filmic character of the piece', while Hartig is struck by the similarity to cinema technique:

> Sergi Belbel divides the simple story into puzzle pieces, which put themselves together after a second glance. Like an artful editor, who cuts up filmscripts and glues the snippets together anew. Set pieces certainly. Film clips. Or uneven reflective surfaces. But at the end there is a picture. ('Everything is Just as it Was')

Hartig (who, unlike the London and Barcelona reviewers, finds the play genuinely and subtly funny) describes the director's setting up of the first half of the production as if it were video sequences, adding: 'black panes broaden and narrow the voyeuristic view of the pathetic rabble'. This effect, he says, ceases in the second half.

Other visual details commented upon include the 'designer bed, a glass monster under alternating stage lights, covered with a ragged, animal skin-like blanket, which someone sometimes wraps around themselves' ('Keen Sense of Rhythm'), and a 'baluster like the German cartoonist Loriot's pug-nosed characters', behind which the couple stand at the beginning of the play ('Everything is Just as it Was'). Such details are often lacking from Catalan, Spanish or London reviews, as (with the notable exception of Joan Casas) is an appreciation that

---

61  For further details see Chapter 2, pp. 89–9.

Belbel's theatre relies on the sort of ensemble performance that was valued by the Bolzano reviewers.[62]

## *Mòbil*

So far, we have observed how reviews of Belbel's plays have varied from enthusiam to indifference to disgust. The play that has provoked the most mixed reactions of all is *Mòbil*, whose reception we shall now consider. It is the only Belbel play to date to have been staged at the Teatre Lliure, which, together with the Teatre Nacional de Catalunya, is one of Barcelona's major theatre venues.[63] The Barcelona press reviews of this play were the most negative Belbel has ever received. Several critics felt that the Lliure should have known better than to try to compete with the commercial sector in what they felt was a dumming-down enterprise. Pérez Olaguer's view is that the play lacks any interest beyond purely commercial ones ('más allá del puramente comercial').[64] Francesc Massip puts it more bluntly when he says:

> The *Mòbil* operation, then, ought to mobilise the theatre profession and the Lliure audience to demand a territorial demarcation of subsidised theatre and to avoid public funds being wasted on shows that would find only on the Paral·lel or on television the type of lazy spectator that the production requires.[65]

---

[62] For example, the *Tribüne* reviewer says that 'rarely has one seen such an ensemble performance at the City Theatre' ('Yawn of the Sexes').

[63] Belbel has also directed just one play at the venue: Benet i Jornet's *L'habitació del nen*, in 2003.

[64] Gonzalo Pérez Olaguer, 'Patinazo del Teatre Lliure' ('Blunder at the Teatre Lliure'), *El Periódico*, 1 January 2007, viewed at http://www.teatre nacional.com/critiques/mobil.html, accessed 17 September 2008.

[65] 'L'operació de *Mòbil*, doncs, hauria de mobilitzar la professió teatral i l'audiència del Lliure per tal de reclamar una delimitació territorial de la creació escènica subvencionada i evitar que es malversin fons públics en espectacles que només trobarien al Paral·lel o a la televisió l'espectador mandrós que requereix el muntatge' (Francesc Massip, 'Camí de crancs', *Avui*, 1 January 2007, viewed at http://www.teatrenacional.com/critiques/ mobil.html, accessed 17 September 2008). The Paral·lel is an avenue in Barcelona with a long tradition of cabaret, music hall, and other popular entertainment venues, some of which are, to say the least, seedy.

The general objection was that a publicly funded theatre should be putting on what was judged to be a poor play, and that a theatre with the Lliure's reputation for quality had committed a serious error in staging it. In Benach's words,

> That's what *Mòbil* is, in fact: a lamentable error. One would not have expected such an entertainment given the standards associated with the Lliure's commitment and the prestige of the playwright and the director. It might have had a modest presence on unambitious commercial circuits, but it has no place in the theatre, established thirty years ago by Pasqual among others, in which quality is normally guaranteed.[66]

Or as Doria has it, 'one wonders what this play is doing on the stage of the Lliure'.[67] Massip feels that the 'cretinisation of society' ('cretinització de la societat') wrought by the venture is reminiscent of the theatre they had to put up with in Franco's times.

The critics' deception is all the greater because of expectations raised by the involvement of two of Catalonia's biggest theatrical names, Belbel and Pasqual, only for the spectators' hopes to be cruelly dashed. Both men incur the critics' wrath. Pérez Olaguer's view is that, by plumping for a strong emphasis on the visual element, Pasqual's production tires the eyes and gives one a headache, while Doria objects to the 'large numbers of lightbulbs that dazzle, and not exactly in a pleasant fashion'.[68] In his view, the premiere was characterised by 'a

---

[66] '*Mòbil*, en efecto, es eso: un lamentable error. Ni de la exigencia derivada del compromiso del Lliure, ni del prestigio del autor y del director cabía esperar un pasatiempo como éste, que tal vez haría una discreta carrera en circuitos comerciales de escasa ambición, pero que no pinta nada en el teatro fundado hace treinta años, entre otros por Pasqual, y que solía asegurar la calidad de su oferta' (Joan-Anton Benach, 'Una lamentable confusión' ('A Lamentable Confusion'), *La Vanguardia*, 1 January 2007, viewed at http://www.teatrenacional.com/critiques/mobil.html, accessed 17 September 2008).

[67] 'se pregunta qué hace esa obra en el escenario del Lliure' (Sergio Doria, 'Bombillitas a todo taco' ('Light Bulbs at Full Blast', presumably a reference to the garish LED lighting employed by Pasqual, while 'taco' is also the Spanish for 'swear word'), *ABC*, 1 January 2007, viewed at http://www. teatrenacional com/critiques/mobil.html, accessed 17 September 2008).

[68] 'muchísimas bombillitas que deslumbran y, no precisamente, de forma grata'.

tedium replete with luminosity and theatricality, in direct proportion to the number of gross expressions that smear its failed dialogues'.[69]

However, it is Belbel himself who comes in for the biggest criticism for what Barcelona critics feel is the exceptionally poor quality of the text. Pérez Olaguer's opinion is that the spectacular production at least serves to distract the audience from the eminently forgettable text. Massip excoriates the text: 'In *Mòbil* everything is mind-numbingly obvious, seemingly designed for adolescents. Jangling dialogues in the mouths of characters who lack dramatic coherence' ('A *Mòbil* tot és d'una obvietat paralitzant que sembla dissenyada per a espectadors adolescents. Unes rèpliques a guisa de matraca posades en boca d'uns personatges mancats de coherència dramàtica'). The harshest criticism came from Marcos Ordóñez, and, significantly, the review appears not in the normal theatre section of *El País* but in its weekly literary review section, Babelia. The following typifies his view of the play:

> If *Mòbil* bores me to death, it's because, in essence, its writing is flat and predictable, with an outpouring of words, unable to separate the grain from the chaff and with one swear word in every three. There is no dramatic tension in the conflicts, which are reduced to carica-ture, nor in the unidirectional speeches that are full of common-places, with no vitality or surprise.[70]

The general critical view from Barcelona was that the only positive feature of the production was the quality of the acting. As Doria puts it, one did not know whether to applaud the professionalism of the actors or to boo the banality produced by Belbel and Pasqual. Fighting against the odds, the actors, it was felt, had made a valiant attempt to rescue an unrescuable play. In Benach's words, 'the best thing about *Mòbil* is the acting: especially the titanic efforts of Marta Marco and Rosa Novell to

---

[69] 'Un tedio repleto de luminosidad y efectismo escenográfico, directa-mente proporcionales a la cantidad de expresiones gruesas que embadurnan unos diálogos fallidos.'

[70] 'Si *Móbil* me aburre a morir es, esencialmente, porque su escritura es plana, previsible y aluvionesca, sin separar el grano de la paja y con un taco cada tres palabras. Sin tensión dramática en los conflictos, reducidos a caricatura, ni en unos parlamentos unidireccionales y cuajados de lugares comunes, sin nervio ni sorpresa' (Marcos Ordóñez, 'Sin cobertura' ('No Coverage'), *El País*, Babelia section, 20 January 2007, p. 21).

ensure that the disastrous and disappointing show would not be wildly catastrophic'.[71] They, opines Pérez Olaguer, 'prove that they are three splendid actresses, far superior to the characters they had to play'.[72] However, even their efforts cannot compensate for the play's deficiencies, a feeling summed up by Doria: 'Neither the efforts of Marta Marco, in her felicitous interpretation of indignation and inebriation, nor the experienced reliability of Maife Gil and Rosa Novell can rescue the audience from boredom.'[73]

As we observed from the German-language productions of *Tàlem*, its reception in Germany was very different from that in London and, to a lesser extent, in Barcelona. The contrast in the case of *Mòbil* is even more striking. According to one review, it received 'great acclaim' at Bremen's Brauhauskeller, while 'the audience at the premiere showed their appreciation for the exciting and successful performance with a long, enthusiastic final round of applause'.[74] This reviewer shared their apparent enthusiasm, as she wrote: '*Mobile* was fun and bubbled over with witty ideas and excellent acting.' A review of the Stuttgart production confirms the esteem in which Belbel is held in Germany: 'the successful Spanish dramatist, Sergi Belbel, who was made famous in Germany with his farces *After the Rain* or *Strangers*',[75] while a reviewer of the Bremen production refers to him as 'one of the most prestigious playwrights of our time: the Catalan Sergi Belbel'.[76] There is no special enthusiasm for the play's content,

71 'lo mejor de *Mòbil* es la interpretación: el esfuerzo titánico, sobre todo, de Marta Marco y Rosa Novell, para que el calamitoso y decepcionante espectáculo no resulte exageradamente catastrófico'.

72 'demuestran que son tres espléndidas actrices, muy por encima del personaje que les ha tocado'.

73 'Ni el esfuerzo de Marta Marco en su feliz interpretación de la indignación y la ebriedad; ni la veterana solvencia de Maife Gil y Rosa Novell pueden rescatar al público del tedio.'

74 Nicole Schaake-Burmann, 'Always Reachable, Ever Lonely', translation of 'Immer erreichbar, stets einsam', *Weser Report*, 7 March 2007. Translated by Julia Summerfield.

75 Inge Bäuerle, 'The Rituals of the Hardworking Telephoners', translation of 'Die Rituale der fleißigen Telefonierer', *Stuttgarter Zeitung*, 30 June 2007. Translated by Chloë Driscoll.

76 Astrid Labbert, 'We Like to Talk – but Only on the Phone', translation of 'Wir reden gern – aber nur am Handy', *Weser Kurier*, 6 March 2007.

but most of the comments on the text itself are fairly neutral, and descriptive rather than analytical. 'In *Mobile* he satirises, sometimes humorously, sometimes analytically, the influence of telecommunications technology on life and the communicative failure of its owners,' writes Astrid Labbert ('We Like to Talk – but Only on the Phone').

Why, then, was the play successful? Of course, it is extremely difficult to quantify why a play can receive such damning criticism in one city or country and be a big success in another. To talk of national taste is tricky, although, as was briefly observed in the discussion of the reception of *Tàlem*, it is one possible explanation. More fruitful, perhaps, although still unquantifiable, is to focus on the direction and the mise en scène. One Bremen review that is less than enthusiastic about the text is clear that the key to its success is the staging. The subtitle is fairly blunt: 'Henrike Vahrmeyer breathes new life into Sergi Belbel's weak play *Mobile* in the Bremen theatre.'[77] He explains: 'Mobiles, globalisation, terrorism and a bit of love. To develop a play from this, you would have to either be quite stupid or particularly clever. […] Ultimately in Sergi Belbel's *Mobile* far too few unexpected things happen. The performance in the Bremen Brauhauskeller Theatre is nevertheless enjoyable, thanks to the sophisticated scenic realisation.' As with the German productions of *Tàlem*, the reviews of *Mòbil* provide quite a lot of detail about what the play actually looked like on stage. According to Schnackenburg, the audience reached their seats via the back of the stage; these seats were revolving stools, surrounded by the sides of the stage, with the actors performing outside while the audience sat inside, a technique that, according to the reviewer, had been used on previous occasions in Bremen's theatres. Schaake-Burmann also mentioned the stools, while Schnackenburg concludes

Translated by Julia Summerfield. It will also be noted that he is referred to as a Catalan rather than a Spanish writer. The play received its German premiere in Hannover. The fact that it was performed in various German centres seems to confirm not only Belbel's popularity in Germany but also the vibrancy of a German theatre scene that is not centred on the capital city (see Marvin Carlson, 'National Theatres: Then and Now', in *National Theatres in a Changing Europe*, ed. S. E. Wilmer, Studies in International Performance (Basingstoke and New York: Palgrave Macmillan, 2008), pp. 21–33, p. 21).

[77] Alexander Schnackenburg, 'Mobile Phone Reception in Bremen's Brauhaus Theatre', translation of 'Handyempfang im Brauhaus', *Kreiszeitung*, 7 March 2007. Translated by Julia Summerfield.

his review by commenting that the performance made the backache caused by the Bremen theatre's stools bearable. This critic also highlights the importance of good direction of this play:

> In a room like that of the Brauhauskeller, which is exactly four metres wide, however, this layout is surprising (stage and costumes: Natascha Steinkamp). The room used as a stage seems therefore to be essential for this play. A large part of the 'dialogues' in *Mobile* form factual monologues: one or another actor is heard or seen talking on a mobile phone, while direct personal encounters are scarce. Obviously it would be quite ridiculous for the actors to repeatedly and obstinately exit stage left or right and then have to come back on. Imaginative stage direction is necessary here.

This sort of detail – which underlines the necessity of imaginative directing – was missing from the Barcelona reviews. Schnackenburg also emphasises that the play was 'staged plainly with a few spotlights'. This contrasts markedly with Pasqual's use of bright LED lighting and video projections in the Barcelona production. Intriguingly, he adds that 'at the author's invitation, she gratefully uses jagged scene changes – appropriate to the shortness of mobile phone conversations'. Other reviewers, too, opine that it was the quality of the directing that made the production a success. To quote Labbert, 'the Bremen ensemble with director Vahrmeyer have made this into an amusing and sometimes touching play' ('We Like to Talk – but Only on the Phone').

To judge from Inge Bäuerle's review, the Stuttgart production of *Mòbil* was very different ftom the Bremen one, but its direction was also highly imaginative:

> [This was also true of] the 'mobile' scenery, designed by Gudrun Schretzmeier, who also took care of the costumes. It is a labyrinth, whose contours are illuminated like a deconstructed runway, and at the same time looks like a pinball machine, due to the revolving glass door in the middle. Sofas, a bed and a plant are able to drop down from the walls – flip-up furniture, an analogy of the garish flip-up phones of the actors.
> **A Waft of Antiquity**
> For Klaus Hemmerle also has the characters rolling in and out like balls through the revolving door. They remain stuck at dead ends accompanied by their phones, roll past each other and collide after

the bomb – 'tilt', while they practise their mobile-telephoning rituals. These are so beautiful that you can easily forget the Spanish guitar notes and snippets of words, which seem somewhat superimposed and repeatedly point to the origin of the piece, just like a waft of antiquity, which is already blowing over the two year old piece as if it were a two year old phone model. ('The Rituals of the Hardworking Telephoners')

The clichéd Spanish guitar seems not to have spoiled the show for this reviewer, although she does fall into another familiar trap when she compares Belbel to iconic Spanish film director Pedro Almodóvar, in that, in this instance, his characters are 'teetering on the edge of a nervous breakdown'. If the guitar is a cliché, the trick used by the director after the performance does appear to be something of a gimmick, although apparently aimed at creating ambiguity over whether the mobile phone is a positive or a negative device. To quote Bäuerle,

The other – deliberate – uncertainty is whether, in the end, mobile phones are a blessing or a curse. This question is probably not to be asked of the dummy mobiles that were distributed among the premiere guests after the performance. They were filled with peppermints and have one advantage over a real mobile: you can neither detonate bombs with them, nor produce electrosmog; they only serve to freshen your breath.

Yet another seemingly quite different German production took place at the Hans-Otto Theatre in Potsdam in June 2007. This time the action was set on two storeys, with a room on the top floor and an airport hotel lobby on the ground floor. Action took place simultaneously on both levels (see Figures 4 and 5). The *Neues Deutschland* reviewer briefly describes the stage, the performance of the actors and the reaction of the audience: the latter, we are told, even applauded at the end of some of the individual scenes.[78] The reviewer goes into some detail on the significance of the play's content, about which he is more positive than other German reviewers and, it goes without saying, their Catalan counterparts. Rather like Heike Marx in his review of *Després de la pluja*, Schutt sees the play as essentially a tragedy emerging from

---

[78] Hans-Dieter Schutt, 'Alone Together', translation of 'Einsam gemeinsam', *Neues Deutschland*, 20 June 2007.

4. Production of *Mòbil*, Hans-Otto Theatre in Potsdam, 2007.

the surface comedy: 'Out of the comedy emerges a tragic, over clouded, existential study, which delivers humour seriously without losing the joke.' He calls the play a 'high-culture critique and yet too clever to amount to nothing more than this'. He underlines the irony and contradictions of the mobile phone, 'this accursed thing which first made self-examination possible', but which ends up as a barrier to conversation and also triggered the terrorist attack. He sums up the contradictions inherent in this ubiquitous object thus: 'The blessing is the curse, and vice versa. As if the author wanted to confirm, in an intricate manner, that these are not two words, but always a single one: happinessandunhappiness, goodandevil, heavenandhell, loveandhate, glamourandmisery.' One final point to note from the Potsdam review is that, as with Labbert's review of the Bremen production, its author refers to Belbel as a Catalan rather than a Spanish playwright.

It almost goes without saying that such an appreciation of *Mòbil* as essentially a profound piece of drama is a world away from the Barcelona critics' disgust with it. The nature of the German productions is likely to have played a part in this respect, although Marx's fulsome praise of the play's content possibly reinforces a sense that it may be more in tune with German than with Catalan sensibilities.

5. Production of *Mòbil*,
Hans-Otto Theatre in
Potsdam, 2007.

From what I have been able to glean from my conversations with Belbel's Danish director, Simon Boberg, the reception of *Mòbil* by Copenhagen audiences and critics was as positive as it was to be in Germany. The play was commissioned by Boberg, and, like Belbel's next play, *A la Toscana*, received its world premiere at the small Plan-B Theatre in Copenhagen. The production seems to have been much more sober than Pasqual's at the Teatre Lliure. There were no marked scene changes, but fluent transitions between the scenes. The design was simple, and was based around suitcases placed at various points on the stage (see Figure 6). These were used to indicate, for example, the cars, driven by Rosa and Jan, which fell as they crashed into each other, a minibar (see Figure 7) and a toilet. There was lots of music, for example a Mozart piece when Jan saw Rosa for the first time. He had filmed himself on Sara's mobile, and his photo became a huge image projected onto a screen at the back of the stage, with Mozart playing, as he fell instantly in love with her. When Jan shouted at his mother over

6. Production of *Mòbil*, Plan B Theatre, Copenhagen, 2006.

the phone, he broke down and took all his clothes off, running around naked on the stage. Belbel loved the production, especially the acting of Ellen Hillingsø, who played Clàudia.[79]

### A la Toscana

Whereas the Barcelona critics almost universally panned *Mòbil*, the reception of *A la Toscana* was much less uniform there, with reactions varying from enthusiastic approval to an almost *Mòbil*-like venom. Like Michael Billington when faced with *Tàlem*, most of the Barcelona critics seemed to want more content and substance from *A la Toscana* than they felt they were getting. *ABC*'s Sergio Doria, one of Belbel's fiercest critics, once more strongly disapproves of the playwright's efforts. Having begun his review by stating that Catalan theatre owes some of its great moments to Belbel the director, he goes on to say that

---

[79] All the information comes from a conversation I had with Boberg in Copenhagen in May 2009. Boberg's company has since moved to the Husets Theatre in the city, but press reviews and photographs of the productions of both *Mòbil* and *A la Toscana* may be found on the Plan-B website, http:// plan-b-teater.dk/. Unfortunately, I have not been able to locate a suitable translator in time for an analysis of the reviews to be included in this book.

7.  Production of *Mòbil*, Plan B Theatre, Copenhagen, 2006.

Belbel the author has for some time been short of ideas and self-satisfied. According to Doria he is guilty of attempting to cover his plays' lack of content with special effects and expensive scenery. Doria mocks *A la Toscana*'s psychological element, claiming that Freud himself would have been bored by its dream sequences. He is scathing about Albert Guinovart's musical score, describing it as 'that Hollywood-kitsch music that Guinovart composes for series on TV3'.[80] He ends with the following damning comment: 'Ultimately, it all becomes a vacuous exercise in style, which appears to be more than it really is, and never actually gets anywhere. Instead of *To Tuscany*, Belbel presents a theatrical journey to nowhere.'[81]

---

[80] 'esa música kitsch-hollywoodense que Guinovart compone para las series de TV3' (Sergio Doria, 'Viaje a ninguna parte' ('Journey to Nowhere'), *ABC*, 20 November 2007, viewed at http://www.teatrebcn.com/critiques/critiques2.asp?Id=4315, accessed 31 December 2008). TV3 is the main Catalan-language television channel.

[81] 'Al final, todo queda en vacuo ejercicio de estilo, que aparenta más de

Ragué-Arias's review is rather more mixed. She sees virtues in the play, especially the scenery (in particular the superb evocation of Tuscany at the end). She strongly praises the acting, and – in complete contrast to Doria – finds Guinovart's score 'beautiful and suggestive' ('bella y sugerente)'.[82] However, she closes on an extremely negative note, highlighting, like Doria, the play's tedious and impenetrable nature: 'Nevertheless, the whole show is sluggish and confused, and the themes do not attract the interest they should, nor does the audience manage to penetrate that textual and thematic magma. And mystery and beauty end up becoming tedium.'[83]

*La Vanguardia*'s critic sees some of the same positives in *A la Toscana* as Ragué-Arias, especially the music. He is also full of praise about Kiko Planas's lighting and the acting. He is more satisfied with the content and structure of the play than she is, considering it, as indicated in the title of his review, 'an intriguing and very well constructed play that works'.[84] Like Ragué-Arias, he detects cinematic qualities: 'in places it resembles a horror film, and demonstrates a deliberate cinematographic progression through scenes and short dialogues and the multiplicity of spaces'.[85] Interestingly enough, the most positive review of the Barcelona production of *A la Toscana* that I have read is by a blogger who admits to never having seen a Belbel play previously. His/her comments are sharp: 'Belbel has really worked the text, has

lo que es y se queda a medio camino de todo. En lugar de *A la Toscana*, Belbel plantea un viaje teatral a ninguna parte.'

[82] María-José Ragué-Arias, 'La inalcanzable utopía', *El Mundo*, 14 November 2008, viewed at http://www.teatrebcn.com/critiques/critiques2. asp?Id=4315, accessed 31 December 2008.

[83] 'Sin embargo, todo el espectáculo resulta moroso y confuso, sin que los temas tratados alcancen su debido interés, sin que el público consiga penetrar en ese magma textual y temático. Y el misterio y la belleza llegan a convertirse en tedio.'

[84] 'una intrigante comedia muy bien fabricada y que funciona' (Santiago Fondevila, 'Una intrigante comedia', *La Vanguardia*, 7 October 2007, viewed at http://www.teatrebcn.com/critiques/critiques2.asp?Id=4315, accessed 31 December 2008).

[85] 'por momentos se acerca a un filme de terror y que muestra una deliberada progresión cinematográfica a través de escenas y diálogos cortos y la multiplicidad de espacios'. Ragué-Arias points to parallels with Ingmar Bergman's films.

polished it, has measured it, has calculated its precise impact.'[86] The blogger is especially impressed by the acting of Lluïsa Castell, and devotes a large part of this review to singing her praises.

The mixed reviews that *A la Toscana* attracted in Barcelona are a reflection of the reception in the press of the play's Catalan premiere as part of Girona's renowned annual Temporada Alta theatre festival in October 2007.[87] Joaquim Armengol is as negative as Sergio Doria, and considers the acting to be the only positive aspect of the production. He criticises the set ('the set is overdone, and it is grandiose and flamboyant'),[88] and, like Doria and Ragué-Arias, finds the play bereft of ideas. The author, he says, attempts to compensate for its lack of content by employing 'a dramatic contrivance that shifts between a touch of surrealism and the most insolent and macabre grotesque'.[89]

In complete contrast, dramatist and academic Jordi Sala's review of the Teatre de Salt production is by far the most enthusiastic of all the ones I have consulted. For Sala, *A la Toscana* is Belbel's most important play since *Morir (un moment abans de morir)*. He comments on its cinematic dimension, detecting echoes of Woody Allen and Ingmar Bergman. He is impressed by its narrative structure: 'what is really powerful is the narrative device (complex and complicated, overpowering, amazing)'.[90] Sala's evaluation of its psychological (and scien-

---

[86] 'Belbel ha treballat i de valent el text, l'ha polit, l'ha mesurat, n'ha calculat l'impacte exacte' (Blog viewed at http://horitzons.blogspot.com /2007/12/la-toscana-sergi-belbel.html, accessed 31 December 2008).

[87] The first staging of the play was at Plan-B in Copenhagen in 2006. Following its Catalan premiere at the Teatre de Salt in Girona (performances on 5 and 6 October 2007), it was staged as part of Catalonia's guest presence at the Frankfurt Book Fair (on 11–13 October), and in Reus, Manresa and Granollers in mid-to-late October before receiving its Barcelona premiere at the Sala Petita of the TNC on 8 November, where it ran until 6 January 2008. In January 2008 it toured to other locations in Catalonia and Mallorca, and in Spanish translation it was performed in Salamanca and Valladolid in February 2008, before running at Madrid's Teatro de la Abadía from 6 to 16 March of that year.

[88] 'hi ha un abús escenogràfic, d'una grandiosa aparatositat' (Joaquim Armengol, 'Contumàcia' ('Obstinacy'), *El Punt*, 7 October 2007, viewed at http://www.teatrebcn.com/critiques/critiques2.asp?Id=4315, accessed 31 December 2008).

[89] 'una artificiositat dramàtica, que vaga des d'un punt de surrealisme fins al grotesc més insolent i macabre'.

[90] 'allò realment poderós és l'artefacte narratiu (complex i complicat,

tific) dimension is far more positive than Ragué-Arias's, as he writes about 'the influence of quantum physics [...] neurolinguistic programming as offering new perspectives on the individual',[91] in a play that offers a multiplicity of possible meanings. In Sala's view, the familiar Belbel ludic element is present – it is a brilliant jigsaw, he says – but it also has a serious underlying purpose.

Sala is as complimentary about the staging, costume, lighting and music as he is about the play's content and structure:

> Max Glaenzel and Estel Cristià again offer a lesson in set design that brilliantly resolves the conflicts that are presented during the short duration of the scenes; the design is also beautiful – and very cold – as required by the play. The lighting design is correct, and the costuming imaginative. Guinovart's music is, as ever, predictably perfect, even though, as ever, it gives the impression of *déjà écoutée*.[92]

Finally, Sala's evaluation of the acting is almost ecstatic, and he ends his review with the following eulogy of Boixaderas: 'there is no longer any doubt that Jordi Boixaderas is not of this world, he's from another planet. A superhuman performance.'[93]

*A la Toscana* seems to have been better received in Madrid than in Barcelona and, Sala apart, Girona. The *ABC* (Madrid) critic clearly liked it much more than his Barcelona counterpart. He writes: 'Sergi Belbel has written a text with some very enjoyable moments.'[94] He is

---

aclaparador, impressionant)' (Jordi Sala, 'Belbel del segle XXI' ('Twenty-first Century Belbel'), *Diari de Girona*, 7 October 2007, viewed at http://www.teatrebcn.com/critiques/critiques2.asp?Id=4315, accessed 31 December 2008).

[91] 'l'ascendent de la física quàntica [...] la programació neurolingüística com a noves mirades sobre l'individu'.

[92] 'Max Glaenzel i Estel Cristià tornen a donar una lliçó amb una escenografia que brilla en la resolució dels conflictes plantejats per la curta durada de les escenes, i que a més és bellíssima – i fredíssima –, com demana l'obra. El disseny d'il·luminació és correcte, i el vestuari, imaginatiu. La música, de Guinovart, és com sempre previsiblement perfecte, encara que, com sempre, faci la sensació de déjà écoutée.'

[93] 'ja no hi ha dubte que Jordi Boixaderas no és d'aquest món, és un extraterrestre. Una interpretació sobrehumana.'

[94] 'Sergi Belbel ha escrito un texto con momentos muy divertidos' (Juan I.

also impressed by the author's skill as a director, as well as by the set: 'The author has directed his text with the lively subtlety of a choreographer, controlling the complicated balance of rhythms and tempos, against Glaenzel and Cristià's shifting and effective set.'[95] He approves of the acting, finding Cristina Plazas outstanding.

*El Mundo*'s reviewer makes perceptive comments on how the repetition of scenes demonstrates 'the spiral of confusion into which some Western inhabitants have sunk through the guilt complex they acquire when they contrast their own comfortable positions with the shortages suffered by other societies that become ever closer to our own'.[96] He also feels that the mirrors help the spectator better to understand Marc's problem in distinguishing what may be true from what is a mere reflection. However, the review concentrates more on the overall achievements of Belbel's career than on the Abadía production of *A la Toscana*. Villora sees Belbel's as the most successful career in contemporary Spanish drama, and views him as the reference point for young Spanish theatre practitioners. He is, says the reviewer, one of our most performed and studied authors, where 'our' presumably means 'Spanish'. He praises Belbel as the complete man of the theatre, 'a complete creative artist, then, and without whom it is impossible to understand contemporary Spanish theatre'.[97] Nowhere is the fact that he is Catalan mentioned, and Villora even Castilianises Belbel's birthplace: 'Tarrasa' instead of 'Terrassa'. This might be expected from a conservative newspaper like *El Mundo*, since traditional forces in the country view Spain very much as a unified whole, not as a loose collection of almost federal autonomous regions. It also recalls the reception of Catalan theatre in Madrid in the late nineteenth and early twentieth centuries,

García Garzón, 'El síndrome de la felicidad' ('The Happiness Syndrome'), *ABC*, 20 March 2008, p. 57).

[95] 'El autor ha dirigido su texto con ágil sutileza de coreógrafo, controlando el complicado equilibrio de ritmos y tiempos, sobre la cambiante y eficaz escenografía de Glaenzel y Cristià.'

[96] 'la espiral de desconcierto en la que están sumidos algunos occidentales por su complejo de culpa al contrastar su buena posición con las carencias de otras sociedades cada vez más próximas' (Pedro Villora, 'Belbel, *En la Toscana*', *El Mundo*, 6 March 2008, viewed at http://www.elmundo.es/papel/2008/03/06/madrid/2340900.html, consulted 31 December 2008).

[97] 'un creador completo, pues, y sin el que no es posible entender el teatro español contemporáneo'.

when the quality of innovative theatre practitioners from Barcelona was fully appreciated in Madrid, but their Catalanness often was not.[98]

Villora's *El Mundo* colleague Javier Villán also brings up the broader Catalonia question as he uses his review of *A la Toscana* at the Abadía to take a swipe at what, according to him, is perceived in Madrid as Barcelona's lack of openness to the staging of theatre in Castilian Spanish. Having referred to the 'powerful presence of Catalan theatre in Madrid', he reports that 'people from Madrid say that, while Madrid is an open city, Barcelona is an impregnable market in which there is room only for Catalan works in Catalan; an accursed market for companies from the rest of Spain'.[99] Despite the swipe, Villora's view is positive on virtually all aspects of the production, especially Belbel's direction and the Glaenzel/Cristià set. Indeed, the 'subtle, complex text' could, in Villán's view, probably work only under Belbel's direction. *La Clave*'s Florentino L. Negrín is equally impressed by the direction and the set, although he is rather more negative than Villora on the quality of the text. For him this is rather confusing, and it requires a skilful director like Belbel himself to make it work onstage. He considers Belbel's dramatic output to be uneven, although he admits to a similar inconsistency in the work of the doyen of the Spanish stage in the first half of the twentieth century, Jacinto Benavente.[100]

Like his previous play, *Mòbil*, *A la Toscana* had received its world premiere in Copenhagen. Its director, Simon Boberg, explained to me that he had commissioned it with specific actors in mind. It was rehearsed simultaneously in Copenhagen and Barcelona; the Catalan cast (except for Lluís Soler) saw the Danish premiere, which changed

---

[98] For further details see David George, *The Theatre in Madrid and Barcelona, 1892–1936: Rivals or Collaborators?* (Cardiff: University of Wales Press, 2002), especially Chapter 5.

[99] 'intensa presencia del teatro catalán en Madrid'; 'la gente del *foro* dice que mientras Madrid es ciudad abierta, Barcelona es plaza inexpugnable en la que sólo hay sitio para lo catalán en catalán; plaza maldita para compañías del resto del Estado' (Javier Villán, 'Lo catalán triunfa en Madrid' ('The Catalan Element Triumphs in Madrid'), *El Mundo* (Cultura), 11 March 2008, p. 57). A discussion of Villán's assertion lies beyond the scope of this study, but Belbel's attitude to the language issue in the Teatre Nacional de Catalunya is discussed in Chapter 5, pp. 167–69.

[100] 'Eso de las vanguardias' ('That Avant-Garde Thing'), *La Clave*, 14 March 2008, p. 95.

aspects of their performance in Barcelona. The Danish cast then went
to see the Barcelona premiere. Belbel commented on how the Danish
production was structured differently from theirs, producing a more
comic effect:

> Ten days before the Girona premiere, Belbel went to Copenhagen
> with the company. 'We liked it a lot, they do it in a very different
> way to us, even though the text is identical. We have gone for the
> little pieces. Each scene is a small piece of a jigsaw that the audience
> has to put together. The pieces are separated by some fifteen seconds
> of darkness, during which the aim is that the spectator puts them
> together, that they do some work, that they think how to fit them
> together. In Copenhagen they do it without a break, they switch
> abruptly from dream to reality. It's harder for them to tie things up,
> but on the other hand they achieve a more comic effect. People
> laughed a lot there, more than here.'[101]

There is an interesting dynamic at play here. Boberg confirmed to me
that the Catalan team were very excited at what they had seen. This sort
of interaction clearly offers Catalan practitioners a new angle on how to
perform a Belbel play, in the hands of someone whose directing style –
as his production of *Mòbil* demonstrates – is sober and intelligent.
From Belbel's comments one also notes that, as in his production of
*Mòbil*, Boberg did not include breaks between the scenes, lending the
production fluidity. The comic element seems also to have featured
strongly, which is logical considering what Boberg told me about both
his view of Belbel's theatre and Danish tastes.[102] Interestingly, Boberg
feels that writing for the Danish theatre represents a kind of liberation

---

[101] 'Deu dies abans de l'estrena a Girona, Belbel es va desplaçar a
Copenhaguen amb la companyia. "Ens va agradar moltíssim, la fan molt
diferent de com la fem nosaltres, tot i que el text és idèntic. Nosaltres hem
optat pels flaixos. Cada escena es una micropeça d'un puzle que el públic ha
d'ordenar. Les peces estan separades per uns 15 segons de fosc, durant els
quals pretenem que l'espectador faci una recomposició, que treballi, que pensi
com les encaixa. A Copenhaguen la fan contínua, passen del somni a la
realitat de cop. Els resulta més difícil de lligar cables, però, a canvi,
aconsegueix un efecte més còmic. La gent reia molt allà, més que aquí"'
(http://www.avui.cat/article/cultura_comunicacio/11566/lobra/teatral/forasters/
sergi/belbel/provoca/polemica/poble/baix/segura.html, accessed 2 January 2009).
[102] See Chapter 1, p. 9.

for Belbel, since he is much less well-known in that country than in Catalonia or the rest of Spain, and therefore does not feel that all eyes are constantly on him. One may recall the phrase from Joan-Anton Benach's review of *Mòbil*, in which he writes of the expectation raised by its presence on the stage of the Teatre Lliure. When Belbel premieres in Copenhagen, it is perfectly natural that he should not experience any of the pressures such expectations inevitably raise. As the final chapter makes clear, Belbel has been even more in the public eye since he became Artistic Director of the Teatre Nacional de Catalunya in 2006, making the relative anonymity he can enjoy in 'neutral' Denmark still more desirable for him.

## Concluding remarks

Overall, this chapter has demonstrated that Belbel is quite justified in looking for relief outside his native Catalonia. Despite his status as the leading Catalan – and possibly Spanish – dramatist of his generation, the reception of his plays at home has, at best, been mixed. Some plays, especially *Després de la pluja*, have been better received than others, particularly *Carícies* and *Mòbil*. The total hostility shown towards the latter in Catalonia does not seem to have a parallel in Germany and Denmark. While the reception of Belbel has often been lukewarm in the UK, in Germany, and, from what I gather, in Denmark, it has been much more positive. The reasons for this belong, of course, within the realms of speculation. It may be that the Catalan critics are not comfortable with an author like Belbel whose plays are often elliptical, ambiguous, and even obscure. On the other hand, it appears that Belbel's fondness for the intellectual game, which seems anathema to British critics, appeals to German critics and audiences, as does the philosophical aspect of his plays. Just as German-language playwrights like Heiner Müller and Peter Handke have influenced Belbel, so he in turn has proved to be popular with German-speaking audiences. As far as Denmark is concerned, Simon Boberg has given one clue to the success of Belbel's plays in that country, namely their comic vein, which, according to the director, chimes well with Danish theatrical tastes.

Another possible reason for the success or failure of productions of Belbel's plays is the direction of individual productions. Although he normally directs his own plays, one of those he did not direct, *Mòbil*, has been the one that has received the fiercest criticism in the press. Pasqual's spectacular, even flashy, production in Barcelona seems to have contrasted with more sober ones in Germany and particularly in Copenhagen. Of course, this would not explain why the text was the main object of the opprobrium of the Barcelona critics, although some of the German reviewers do also have reservations about the quality of the text. One must remember that the director in Germany fulfils an essentially different role from that of the director in other countries. Whereas in the UK it tends to be to 'serve' the text, in Germany he/she is essentially a creative artist, with much greater power, and playing a key role in 'creating' a production. The visionary German director often works with new plays, and is free to do much more with them than, say, a UK director. Also, the more realistic vein of English playwriting is very different from that of Belbel. Finally, there is more of a sense of intellectual debate around theatre in Germany than in many other countries, and, correspondingly, German reviews tend to be longer and more detailed than is the custom in countries like Spain.

# 5

# Belbel and the Teatre Nacional de Catalunya

> It is so necessary that I now think that it would be a great
> loss to spectators in Catalonia to have to do without the
> TNC. It fulfils a specific function, namely the safekeeping
> of the Catalan theatrical patrimony, both classical and
> contemporary.[1]

The development of a culture of national theatres in Europe is complex
and varied. Marvin Carlson evokes the established picture of a national
theatre, and adds a warning:

> The common image of a National Theatre is of a monumental edifice
> located in a national capital, authorized, privileged and supported by
> the government, and devoted wholly or largely to productions of the
> work of national dramatists. Naturally some National Theatres
> adhere closely to this ideal model, but the vast majority depart from
> it in one way or another.[2]

Some countries have a building or buildings that bear the name
National Theatre, while others, such as Germany, Italy and the Nether-
lands, possess a national theatre network. As will be observed in this
chapter, the National Theatre of Catalonia fits the 'ideal' model evoked
by Carlson in some respects but not in others. Various attempts were
made to establish a Catalan National Theatre in the early twentieth
century, and, in effect, the Teatre Romea in Barcelona was a *de facto*

---

[1] 'És tan necessari que ara crec que seria una gran pèrdua per als
espectadors de Catalunya prescindir del TNC. Fa una funció específica de
tenir cura del patrimoni teatral català, tant clàssic com contemporani' (email
correspondence with Sergi Belbel, 12 November 2008).

[2] Marvin Carlson, 'National Theatres: Then and Now', in *National
Theatres in a Changing Europe*, ed. S. E. Wilmer, Studies in International
Performance (Basingstoke and New York: Palgrave Macmillan, 2008), pp.
21–33, p. 21.

National Theatre, putting on many plays in Catalan during the first decade of the twentieth century. However, the development was never fully solidified and, between 1911 and 1917, the Romea's repertoire was exclusively in the Spanish language.[3] Similar efforts to establish a national theatre in Wales also belong to the period around the First World War. Anwen Jones's comments on the situation in Wales are apposite to what was occurring in Catalonia at the time:

> Self-awareness had brought about an impasse, a polarization of those who opted for cultural and linguistic promotion and preservation and those who advocated an ecumenical acceptance of the variety of different cultural and linguistic perspectives and experiences that combined to constitute twentieth-century Wales and, ultimately, put the nation in touch with a wider world, beyond its own national boundaries. Both viewpoints were valid and valuable.[4]

While the Abbey Theatre, the first state-subsidised theatre in the English-speaking world, was established in 1903,[5] moves to set up a national theatre in both Catalonia and Wales did not bear fruit in the early twentieth century, and it was not until the end of the century or in the early twenty-first that, in very different ways, their efforts were successful.

However, they were not alone in finding such efforts long and arduous. A British national theatre did not come to fruition until the National Theatre Company's first performance at the Old Vic on 22 October 1963. As Dominic Shellard puts it, 'it had taken over a century of procrastination before Peter O'Toole took to the stage in an uncut *Hamlet* – directed by Laurence Olivier'.[6] What is more, the South Bank

---

3 For further details on this emblematic Barcelona venue, see *Romea, 125 anys*, ed. Ramon Bacardit et al. (Barcelona, Generalitat de Catalunya, 1989).

4 Anwen Jones, *National Theatres in Context* (Cardiff: University of Wales Press, 2007), p. 180.

5 See Christopher Fitz-Simon, *The Abbey Theatre: Ireland's National Theatre, The First Hundred Years* (London: Thames & Hudson, 2003); Robert Welch, *The Abbey Theatre (1899–1999): Form and Pressure* (Oxford: Oxford University Press, 1999); Ben Levitas, 'The Abbey Opens: A First Night Revisited', in Wilmer (ed.), *National Theatres in a Changing Europe*, pp. 73–83.

6 Dominic Shellard, *British Theatre Since the War* (New Haven and London: Yale University Press, 2000), p. 100.

complex that houses the three spaces of the National Theatre was not completed until 1976, and the National became the Royal National Theatre in 1988.[7]

Catalonia's attempts to establish its own National Theatre finally yielded the desired result in 1996,[8] when the Catalan actor-manager Josep Maria Flotats, who had previously been based at the Comédie-Française, became its first Artistic Director. His reign was short lived: a month after the official opening of the TNC he was sacked because of disagreements with the Generalitat de Catalunya, supposedly for being a bad manager, and replaced by Domènec Reixac in July 1998. Reixac had previously been Director of the Centre Dramàtic de la Generalitat de Catalunya (CDGC), based at the Teatre Romea, which did much to promote the work of Catalan playwrights, and was, in effect, a prototype National Theatre of Catalonia. He held the TNC post until 2006, when he was succeeded by Belbel as Artistic Director. For one critic, the appointment was the logical culmination of a process for a 'multifaceted man of the theatre' ('home de teatre polifacètic').[9] As has been demonstrated in previous chapters, Belbel's reputation as a writer and director had been firmly established well before his appointment, while his close involvement with his predecessor at the TNC could be expected to ensure a smooth transition and continuity. As was illustrated in Chapter 2, Belbel understands and is understood by theatre people, and likes to work in a calm, organised and conflict-free way, which would seem to make him the ideal person to head a sometimes contentious venture like the TNC. Also, as has been demonstrated, Belbel's commitment to the text is unquestionable, and he has an interest in maintaining text-based theatre at the TNC. The current chapter discusses the period of Belbel's as yet brief stewardship of the theatre, considering such questions as the objectives of his appointment, the TNC and Catalan politics and national identity, the building in which the TNC

---

[7] For a potted history of national theatre in Britain, see http://www.nationaltheatre.org.uk/1403/faqs/history.html, accessed 23 October 2008.

[8] The official opening was on the Catalan National Day, 11 September 1997.

[9] Marçal Lladó, 'Sergi Belbel, nou director del TNC', *Lamalla.cat*, 18 March 2005, http://www.lamalla.cat/actualitat_cultural/teatre/article?id=98481, accessed 13 October 2008.

is housed, and the programming since Belbel took over. Using interviews and my own email correspondence with Belbel, I attempt to establish the principal features and challenges of his period of office. It is not within the competence of the present study to offer value judgements on what a National Theatre should or should not be, but, through the headings outlined above, to present what seem to me to be the salient characteristics that are relevant to this particular aspect of Belbel's multifaceted career in the theatre.

## Objectives of Belbel's appointment

According to a press article written at the time of his appointment, Belbel's brief was to develop Catalan playwriting and dance, with contemporary classics and traditional Catalan theatre further priorities.[10] Belbel himself is clear that, although dance, music and multidisciplinary spectacles should be an integral part of the TNC's activities, its main focus had to be 'text-based theatre and Catalan drama'.[11]

As was to be expected given that he had formed part of Domènec Reixac's advisory team, continuity rather than radical change was to be the tone of Belbel's artistic directorship. As he said in a 2005 *El Temps* interview with Andreu Sotorra, the only way he could have accepted the role within an institution as large as the TNC was if it were a gradual process.[12] In the same interview he explains that, through having premiered in the three spaces of the TNC and already having worked there as part of the advisory team, he knew well how the theatre functioned. Even in 1998, when he was one of Domènec Reixac's advisors, Belbel was articulating the delicate balances that have to be struck in a publicly funded theatre like the TNC:

> We are working hard to agree on the philosophy of the project. How to get through to the public without making any commercial

---

10   See Marçal Lladó, 'Sergi Belbel, nou director del TNC'.

11   'El teatre de text i la dramatúrgia catalana' (César López Rosell, 'El TNC a examen', http://blogs.que.es/6527/2006/11/11/el-tnc-fa-10-anys-amb-repte-d-assentar-dramaturgia, accessed 13 October 2008).

12   Interview published in *El Temps*, 31 May 2005, consulted at http://www.andreusotorra.com/teatre/entrevista118.html, accessed 22 October 2008.

concessions. How to act without competing with the private sector. [...] The aim of the programming is to find a balance, not all Catalan playwrights, not all foreign ones, juggling with a rational budget, and giving plenty of work to the actors ... It's a slow process [...] If because of the two great public centres [the TNC and the Theatre City][13] the subventions to smaller venues are lost, it will be a mistake. [...] If an actor wants to get rich, he should go to the private sector. Taxpayers mustn't pay for anybody's profit. [...] Theatre is a luxury, not a necessity.[14]

## The TNC, Catalan politics and national identity

Lourdes Orozco has detailed how party politics exercised a key influence on the theatre in Barcelona in the post-Franco period. Although she recognises that 'the three institutions examined have made explicit their common concern for the theatre, in spite of the differences that separate them', she asserts that they are 'affected by the political ideologies of the parties that govern them'.[15] I put to Belbel two questions concerning theatre and politics as far as the TNC is concerned: his answers are revealing. My first question was about the traditional

---

[13] The Theatre City (Ciutat del Teatre) is a complex in the Montjuïc area of Barcelona, containing the Teatre Lliure, the Mercat de les Flors and the Institut del Teatre (Theatre Institute).

[14] 'Estem treballant molt per posar-nos d'acord en la filosofia del projecte. Com arribar al públic sense fer concessions comercials. Com actuar sense fer competència al sector privat. [...] La programació vol buscar un equilibri, que no siguin tot autors catalans, que no siguin tot estrangers, jugant amb un pressupost racional, que doni molta feina als actors ... És un treball lent [...] Si per culpa dels dos grans pols públics [TNC i Ciutat del Teatre], es perden els ajuts als més petits, serà un error. [...] Si un actor es vol fer ric, que se'n vagi al teatre privat. Els contribuents no han de pagar el benefici de ningú. [...] El teatre és un luxe, no una necessitat' (Andreu Sotorra, 'Belbel a la Tarantino', *Avui* DDD, 17 April 1998, viewed in http://www.andreusotorra.com/teatre/entrevista3.html, accessed 20 October 2008).

[15] 'las tres instituciones examinadas han hecho explícita, pese a las diferencias que las separan, una preocupación común por el teatro'; 'afectadas por las ideologías políticas de los partidos que las gobiernan' (*Teatro y política: Barcelona (1980–2000)*, Serie Debate, 12 (Madrid: Publicaciones de la Asociación de Directores de Escena, 2007), p. 269). The institutions in question are the Generalitat de Catalunya, the Barcelona City Council, and the Diputació de Barcelona.

association between the TNC and the centre-right Catalan nationalist party the CiU, which ran the Catalan Autonomous Government (Generalitat de Catalunya) from 1980 to 2003 under their charismatic leader Jordi Pujol, and between the Teatre Lliure and the Catalan Socialists (PSC), and whether the advent of the coalition government (between the PSC, the Catalan Republican Left Party (ERC) and the Initiative for Catalonia/Green Party (Iniciativa per Catalunya/Els Verds) alliance, which has run the Generalitat since 2003, has affected the political balance as far as theatre is concerned. Belbel's response was that the situation has changed dramatically since the days of the intense rivalry between the Generalitat (controlled by the CiU) and the Socialist-run Barcelona City Council.[16] In reply to my question of whether or not there has been political interference in his work as Artistic Director of the TNC, Belbel makes it clear that there is none:

> At this time I can't speak of political interference as far as my work is concerned (Artistic Director of the TNC). There does exist a 'contract-programme' agreed with the Administration in order to establish, amongst other things, the strategic objectives (duties, obligations, etc.) of the TNC's activity. It is the theatre's Administrator and not I who deals with the political link with the Generalitat. And I have to say that there is absolutely no political interference in artistic questions, which makes my job much easier.[17]

[16] 'One can no longer associate the TNC with any political party nor the Lliure (which is a consortium) with any other specific party. It was like that when there was a bipolarisation of power in Barcelona and Catalonia (the Generalitat run by CiU and Barcelona City Council by the Socialists' ('Ara ja no es pot associar el TNC a cap partit polític ni el Lliure (que és un consorci) a cap altre partit determinat. Això era així en un moment en què a Barcelona i a Catalunya hi havia una bipolarització del poder (Generalitat convergent i Ajuntament de Barcelona socialista)' (email correspondence with Belbel, 12 November 2008).

[17] 'De moment, no puc parlar d'interferència política pel que fa a la meva feina (direcció artística del TNC). Sí que, efectivament, existeix un 'contracte-programa' pactat amb l'Administració per a establir, entre d'altres aspectes, els objectius estratègics (deures i obligacions, etc.) de l'activitat del TNC. L'enllaç polític del teatre amb la Generalitat no el personalitzo jo sinó l'administrador del teatre. I he de dir, per aquesta banda, que no hi cap mena d'interferència en les qüestions artístiques. La qual cosa em facilita molt la feina.' The situation seems to have been very different when the TNC was first

A key question is the extent to which the TNC is or should be a mark of national identity, and, by extension, a medium for the promotion of the Catalan language. Should Catalan be the language of this national institution (which is, of course, related to the whole question of Catalonia's status as a nation), or should a balanced programme of plays in Castilian and Catalan be sought? Orozco is in no doubt about the reality:

> The TNC has to be understood as the central plank in the theatre planning that the Generalitat created for Catalonia, and as a reflection of the aims of the nationalist theatre policies of that institution. [...] Of equal importance is the word 'identity', which redefines the TNC as a symbol of national identity, thus conditioning its programming and, to an extent, its artistic objectives.[18]

Belbel's predecessor as Artistic Director of the TNC is firmly of the view that language and identity are at the root of the establishment of the TNC: 'The origins [of the TNC] are to be found in the recognition of the importance of theatre, of the importance of language and identity, so that people may recognise themselves through a public institution.'[19] There is a clear parallel with the situation in Wales. As David

inaugurated and Josep Maria Flotats was sacked, clearly through political interference by the Generalitat.

[18] 'El TNC deberá entenderse como la pieza central en la planificación teatral que la Generalitat creó para Cataluña, y como reflejo de las intenciones de la política teatral nacionalista de esta institución. [...] De igual importancia es la palabra identidad, la cual redefine al TNC como símbolo de identidad nacional condicionando así su programación y, hasta cierto punto, sus objetivos artísticos' (Lourdes Orozco, *Teatro y política: Barcelona (1980–2000)*, pp. 104–05). Kathryn Crameri is also of the opinion that the TNC was 'an institutional rather than an artistic project' (*Catalonia: National Identity and Cultural Policy, 1980–2003*, Iberian and Latin American Studies (Cardiff: University of Wales Press, 2008), p. 95; see pp. 92–99 for Crameri's astute analysis of theatre within the overall cultural policy of CiU, the ruling party in the Generalitat de Catalunya at the time of the establishment of the TNC.

[19] 'Los orígenes [del TNC] se encuentran en el reconocimiento de la importancia del teatro, de la importancia de la lengua y de la identidad, para que la gente se reconozca a través de una institución pública' (Interview with Reixac in Orozco, *Teatro y política: Barcelona (1980–2000)*, pp. 287–93, p. 287).

DAVID GEORGE

Adams puts it, 'the Great National Theatre Debate is really about more than theatre. It is about the state of Wales, about cultural identity, about nationalism and internationalism. But the debaters talk only about theatre.'[20] As for Catalonia, Orozco feels that, in its early years, the TNC's ideological base (Catalan nationalism), driven by the political make-up of its principal financier, the Generalitat, did not respond to the needs of the theatre within Barcelona, particularly its multicultural nature (*Teatro y política*, p. 117). Crameri, however, takes a somewhat different view on Catalan theatre as a whole in the post-Franco period:

> The contemporary development of Catalan theatre has primarily been about exploring the rich possibilities of theatre as a genre, not about exploring Catalan identity. This made the theatre less suscep- tible to the nationalizing and institutionalizing pressures coming from the *Generalitat*, although of course it did not exempt theatre professionals from having to engage with them.[21]

Dragan Klaic suggests that, in any case, any attempt to establish the TNC as a plank in the development of a specifically Catalan culture would be doomed to fail in the multicultural world that is modern Barcelona.[22]

Belbel (or any Artistic Director of the TNC for that matter) clearly has a difficult balance to strike. As well as the question of whether or not to concentrate on experimental offerings or plays with a wider audience appeal, the Artistic Director of the TNC has to decide what percentage of the productions should be by Catalan playwrights, and what presence foreign theatre should have. This is obviously a question that faces any national theatre, but, as we have seen, this is complicated in Catalonia by the language issue. Orozco is highly critical of the

[20] David Adams, *Stage Welsh: Nation, Nationalism and Theatre: the Search for Cultural Identity*, Changing Wales (Llandysul: Gomer, 1996), p. 5. Having said that, a little later in his book Adams writes: 'Nationalism, nation- hood and cultural identity are slippery concepts and ones of which I wouldn't want to pretend to have a confident grasp' (p. 9).

[21] Crameri, p. 100.

[22] 'National Theatres Undermined by the Withering of the Nation-State', in Wilmer (ed.), pp. 217–27, p. 219. One of Klaic's general conclusions is that 'the term National Theatre has become a rather arbitrary, almost meaningless label, an anachronistic, exhausted ideological construct' (p. 220).

TNC's emphasis on the use of the Catalan language as opposed to Castilian Spanish during the first four years of its existence, and prior, of course, to the beginning of Belbel's tenure, feeling that it 'produces a false representation of Catalonia, a nation in which Catalan and Castilian dynamically coexist'.[23] She contrasts the practice at the TNC with trends in the rest of Europe, which

> reduced the spoken word's significance in favor of other means of performative expression and enhanced multilingual performance. Similarly, an alternative to the translation of text-based performances was found in the use of subtitles, which were increasingly employed as a means of preserving the text's original sound as well as meaning.[24]

In a 2003 interview with Orozco, Belbel says that language is not an issue in the theatre, and the fact that a show is performed in either Catalan or Spanish will not influence its success or otherwise.[25] However, he opines that Catalan should be the preferred language of the TNC, as 'the language of Catalonia is Catalan, and I'm not a nationalist'. He links his views with the fact that he is a linguist, and for him 'the loss of a language is very sad because it is a cultural benefit, a sign of identity and, therefore, it must be protected, nurtured,

[23] Lourdes Orozco, 'National Identity in the Construction of the Theater Policy of the Generalitat de Catalunya', in *Catalan Spaces*, ed. P. Louise Johnson, special issue of *Romance Quarterly*, 53:3 (2006), 211–22, p. 217.

[24] 'National Identity in the Construction of the Theater Policy', p. 218. Orozco gives as an example of the use of subtitles a Romanian production of *The Seagull* at the 2005 Edinburgh Festival, and makes the point that they are used in Barcelona's Teatre Lliure. In email correspondence with me, Belbel asserts that surtitles are now regularly used at the TNC. He says that the original language is always respected when foreign companies perform there, adding that two or three foreign spectacles are programmed annually, and are always large-scale productions, to fit the specific conditions of the TNC's Sala Gran (email correspondence with Belbel, 12 November 2008).

[25] Orozco, *Teatro y política*, p. 305. As Adams writes, 'there is more to theatre than language, [...] and the first language of theatre is the *lingua franca* of performance' (p. 15). Adams also feels that one could identify something called 'Welsh theatre' independently of whether it is through the medium of English or Welsh (p. 47).

especially if making products in Catalan does not mean that people stop consuming them'.[26] None the less, in response to Orozco's next question, he accepts that Castilian Spanish can have a role at the TNC, and explains that shows are put on in that language when relevant. It does not, he says, make sense for a Calderón play to be translated, but Shakespeare, he feels, should always be performed in Catalan rather than Castilian, unless it is a question of ensuring that there is room for a quality Spanish-language production coming from outside Catalonia. For him, 'theatrical quality is the number one consideration, but public theatres in Catalonia have to programme in Catalan, just as public theatres in Spain must programme in Castilian'.[27]

When I asked Belbel how he views the solution to the language question within the two National Theatres of Wales, where Welsh-language theatre is performed within Theatr Genedlaethol Cymru, and English-language theatre in the confines of the National English Language Theatre,[28] he said that he does not favour such a separation for national theatre in Catalonia:

> It's a slightly 'segregationist' solution. At least that's how it would be read here. I don't see the need for it. In any case, if you wanted to open a kind of 'Spanish National' theatre in Barcelona, it would have to be a question of State rather than Catalan bodies, wouldn't it? In fact, the TNC has hosted shows from the two main Spanish public theatres, the CDN [Centro Dramático Nacional] and the

---

26 'la lengua de Cataluña es el catalán, y eso que no soy nacionalista'; 'la pérdida de una lengua da mucha pena porque es un bien cultural, es un signo de identidad y, por lo tanto, hay que protegerla, hay que mimarla, sobre todo si hacer productos en catalán no implica que la gente deje de consumirlos' (*Teatro y política*, p. 305). On the language and identity issue, Belbel makes the interesting point that, since the huge rise in the profile of Barcelona in recent years, he is now known outside Spain as a Spanish rather than a Catalan writer (see Sotorra, *El Temps* interview, and see Chapter 4, for variations on this perception).

27 'prima más la teatralidad que otra cosa, pero los teatros públicos de Cataluña tienen que programar en catalán, de la misma manera que los teatros públicos de España tienen que hacerlo en castellano' (*Teatro y política*, p. 305).

28 For details of the former see http://www.theatre-wales.co.uk/companies/company_details.asp?ID=125, and for the latter see below, p. 172.

CNTC [Compañía Nacional de Teatro Clásico), and others from the Community of Madrid: the Teatro de la Abadía.[29]

In short, Belbel's attitude to the language issue is, as with most other things, pragmatic.[30] He views the identity question too as a subtle, complex one. In answer to my question about the extent to which the TNC has a duty to reflect Catalonia's ever more varied cultures, Belbel said the following:

> It's a difficult question to answer. As a public theatre, the TNC is obliged to try to cover all sections of our community. But at the same time it has priorities, fixed in the contract-programme, which are plays from the Catalan repertory. That said, in all the TNC's programming there are plays in Castilian by classical and contemporary authors. And there have been playwrights from the T6 who have come from outside Catalonia, and who have written plays in Castilian. As far as immigration from other cultures is concerned, I recognise that this is a topic we often discuss and some of the plays

---

[29] 'És una solució un pèl "segregacionista". Almenys es llegiria així a casa nostra. No en veig la necessitat. En qualsevol cas, si es volgués obrir a Barcelona un teatre diguem-ne 'Nacional-Espanyol' hauria de ser una qüestió de les administracions de l'Estat, no pas de les administracions catalanes, no? De fet el TNC ha acollit espectacles dels dos principals teatres públics de l'Estat: CDN i CNTC, i d'altres de la comunitat de Madrid: Teatro de la Abadía' (email correspondence with Belbel, 12 November 2008).

[30] One may observe a contrast with the much more theoretical approach of the first Artistic Director of the TNC, Josep Maria Flotats. Helena Buffery's article on theatre space and cultural identity in Catalonia is structured around her analysis of the following key paragraph from Flotats's *Un projecte per al Teatre Nacional* (Barcelona: Edicions de la Revista de Catalunya, 1989): 'Universality and Catalonia. Language and history. Tradition and modernity. Proximity and communication. A cultural village within the city. Creators and artisans. National and European. The theatre within and the architectural symbol without. The public, the city and their district. Research and adventure. Team, independence and freedom. Risk and continuity. Adventure and classical references' ('Universalitat i Catalunya. La llengua i la història. Tradició i modernitat. Proximitat i comunicació. Una vil·la cultural dins la ciutat. Creadors i artesans. Nacional i europeu. El teatre de dins i el símbol arquitectònic exterior. El públic, la ciutat i el seu barri. Recerca i aventura. Equip, independència i llibertat. Risc i continuïtat. Aventura i referències clàssiques') (quoted in Helena Buffery, 'Theater Space and Cultural Identity in Catalonia', in *Catalan Spaces*, ed. P. Louise Johnson, 195–209, p. 199).

we have premiered are connected to that, but I would say that this is
an unresolved issue not only for the TNC but for the great majority
of the theatres in the country.[31]

Belbel's pragmatic approach to his task as Artistic Director of the
TNC is closely allied to another feature of his approach to the tricky
world of Catalan theatre politics (and, indeed, cultural politics more
generally): his caution and his avoidance of a polemical attitude. In
contrast to some of the more outspoken and proselytising critics of the
TNC, such as Jordi Coca or Albert Boadella, Belbel tends to steer what
might be termed a middle course. Some revealing examples of his
approach occur in his 2005 *El Temps* interview with Andreu Sotorra.
He expresses his admiration for the hardworking, step-by-step
approach of his predecessor, Domènec Reixac, which resulted in what
Belbel views as a very acceptable 80% seat occupation by the end of
his period at the TNC.[32] His cautious approach, he says, is due, at least
in part, to having to run a company the size of the TNC: 'It's a question
of balancing.' The key word here is the last one, which sums up
Belbel's approach to the forthcoming task. When asked about the
budget, he again demonstrates discretion: 'I think that the budget is
sufficient, but we theatre people never have enough.'[33] However, in
email correspondence with me, he was more critical of the level of
financial support received by Barcelona theatres in comparison with

31 'És una pregunta difícil de respondre. El TNC, com a teatre públic, està
obligat a intentar abarcar tots els sectors possibles de la nostra població. Però
al mateix temps, té unes prioritats, fixades en el contracte-programa, que són
les obres de repertori català. Tot i així, a totes les programacions del TNC hi
ha espectacles en castellà d'autors clàssics i contemporanis. I hi ha hagut
autors del T6 vinguts de fora de Catalunya que han escrit les seves obres en
castellà. Pel que fa a la immigració d'altres cultures, reconec que és un tema
que sovint ens plantegem i algunes de les obres que hem estrenat s'hi
refereixen, però diria que és un tema pendent no només del TNC sinó de la
gran majoria de teatres del país' (email correspondence with Belbel, 12
November 2008).
32 A note of caution should be struck here, due to the high percentage of
seats that are invitations (20% in 1999); see Orozco, *Teatro y política: Barcelona (1980–2000)*, p. 114.
33 'Es tracta d'anar fent equilibris'; 'el pressupost crec que és suficient,
però la gent de teatre no en tenim mai prou' (both citations are from the
Sotorra interview).

their Madrid counterparts, comparing the situation unfavourably with that of other European countries:

> From what I know, we have a very high quality infrastructure, absolutely competitive with any theatre in the rest of Spain and any other European country (even superior to some of them), but unfortunately that is not reflected in the budgets. I mean that, while we have the most generous budget of the Catalan theatres, it's lower than that of other public theatres I know outside Catalonia. It's a really odd situation. In the Madrid public theatres, for instance, the level of salaries and budgets for shows is quite a bit higher than ours. That creates a really strange situation: we have a reputation for doing 'good theatre', but we have less money. I don't understand how in a city like Barcelona, just because we are not the state capital, and with such an intense theatre activity as our own, we should have less money. Do theatre professionals from Milan earn less than their counterparts in Rome? Do Berlin professionals earn less than those from Munich, Hamburg or Frankfurt? Do they get less money for their shows? I would have thought not.[34]

## The building

Does a national theatre need a designated building? Helena Buffery associates having one with the nation-state: 'In England, France, Germany and other nation-states, "national theater" means a particular

---

[34] 'Bé, pel que sé, tenim una infraestructura d'altíssim nivell, absolutament competitiva amb qualsevol teatre de la resta de l'estat i de qualsevol país europeu (fins i tot superior a alguns d'ells) però malauradament això no es reflecteix en els pressupostos. Vull dir que tot i tenint el pressupost més generós dels teatres de Catalunya, és menor que el dels altres teatres públics que conec de fora. És una situació ben peculiar. Als teatres públics de Madrid, per exemple, el nivell de sous i de pressupostos per espectacles és bastant superior al nostre. Això crea una situació ben estranya: nosaltres tenim fama de fer 'bon teatre' però disposem de menys diners. No entenc com en una ciutat com Barcelona, pel fet de no ser la 'capital de l'estat', i amb l'activitat teatral tan intensa que tenim, haguem de disposar de menys diners. ¿Cobren menys els professionals que fan teatre a Milà que els de Roma? ¿Cobren menys els professionals de Berlín que els de Múnic, Hamburg o Frankfurt? ¿Tenen menys diners per fer els espectacles? Jo diria que no' (mail correspondence with Belbel, 12 November 2008).

institution, or the building in which that institution is housed.'[35] The
Welsh and Scottish versions do not have one, which is viewed as
advantageous by Vicky Featherstone, Artistic Director and Chief Executive of the National Theatre of Scotland (NTS), who refers to 'our
innovative building-free model, which means we can put on a great
variety of work all over Scotland which we hope appeals to the hugely
diverse individuals who make up our audience'.[36] NTS's Chairman's
view is that 'the rural areas are just as important as the towns and cities
of Scotland, given our geography. We would not wish to replicate the
work of existing theatre networks and theatre organisations, so we will
work with those networks and organisations as appropriate. There are
existing regional and national networks, for both amateur and professional theatre, and I would seek to work with them rather than
re-inventing the wheel.'[37] To quote Featherstone, 'in two years, we
have reached audiences of over 235,000, created 59 productions in 101
different locations, spanning three continents'. According to Phil
George, its Chair, a similar idea lies behind the decision not to house
the new English-language Welsh National Theatre in a building: 'this
will give it the freedom to commission and create productions', while
the aim was to 'reach wider audiences than currently go to the theatre.
Sometimes that will take us to unexpected and unconventional
spaces.'[38] One might add, of course, that buildings are also a huge
financial drain.

Despite the obvious advantages of having a building, it can also
prove to be something of a burden. The long awaited South Bank
complex in London drew criticism, as Dominic Shellard explains:

> Over the years, the physical appearance of the new National Theatre
> has attracted almost as much comment as some of the productions,

35 Buffery, 'Theater Space and Cultural Identity in Catalonia', p. 196.
36 http://www.nationaltheatrescotland.com/content/, accessed 24 October
2008.
37 http://64.233.183.104/search?q=cache:ZFy89rgloUgJ:www.british
theatreguide.info/news/NToSpublicmeetingsreport%2520updated%252016%
2520July%25202004.doc+national+theatre+of+scotland+public+meetings&hl
=en&ct=clnk&cd=1&gl=uk, accessed 4 November 2008.
38 http://www.artswales.org.uk/viewnews.asp?id=731, accessed 15 December 2008.

but its concrete brutalism was of less concern to [Peter] Hall [Director of the NT between 1973 and 1988] than its eventual inhabitation. [...] Although the delays were immensely frustrating for Hall and the company at the time, a fine theatre building had actually been created, at least for audiences, who have grown to appreciate the complex as the years have passed.[39]

To an extent, something similar seems to have happened with the TNC. Its striking home, designed by the internationally renowned Catalan architect Ricard Bofill, has proved to be one of the most controversial aspects of the whole project. The building that houses its three theatre spaces has been criticised for its excessively grand design (as well as for the poor acoustics of the Sala Gran). Maria Delgado sums it up thus: 'Standing like a grand mausoleum [...] the Catalan National Theatre presents an imposing sight. Grounded on an island circled by traffic, surprisingly inhospitable and austere, it stands out like an unreachable white stone temple,'[40] while the leader of Els Joglars, Albert Boadella, has scathingly described the building as a Catalan Valley of the Fallen.[41] In an interview she conducted with Belbel at the TNC in June 2007, Zeneida Sardà refers to 'the aseptic immensity of the National Theatre of Catalonia'.[42]

In the Sotorra interview in *El Temps*, Belbel expresses some interesting and, as usual, nuanced opinions on the building and its theatre

[39] Shellard, *British Theatre Since the War*, p. 167.

[40] Maria M. Delgado, *'Other' Spanish Theatres: Erasure and Inscription on the Twentieth-Century Spanish Stage* (Manchester: Manchester University Press, 2003), p. 166.

[41] Cited in Joan de Sagarra, '¿Quién le paga el mármol?' ('Who Pays for the Marble?'), *El País* (Edición Cataluña), 13 September 1997, p. 31. The Valley of the Fallen, or Valle de los Caídos, is a grandiose monument situated in the spectacular scenery of the Sierra de Guadarrama and inaugurated in 1959. Its aim was ostensibly to commemorate the fallen of both sides during the Spanish Civil War. However, it quickly became a symbol of the regime of General Franco, and was largely built using the forced labour of Republican soldiers and political prisoners.

[42] 'la immensitat asèptica del Teatre Nacional de Catalunya' ('Sergi Belbel, dramaturg i director del Teatre Nacional de Catalunya', *Serra d'Or*, 570 (June 2007), 54–58). I consulted an extract from the interview at http://www.escriptors.cat/autors/belbels/pagina.php?id_sec=2716, accessed 14 October 2008.

spaces. Although the Sala Gran is, in principle, a very inhospitable space, if one chooses works that connect with people, 'the space ends up being pleasant, a place where all social sectors can meet'.[43] He gives as examples of what he means Dagoll Dagom's *Mar i cel* (*Sea and Sky*) (during the 2004–05 season) and Eduardo de Filippo's *Sabato, domenica e lunedì* (performed as *Dissabte, diumenge i dilluns*) (2002), which was one of his own most successful ever productions, both of which were performed in the Sala Gran. He admits that there were design problems with that space, and the acoustics were poor, although the insertion of panels to reflect sound from the ceiling back to the audience has improved the situation. Be that as it may, Belbel is in no doubt that possessing its own building is more advantageous to the TNC than not having one. I put it to him that not having one – the case with the Scottish and the Welsh National Theatres – might allow more flexibility, but he replied: 'It's got disadvantages but many advantages. The main advantage is the very infrastructure, which allows us to have a group of magnificent professionals who are perfectly familiar with the installations and can make the most of them.'[44]

**The programme**

The most consistent, and fiercest, critic of the TNC's programming is Catalan writer, theatre director and academic Jordi Coca. In a 2007 article Coca cites the avant-garde Catalan poet, playwright and artist Joan Brossa (1919–98) as symptomatic of the Franco generation of Catalan theatre practitioners, who have, in his view, been systematically ignored by the Catalan public theatres since the restoration of democracy in Spain in the late 1970s and the subsequent establishment of autonomous governments in the country.[45] His criticism centres on what he views as the unjustifiable, wilful even, neglect of the

[43] 'la sala s'acaba fent amable, un lloc de trobada de tots els sectors socials'.

[44] 'Té inconvenients però molts avantatges. L'avantatge principal és la pròpia infraestructura, que permet tenir un conjunt de professionals magnífics que coneixen perfectament les instal·lacions i en treuen un profit excel·lent' (email correspondence with Belbel, 12 November 2008).

[45] Jordi Coca, 'Brossa and the Others', translated by Simon Breden, Maria M. Delgado and David George, in *Catalan Theatre, 1975–2006: Politics,*

generation of playwrights, directors and stage designers who struggled to keep Catalan theatre afloat in the difficult late Franco years. In this article he lists some of the 'neglected' theatre practitioners, dealing with Catalan public theatre in general, and, in essence, covering the pre-Belbel period. Coca develops his ideas in an article published in the Catalan language daily *Avui* in November 2007. He used a forthcoming production of a work by a playwright from that generation at the Teatro Español in Madrid to mount a vitriolic attack on the programming ethos of the TNC, which he describes as Stalinist:

> Hermann Bonnín will direct at Madrid's Teatro Español a selection from the plays that Palau i Fabre wrote on the Don Juan theme.[46] A few days ago the veteran director declared to Andreu Gomila and to this newspaper that 'the country is as it is', and that he didn't want to 'have a go at anyone'. On the other hand, it seems to me that it must be said that Sergi Belbel has altered very little the Stalinist National Theatre model (manipulator of history) that CiU imposed on us through Domènec Reixac. Belbel has made a few aesthetic adjustments, as for example putting on a Brossa, but he continues to produce commercial spectacles with public money, with blatant and lazy programming, from a magic circle of the initiated. Belbel is not aware of the rich variety of the names who are vegetating in the giant shadow of Catalan public theatre.[47] Continuing stubbornly to re-read our classics with sentimentality and evanescent superficiality, he still denies us the right to the great Greco-Latin tradition and enjoys spending madly on lightweight scenographic trappings, always determined not to put on plays by great authors, preferring instead commercial hits.[48]

*Identity, Performance*, ed. Maria M. Delgado, David George and Lourdes Orozco, special issue of *Contemporary Theatre Review*, 17:3 (2007), 446–52.

[46]  Josep Palau i Fabre (1917–2008) was a poet and playwright, much influenced by French culture, and translated Catalan poetry into French. He was a friend of Picasso, on whom he wrote a number of studies in the 1960s and early 1970s. The production to which Coca refers was *Príncep de les tenebres* (as *Don Juan, Príncipe de las tinieblas*, *Don Juan, Prince of Darkness*), which contained extracts prepared by Bonnín from five plays Palau wrote on the Don Juan theme in the late 1940s.

[47]  One is reminded of Coca's viewing Brossa as 'the tip of an enormous iceberg' in his 'Brossa and the Others' (p. 449).

[48]  'Hermann Bonnín dirigirà al Teatro Español de Madrid una dramatúrgia de les obres que Palau i Fabre va escriure sobre Don Joan. El veterà director

A similar view had been expressed (less vehemently) a year earlier by
Iolanda G. Madariaga. Discussing the presence of Espriu's *Primera
història d'Esther* during the TNC's 2006–07 season, she writes:

> Salvador Espriu's *Primera història d'Esther* is on the programme (it
> was about time that the TNC decided to put on a play by such an
> important writer for the Catalan language as Espriu!), but the name
> of Ricard Salvat, associated historically with the poet, is nowhere to
> be seen. If the Nacional is to be a reference theatre and broadly
> representative of the tradition and the current theatrical reality of
> Catalonia, then we're starting off with a few lacunae.[49]

declarava fa uns dies a Andreu Gomila i a aquest diari que 'el país és com és' i
que no volia 'retreure res a ningú'. En canvi, a mi em sembla que cal dir que
Sergi Belbel ha retocat ben poc el model de Teatre Nacional estalinista
(manipulador de la història) que ens va imposar CiU de la mà de Domènec
Reixac. Belbel ha sabut fer alguns retocs estètics, com per exemple estrenar
un Brossa, però continua produint espectacles comercials amb diner públic,
programant des de l'obvietat i l'esbarjo, i des d'un cercle màgic d'iniciats.
Belbel no s'adona de la varietat i riquesa dels noms que vegeten a l'ombra
gegantina del teatre públic català, continua entossudit a rellegir els nostres
clàssics des del sentimentalisme i la superficialitat evanescent, ens nega
encara el dret a la gran tradició grecollatina i gaudeix fent despeses boges en
parafernàlies escenogràfiques que són insubstancials, sempre decidit a no fer
les obres dels grans autors i a preferir les obres d'èxit' (Jordi Coca, 'Don Joan
a l'exili', *Avui* online, 23 November 2007; http://paper.avui.cat/article/cultura
/106640/don/joan/lexili.html, accessed 28 June 2008). Coca's view is that the
obligation of any National Theatre is to showcase national writers (understanding 'national' in this case as Catalan), and to offer critical interpretations
of their work as part of their evaluative function.

[49] 'Se programa *Primera història d'Esther*, de Salvador Espriu (¡Ya era
hora que el TNC se decidiera a programar a un autor tan importante para la
lengua catalana como Espriu!), pero el nombre de Ricard Salvat, histórica-
mente asociado al del poeta, no aparece por parte alguna. Si se trata de hacer
del Nacional un teatro de referencia y ampliamente representativo de la
tradición y de la actualidad teatral en Cataluña, empezamos con algunas
lagunas' (Iolanda G. Madariaga, 'Una fulgurante trayectoria: Sergi Belbel en
la cumbre del teatro catalán' ('A Brilliant Trajectory: Sergi Belbel at the
Summit of Catalan Theatre'), *Primer Acto*, 315:4 (2006), 8–13, p. 13).
Salvador Espriu (1913–85) was the leading Catalan poet of the Franco era, and
his *Primera Història d'Esther*, premiered in 1957, was a linguistically rich and
complex puppet farce, which contained considerations on the themes of power
and civil war, all from a profoundly humanist perspective. For a bilingual

The generation whose perceived absence so preoccupies Madariaga and Coca is, for Belbel, just one element of a wider programming consideration. In email correspondence with me, Belbel has offered a practical reason for the limited number of opportunities offered to practitioners from the generation endorsed by Coca, saying that 'as far as all the other demands Coca makes in his articles are concerned, although he is absolutely right, I have to say that we can't fit them all in during one season'.[50] Because of his age, Belbel is much more distant from the generation with which Coca feels so much affinity. As Chapter 1 demonstrated, Belbel himself represented a real break with that generation when he emerged onto the Catalan stage in the 1980s and 'Operation Belbel' began. Although he grew up under the Franco regime, democracy had already been re-established when he began working in the theatre. As was observed in the Introduction (p. 6), Benet i Jornet made clear in my interview with him that Belbel was not familiar with the Catalan theatrical tradition when he began his career, and the early influences on his work were writers he had discovered through Sanchis Sinisterra or his own knowledge of the theatre beyond Catalonia, especially that of France. Subsequently, of course, Belbel has developed a broader knowledge of Catalan theatre, and his directing career has included two plays by Àngel Guimerà.

Significantly, in response to Orozco's question 'how do you see the evolution of the theatre in Barcelona since the 80s?' ('¿cómo has visto la evolución del teatro en Barcelona desde los años 80?'), Belbel says:

> Fantastic. Previously I used to go to Paris, Germany or the Avignon Festival to see theatre, and I used to return terribly depressed. When

Catalan/English version of the play, see Salvador Espriu, *Primera Història d'Esther/ The Story of Esther*, trans. Philip Polack, Anglo-Catalan Society Occasional Publications, 6 (Sheffield: Anglo-Catalan Society, 1989). The director Ricard Salvat (1934–2009) was one of the key figures in the renovation of the Catalan stage during the Franco period. Having worked extensively in Germany, he was one of the main promoters of Brechtian theatre in Catalonia and in Spain more widely. He was one of the founders of the Escola d'Art Dramàtic Adrià Gual in 1960 and Director of the Sitges International Theatre Festival from 1977 to 1986.

[50] 'en relació a totes les altres reivindicacions que en Coca fa en els seus articles, si bé té tota la raó del món, he de dir que tampoc podem donar cabuda a totes elles en una sola temporada' (email correspondence with Belbel, 12 November 2008).

I returned and saw what was being done here I used to think that we were lacking a lot. Now the opposite happens to me, or at least I think we have nothing to be envious about.[51]

This is not to say, of course, that Belbel has a prejudice against what was happening in Catalan theatre in the late Franco period or during the transition to democracy, but he inevitably looks at the pre-democracy generation from a greater distance and from a different perspective than Coca does. Belbel's theatrical models are international,[52] while his training as a French philologist evidently influences his cultural thinking and his choice of repertoire. In short, the key is that he does not come from the Catalan tradition. He makes the point, in the Orozco interview, that his plays are performed in Germany before Madrid, and says: 'I am just finishing my latest play and I'm translating it into Spanish not to send it to Madrid but to send it to France, Germany, Sweden'.[53] As we saw in Chapter 4, Belbel's two latest plays were premiered in Denmark before Barcelona, let alone Madrid. This is the international context, I feel, in which we must view his programming in the TNC, and it is perhaps inevitable, given the international environment in which he moves, that he will not feel the same visceral attachment as Coca does to the generation of theatre practitioners who kept Catalan theatre alive during the difficult Franco period.

This said, it is interesting that a number of these practitioners have already featured at the TNC during Belbel's short artistic directorship. They include the playwrights Carles Soldevila and Salvador Espriu, as

---

[51] 'Bestial. Yo antes iba a ver teatro a París, a Alemania, al Festival de Avignon y volvía con unas depresiones increíbles. Cuando volvía y veía lo que se hacía aquí pensaba que nos faltaba mucho. Ahora me pasa al revés o, por lo menos, pienso que no tenemos nada que envidiar' (*Teatro y política*, p. 303).

[52] Coca, too, has directed foreign theatre, for example, Maeterlinck's *L'Intruse* and Beckett's *Krapp's Last Tape*, while I was present at a production of his own *Black Beach* (translation of *Platja negra*) at the Chapter Theatre in Cardiff in November 2008, as part of a three-day celebration of new Catalan and Welsh drama.

[53] 'ahora mismo he terminado mi nueva obra teatral y la estoy traduciendo al castellano no para enviarla a Madrid sino para enviarla a Francia, a Alemania, a Suecia' (*Teatro y política*, p. 307). Interestingly, David Adams feels that Welsh theatre's connections 'have been more with European cultures that relate to Wales more than England, like Catalonia and Macedonia' (p. 51).

well as Brossa himself, the directors Esteve Poll, who at the age of eighty-five directed Josep Maria de Sagarra's *El poema de Nadal* (*Christmas Poem*) in December 2007, and Lluís Pasqual, who also directed at the TNC in the same season. His production of García Lorca's *The House of Bernarda Alba* (*La casa de Bernarda Alba*), in Castilian and in a co-production with the Teatro Español, included the internationally renowned Catalan actress Núria Espert, another figure who, according to Coca, 'has been ignored by our nation's official theatres'.[54] As Belbel has explained to me:

> Jordi Coca is an intellectual who has been very critical of the work of the TNC for a long time. Even so, some of his demands have been met: we premiered a Brossa last year, and Espriu two seasons ago, and this year we have staged a play by a little-known playwright, Ambrosi Carrion. One of Coca's other demands, Manuel de Pedrolo, has not been possible, since we wanted to stage a dramatisation of one of his representative novels (as is done in practically all the theatres of Europe – Dostoevsky in Russia is a good example), and we were denied the rights, and told that either we performed one of Pedrolo's plays or nothing.[55]

The second criticism in Coca's *Avui* article – that the TNC uses public money to fund commercial spectacles – seems to me to be complex, and a problem that is probably faced by any publicly funded

---

[54] 'Brossa and the Others', p. 452.

[55] 'Jordi Coca és un intel·lectual molt crític amb la tasca del TNC des de fa molt de temps. Tot i això, algunes de les seves reivindicacions han sigut realitat: vam estrenar una obra d'en Brossa la temporada passada, una d'Espriu fa dues temporades, enguany hem estrenat l'obra d'un autor poc conegut, l'Ambrosi Carrion. Una altra de les seves reivindicacions, Pedrolo, no ha estat possible perquè volíem fer-ne una adaptació dramàtica d'una de les seves novel·les emblemàtiques (com es fa pràcticament a tots els teatres d'Europa – Dostoievski a Rússia n'és un bon exemple) i se'ns van denegar els drets adduint que o es feia directament una obra teatral de Pedrolo o res' (email correspondence with Belbel, 12 November 2008). Manuel de Pedrolo (1918–90) was a well-known Catalan novelist and playwright. On his theatre, see David George and John London, 'Avant-Garde Drama', in *Contemporary Catalan Drama*, ed. David George and John London, Anglo-Catalan Society Occasional Publications, 9 (Sheffield: Anglo-Catalan Society, 1996), pp. 73–101, pp. 83–89. On adaptations of novels at the TNC, see below, pp. 187–88.

theatre or other organisation for that matter.[56] In his analysis of Kenneth Tynan's period as dramaturg in the British National Theatre, Dominic Shellard writes:

> Identifying the problems involved in building a company in an environment where commercial theatre could offer much higher salaries, he [Tynan] argued that the company needed 'actors who passionately believe in the repertory idea, who feel evangelical and idealistic about it' – thereby articulating the constant tension that would exist from now on between state subsidised enterprises, or noncommercial ventures, and the monolithic West End groups.[57]

Belbel's view is that an Artistic Director of a publicly funded theatre has an obligation to give the public what it wants. He has reiterated this point in interviews, for example: 'At the Nacional I have more responsibility. In the private sector I also have freedom because I think that, if it doesn't go well, they won't offer me another contract. I am more upset if a show goes badly at the Nacional, I have a moral duty, I am working with the spectator's money.'[58] Of course, this begs the question of whether a national theatre's primary function should be to fill its halls, or to stage plays that will never find their way onto the commercial stage. As Orozco puts it, 'the problem faced by the director of the TNC was to find a balance between the presentation of innovative dramatic forms and a theatre programme that would fill the halls'.[59] Belbel's own view, expressed in a 2005 interview, is that the principal philosophy of the TNC was 'not to look for money, but to search for an identity and to watch over the artistic and cultural

---

[56] Coca had voiced the same criticism in 'Brossa and the Others', claiming that Catalan public theatres 'value bums on seats over any cultural criteria' (p. 452).

[57] Shellard, *British Theatre Since the War*, pp. 108–09.

[58] 'En el Nacional tengo más responsabilidad. En la privada, tengo también libertad porque pienso que si no va bien no me volverán a contratar. Me duele más que vaya mal un espectáculo en el Nacional, tengo un deber moral, estoy trabajando con el dinero del espectador' (Orozco, *Teatro y política*, p. 307).

[59] 'el problema con el que se encaró el director del TNC fue el de encontrar un equilibrio entre la presentación de formas teatrales innovadoras y una programación teatral que llenara las salas' (*Teatro y política*, p. 111).

heritage'.[60] For Coca, the pursuit of commercial goals has led to a conservative approach and a reluctance to take risks on the part of Catalan public theatres. Having said that, he accepts that increasing the size of audiences is positive: 'it would be wrong not to acknowledge that the consolidation of audiences and adaptation of programming policy to more conservative, insipid sensibilities has led to an increase in ticket sales and an increase in the strictly economic level of theatre business'.[61]

Apart from the delicate and complex task of trying to appeal to a wide sector of the public (who pay the taxes that finance public theatre) while not compromising standards or artistic principles, trying to put together a balanced, interesting and appealing programme is a challenging task for the artistic director of any public theatre. It is not my purpose here to offer qualitative judgements on the TNC's programme, but to try to identify some of its characteristics and patterns during Belbel's as yet short tenure.[62]

Belbel's online presentation of the 2008–09 season identifies the following priority areas:

> The principal axes of the programming are organised around author's theatre (Racine, Mayorga, Rodoreda, Carrion, Gogol, Villalonga, Mankell, Lorca, Shaw, Oliver, Riba), the great names of the international stage (Donnellan, Decouflé, Lepage, Sylvie Guillem, and our 'own' Pasqual, Espert and Sergi López), shows for all the family (Andersen, Los Excéntricos, Buka, El teatre de l'home dibuixat, Boni & Cia), the best of contemporary dance (Colomé, Sempere, Vergés, Corchero) and the T6 Project (Aymar, Hibernia, Miró, Sarrias).[63]

---

[60] 'no buscar diners, buscar una identitat i vigilar pel patrimoni artístic i cultural' (interview with Andreu Sotorra in *El Temps*).

[61] Jordi Coca, 'Introduction', in *Black Beach and Other Plays*, ed. Jeff Teare and Jordi Coca (Cardigan: Parthian, 2008), pp. vii–xii, p. x.

[62] Marvin Carlson's view is that 'the TNC is still building its reputation and attempting to find a middle ground between a national and a European theatre' ('National Theatres: Then and Now', p. 31).

[63] 'Els eixos principals de la programació s'articulen entorn del teatre de l'autor (Racine, Mayorga, Rodoreda, Carrion, Gogol, Villalonga, Mankell, Lorca, Shaw, Oliver, Riba), els grans noms de l'escena internacional (Donnellan, Decouflé, Lepage, Sylvie Guillem, i els també "nostres" Pasqual, Espert i Sergi López), els espectacles per a tota la família (Andersen, Los

What follows is a description of the TNC's programme in the three seasons of Belbel's stewardship. It would seem appropriate to begin with the two strands identified as priority by the TNC Board: Catalan playwriting and dance. The former has been promoted mainly through the T6 project. Belbel was already one of the prime movers behind it before his appointment as Artistic Director. In a 2005 interview, he explained how he viewed this project in the context of the need to re-establish the position of the playwright in contemporary theatre: 'We must restore the figure of the playwright to the stage. The T6 project is a step in that direction.'[64] He explains and amplifies on the project:

> The next [stage] will consist of taking six authors and proposing that they each do two plays over a three-year period, one to be staged in the TNC and the other outside the TNC, in an alternative venue. The author is asked to conduct a double strategy: for the one, a more popular piece, and for the other, a more personal one, in order to break the grandiose requirements imposed by the TNC.[65]

This is a strategy designed not only to offer opportunities to new writers but also to develop links with the alternative theatres, which are under constant threat, and to have playwrights thinking about different types of audiences. It is also an attempt to overcome the perceived grandeur of the building, which is acknowledged as a problem by Belbel. He has refined his analysis in correspondence with me:

Excéntricos, Buka, El teatre de l'home dibuixat, Boni & Cia), les millors veus de la dansa contemporània (Colomé, Sempere, Vergés, Corchero) i el Projecte T6 (Aymar, Hibernia, Miró, Sarrias)' (http://www.tnc.cat/ca/programacio-i-gires, accessed 31 October 2008).

    64 'Hem de tornar a reivindicar la figura de l'autor a l'escenari. El projecte T6 és un pas en aquesta direcció' (Andreu Sotarra, interview in *El Temps*). In fact, this was a project run jointly by the TNC, the Sales Alternatives de Catalunya (COSACA) and the Sociedad General de Autores y Editores (SGAE), although, COSACA no longer participates in it.

    65 'La següent [etapa] consistirà a agafar sis autors i proposar-los, durant tres anys, dues obres a cadascun. Una per ser estrenada al TNC i l'altra per ser estrenada fora del TNC, en una sala alternativa. Se li demana a l'autor que faci un joc doble, una dramatúrgia d'abast més popular, per una banda, i una més personal per l'altra, per trencar les necessitats de grandiositat que sembla que imposa el TNC.'

Over the years the T6 has been shown to be a necessary project. The collaboration with other theatres is important so that the TNC does not become a kind of 'palace', inaccessible to our new playwrights. Contemporary authors who work at the TNC have budgets and stage conditions that are superior to those of other theatres. And they can work with freedom and without any kind of aesthetic, political or commercial restrictions.[66]

Several new, or relatively new, playwrights have had their plays performed, most of whom have connections with theatres in the alternative sector. For example, Albert Mestres, who has premiered two plays within the T6 project – *Temps real* (*Real Time*) (2007) and *Dos de dos* (*Two from Two*) (2008) – has been involved for a number of years as writer and director with theatres such as Brossa Espai Escènic. In accordance with the T6 philosophy, Mestres's *Dos de dos* was performed at that theatre in June–July 2008, following its premiere at the TNC in May of the same year. The young Barcelona playwright Pau Miró has also featured prominently in the T6 programme. Like Mestres, Miró has also been involved in other productions, including, in March–April 2008, *Los persas: réquiem por un soldado* (*The Persians: Requiem for a Soldier*) – his updated version of the Aeschylus play – with Calixto Bieito at the Romea Theatre, while all of his works have been produced, at the TNC, the Teatre Lliure or in Barcelona's alternative theatre venues. So, one can at least begin to see a spin-off from, or, perhaps more to the point, an interaction between T6-featured authors and other areas of Barcelona theatre, including the private (Bieito's Romea-based production company) and alternative (Brossa Espai Escènic) sectors. Hopefully, this will break down a sense that the TNC is a Catalanist, isolated bastion, cocooned in its Bofill-designed ivory tower and privileged by a traditional CiU elite. This

---

[66] 'El T6 s'ha revelat al llarg dels anys com un projecte necessari. La col·laboració amb la resta de teatres és important per no fer del TNC una mena de 'palau' inaccessible per a les noves veus de la nostra dramatúrgia. Els autors contemporanis que treballen al TNC disposen de pressupostos i condicions escèniques superiors als altres teatres. I es treballa amb llibertat i sense condicionaments ni estètics ni polítics ni comercials ni de cap mena' (email correspondence with Belbel, 12 November 2008).

greater fluidity may be in embryonic form, but at least there are promising signs.[67]

As for dance, there have been regular performances, showcasing both Catalan dance (under the T6 dance project) and international artists. Among the former are Toni Mira and Nats Nus, while international dance at the TNC is centred on ballet, and companies to perform there include the French director/choreographer Philippe Decouflé, the Aix-en-Provence-based Ballet Preljocaj, Cullberg Ballet from Sweden, and Robert Lepage directing *Eonnagata*, a hybrid spectacle as part of the Grec 2009 summer festival and described in the following terms:

> The project brings together an intriguing variety of creative imaginations and performers: Lepage, contemporary choreographer Russell Maliphant, and Sylvie Guillem, former principal dancer of Ballet de l'Opéra de Paris. Beyond the usual demands of dance, their collaboration presents the challenge of linking together abstraction, contemporary dance, and the narrative tendencies of the theatre. To what point is it possible to tell a story through movement?[68]

This does seem to represent some kind of departure from the 'enclosed environment in which Catalonia's performing arts had to develop' that Orozco attributes to the TNC in the period up to 2000.

As far as other features of TNC programming under Belbel are concerned, I will consider the following areas: performance, circus, puppets and magic; adaptations of European classics, ancient and modern; contemporary American and European drama; Catalan classics; and adaptations. As throughout this chapter, my objective is not to evaluate but to present, so that readers may be familiar with what Catalan spectators have available at their National Theatre. Performance groups have included the internationally renowned La Fura dels Baus, with their version of *Boris Godunov* (2008), where they attempt

---

67 The latest information I have is that, in the future, the T6 will be exclusively a TNC project, without the collaboration of the *sales alternatives* although, in early 2010, SGAE was still a participant. In addition, the T6 will have its own company of actors; hence the T6 playwrights will write their plays knowing that a specific group of actors will be performing them.

68 http://lacaserne.net/index2.php/work_in_progress/eonnagata/, accessed 29 October 2008.

to re-create the situation in the Dunrovka Theatre in Moscow in 2002 in which the audience was taken hostage by terrorists and many of them killed. An older Catalan group, Comediants, have also had one show under Belbel's tenure: the double bill *El gran secret/ El petit secret* (*Big Secret/ Little Secret*) (2006–07), the first for adults, the second for children, while another planned spectacle by La Cubana had to be abandoned due to lack of finance.[69] Indeed, the inclusion of puppets, marionettes and circus illustrates Belbel's desire to broaden the potential audience at the TNC, in particular by introducing the next generation of theatregoers to the habit at an early age. A particularly innovative venture was the production in May 2007 of a double bill by the street performance group Artristras to celebrate their twenty-fifth anniversary, *Medusa* and *Pluges d'estiu* (*Summer Rains*).[70] The shows, put on in the gardens of the TNC, were organised by Joan Font, who was responsible for the Family Theatre Group of the TNC until his dismissal (apparently as part of a financial cutback) in September 2008.[71]

As for what might be termed European classics, the following have been staged at the TNC to date during the Belbel period. With the exception of two Spanish plays, Tirso de Molina's late sixteenth-century play *Don Gil de las calzas verdes* (*Don Gil of the Green Breeches*) (2007) and Federico García Lorca's 1930s' drama *La casa de Bernarda Alba* (*The House of Bernarda Alba*) (2009), they have been exclusively performed in Catalan. Just one Shakespeare play has been performed at the TNC since its inauguration (*King Lear*, in 2008, adapted by Spanish playwright Juan Mayorga, whose own *La paz*

---

[69] Email correspondence with Belbel, 12 November 2008.

[70] The group's spokesman outlined the interdisciplinary element of the spectacles, describing them as 'a compendium of live dance and music, popular and Mediterranean festive iconography, with a contemporary language' ('un compendio de danza y música en directo, de iconografía popular y de fiesta mediterránea, con un lenguaje contemporáneo') (http://www.acceso.com/display_release.html?id=36000, accessed 29 October 2008).

[71] The puppet show has a long and vibrant history in Catalonia. For an analysis of its significance over the last forty years, see Cariad Astles, 'Catalan Puppet Theatre: A Process of Cultural Affirmation', in *Catalan Theatre, 1975–2006: Politics, Identity, Performance, Contemporary Theatre Review*, 17:3 (2007), 323–34.

*perpetua* (*Perpetual Peace*) was included in the 2008–09 programme). One French classical play has been staged there: Jean Racine's *Andromaque* (2008), directed by Declan Donnellan in the original language. The virtual absence of French playwrights at the TNC is perhaps surprising given Belbel's own interest in French theatre (see Chapter 2),[72] but other European theatre is represented by a variety of well-known dramatists, including Strindberg's *Ensam* (as part of the Grec 2008 summer festival), Dürrenmatt's *Play Strindberg* (2007) and Pirandello's *Man, Beast and Virtue* (2008). The Piccolo Theatre performed Goldoni's *Il ventaglio*, while a sign of the times, perhaps, is that there was only one Brecht during the period, *The Caucasian Chalk Circle* (2008). Pinter's *The Homecoming* featured during Belbel's first season in charge of the TNC, in 2007, while Jordi Galceran's adaptation of Gogol's *The Government Inspector* was Belbel's contracted directorial venture for the 2008–09 season. Writing in the online presentation of the 2008–09 season, Belbel himself feels that one of its surprises will be Swedish crime writer Henning Mankell's *Antilopes*.[73] Wilde and Shaw, two of several Irish 'classic' playwrights who have achieved universal status, at least in the English language, have each received productions at the TNC, with the former's *Lady Windermere's Fan* (2007), and the latter's *Heartbreak House* (2009). As for an older generation of Catalan playwrights, the following have been staged under Belbel's stewardship: Àngel Guimerà's *En Pólvora*, which was Belbel's choice for his first directorial venture of his TNC tenure (see Chapter 2), Josep Maria de Sagarra's Christmas piece *El poema de nadal* (*The Christmas Poem*) (2007), a version for puppets of *noucentista* poet Carles Riba's *Sis Joans* (*Six Johns*) (2008), Carles Soldevila's *Valentina* (2006), and Salvador Espriu's *Primera història d'Esther* (2007).

[72] Belbel may have been mindful of the criticism levelled at Josep Maria Flotats because of what was considered his excessive emphasis on foreign – in particular French – theatre at the expense of Catalan drama. The criticism referred specifically to the period in which his company had its headquarters at the Poliorama Theatre in Barcelona (1985–94), and prior, of course, to his brief tenure as Artistic Director of the TNC; see Enric Gallén, 'Catalan Theatrical Life', in *Contemporary Catalan Drama*, ed. George and London, pp. 19–42, p. 34; and Lourdes Orozco, *Teatro y política: Barcelona (1980–2000)*, pp. 99–100.

[73] http://www.tnc.cat/ca/programacio-i-gires.

While the Catalan dramatic canon – including the Franco generation so vigorously defended by Jordi Coca – has not had an especially strong presence at the TNC,[74] under Belbel a number of representatives of the generation have been represented there. Joan Brossa's *El dia del profeta* (*The Day of the Prophet*) was put on in the 2007–08 season, while exiled playwright Ambrosi Carrion's 1949 *La dama de Reus* (*The Lady of Reus*) formed part of the 2008–09 programme. If one adds this to Esteve Poll's direction of Josep Maria de Sagarra's *El poema de Nadal* during 2008–09 and Lluís Pasqual's of *La casa de Bernarda Alba* in the same season, then it seems clear that, in part at least, Coca's objections are being met. In addition, in 2006–07 and 2008–09 a number of adaptations of well-known Catalan novels have been staged. In this respect Belbel seems to be one of Dragan Klaic's 'clever producers who know or just feel that repertory as a *smorgas-bord*[75] does not work any longer [and who] seek to attract their audience with a dramatization of a bestselling novel' (p. 223). Partly, however, the adaptations staged at the TNC stem from the centenary celebrations of perhaps the major Catalan novelist of the post-Civil War period, Mercè Rodoreda. Josep Maria Benet i Jornet's adaptation of her most famous novel, *La Plaça del Diamant*, was staged during the 2007–08 season, while one of her early works, *Aloma*, was included in the 2008–09 repertoire. Another adaptation of a well-known Catalan novel to be staged under Belbel's artistic directorship of the TNC was Marc Rosich and Rafel Duran's version of the Mallorcan novelist Llorenç Villalonga's *Mort de dama*, in a co-production with the Teatre Principal de Palma de Mallorca (staged in 2009). These adaptations have allowed directors to devise imaginative solutions to storytelling and to discover broader ways to interrogate the Catalan literary heritage.

---

[74] Dragan Klaic's view is that 'national classics in the national language […] once perceived within their own national culture as formative assets to be read and seen several times in a lifetime by everyone of average education, thus expected to become familiar and almost proverbial references, have become dusty icons for the generations that grew up on MTV, even if they ultimately acquire a masters degree in facility management or human resources' (p. 223).

[75] Swedish word meaning 'buffet' or 'open table'.

## Concluding remarks

> In general, theatre matters less across Europe as a cultural force and
> as a public platform than it did a century or two ago and is thus of
> much less interest to nationalists, or any other militant ideology, than
> before. Politics has become primarily a master of media control and
> its impact – as Berlusconi's career symbolizes. Nationalist pressures
> and appropriations are not the primary concern of theatres in Europe
> today. While commercial theatre thrives and will continue to thrive,
> quality theatre depends on the continuity of public subsidy and
> therefore faces the indifference of politicians and a cultural
> distancing from many potential audiences as its main challenges.
> Theatres that grasp these challenges will drop the National Theatre
> label as an anachronistic status symbol and stop hiding behind its
> supposed prestige. They will lose credibility if they perpetuate indif-
> ference towards the cultural diversity issues and continue to evade
> the inclusion of other ethnic, cultural and linguistic groups on stage,
> behind the stage and in the auditorium. However, if they transform
> their repertory system to a variety of alternative organizational
> models and production patterns and replace the *smorgasbord* notion
> of the repertory with more focused and profiled programming,
> derived from a critical analysis of the reality rather than from a
> bookshelf of old plays, those theatres can hope to reconnect with
> their culturally diverse local constituencies and creative peers across
> Europe and serve as a platform for reflection and critical thinking in
> an emerging Europe-wide civil society. By recognizing the with-
> ering of the nation-state and recognizing their own capacity to
> enhance intercultural competence over national tradition, such thea-
> tres may become a force shaping the notion of European citizenship,
> especially in the growing practice of bilateral and multilateral inter-
> national co-productions. (p. 227)

I have quoted this passage from Klaic at length, as it encapsulates some
of the challenges facing any national theatre, the TNC included, in the
global age. To an extent, the TNC is still a symbol of Catalan nation-
hood, its imposing structure a statement of a grand(-iose) project. But
the building also fulfils a purpose and allows a focal point for the
development of theatre in Catalonia in a way that the new English-
language Welsh and Scottish National Theatres do not. On the other
hand, their models perhaps allow them a flexibility that Catalonia's
model does not possess, while the cost of maintaining such a large

complex as the TNC is a major factor. The danger is that Catalan theatre becomes over-centralised in Barcelona. However, considerable effort is being expended in order to develop – or re-develop – theatres outside the city, with touring productions from the TNC that are helping to revitalise theatres in Catalan towns such as Manresa and Reus. Moreover, for Belbel the TNC is not so much a national status symbol as an attempt to attract as broad an audience as possible. The T6 sems to me to belong to Klaic's 'balanced and profiled programming', but, to an extent, what he calls the *smorgasbord* approach still persists – perhaps inevitably – at the TNC as Belbel attempts to expose Catalan audiences to a range of theatrical experiences that emanate from within Catalonia and from outside. The current programme is certainly not a 'bookshelf of old plays', but includes a variety of performance models. For some critics (most notably Jordi Coca) the programme is not sufficiently rooted in the Catalan theatre tradition, while, on the other hand, it could be criticised for lagging behind the fast-changing make-up of Catalonia, where immigration from Latin America, Africa and Eastern Europe quickly renders obsolete established cultural and linguistic models. Keeping pace with demographic changes and rapidly changing cultural tastes would seem to be one of the major challenges facing Belbel or any future Artistic Director of the TNC. Trying to satisfy a wide range of audiences may also mean that the TNC has not perhaps explored cutting-edge performative practices as the Teatre Lliure has done. One may ask whether there will continue to be room in Barcelona for both theatres, another of the challenges facing Belbel.

# CONCLUSION

In the quarter of a century since Belbel first began his playwriting career much has changed in Catalan theatre. He has formed part of these changes and helped in no small way to shape them. In his early career he was instrumental in restoring the primacy of the text in a Catalonia dominated by internationally renowned performance groups, yet always respecting the work of these groups. His 1980s plays were very different from the realist idiom favoured by the Franco generation of Catalan playwrights and helped forge a new minimalist style of Catalan writing that proved to be hugely influential. Although some of the plays he has written in the past decade conform, to a limited extent, to what Carles Batlle has identified as a new concentration on local issues in Catalan drama,[1] as *A la Toscana* clearly demonstrates, this can in no way be considered to be a firm trend in his writing. Although a number of his plays tackle recognisably contemporary issues, such as the sexual and social outsider, the dysfunctional family and domestic and terrorist violence, it is difficult to detect specific local settings and they are rarely set in recognisable locations. *La sang* was inspired by an ETA kidnap and murder, but it is not a play *about* Basque terrorism, while *Forasters* is in no way a detailed study of the social phenomenon of immigration, despite the fact that Belbel is the son of Andalusian immigrants to industrial Catalonia. Socio-political issues are often linked to what one might term broader, more philosophical, questions surrounding life and death, and modes of thinking through the ethical and social decisions taken by the characters that inhabit the plays.

---

[1] Carles Batlle i Jordà, 'Contemporary Catalan Theatre: Between the Desert and the Promised Land', in *Catalan Theatre, 1975–2006: Politics, Identity, Performance*, ed. Maria M. Delgado, David George and Lourdes Orozco, special issue of *Contemporary Theatre Review*, 17:3 (2007), 416–24, p. 423.

Belbel's work is particularly concerned with the subjectivity of time and the irrationality of the human mind, while, on the other hand, his fascination with science reflects his interest in rational phenomena and in dissecting the composition of the material world. In contrast to the stage plays, Ventura Pons's film versions of them are firmly set within Barcelona locations that enhance a sense of period and place. Their international projection in film festivals and retrospectives has indirectly enabled Belbel's work to become accessible to a wider audience, and has arguably served to gain it new audiences in another medium.

Just as Belbel epitomises the 'return to the text' in Catalan theatre of the 1980s, so his directing is characterised by a 'respect' for the text. As a director he has facilitated the career of fellow Catalan Jordi Galceran, whose *El mètode Grönholm* is the most successful Catalan play of the post-Franco era in box-office terms.[2] Belbel has helped Josep Maria Benet i Jornet to reshape his dramatic trajectory, and his direction of several Benet plays has undoubtedly been highly significant in that dramatist's success in moving away from social realism and embracing a much more suggestive and spare theatrical language. He has also played a major role in developing the career of several actors and other practitioners and, to judge from my interviews with them, he is respected within the profession for his inclusive, encouraging directing style. Belbel habitually directs his own plays, and, perhaps not entirely coincidentally, his most criticised work within Catalonia to date has been *Mòbil*, one of only three he has not directed himself.[3] Aside from two plays by Àngel Guimerà, Belbel has not directed any Catalan 'classic', and the majority of the directing has been of playwrights from outside Catalonia, be they Spanish or foreign. These represent a wide range of styles and periods, ranging chronologically from the French classical period to modern European and North American writers. He has directed in a variety of spaces, although his more recent work has been at the Teatre Nacional de Catalunya, where he is contracted to direct one work annually. Like his fellow Catalans Lluís Pasqual and Calixto Bieito, he has also ventured into opera, directing

---

[2] The play enjoyed some 800 performances attended by around 600,000 spectators.

[3] In fairness, one should add that the other two were, in critical terms, much more successful: *Elsa Schneider*, directed by Ramon Simó, and *La sang*, directed by Toni Casares.

Rossini's little-known *Il viaggio a Reims* at Barcelona's Teatre Liceu in 2003. While Pasqual, Bieito and Álex Rigola are undoubtedly better known directors abroad, like Carol López, the new Director of Barcelona's Teatre Villarroel, Belbel has shown that writers can also be directors.

Numerous aspects of Belbel's relationship with Catalan theatre professionals have been considered in this book, including actors, composers and designers. He may have begun as a playwright on the 'fringes', working at the Sala Beckett, but he is now at the centre of the nation's cultural establishment. As Artistic Director of the TNC, he occupies one of the most important positions in Catalan theatre, while the premiere of any Belbel play attracts immediate media attention.

Although, unlike Bieito and Pasqual, he does not direct outside Spain, in many ways Belbel may be described as an internationalist. Unsurprisingly for a languages graduate, the early influences on his work were French and German, while his writing often seems to belong to a Western, rather than a Spanish or Catalan, theatrical tradition. Likewise, his own plays (particularly *Mòbil*) have often received a more positive reception abroad than at home. This seems especially to be the case in Germany, although much less so in the English-speaking world. The Germans clearly appreciate his theatrical language, possibly seeing in Belbel a reflection of their playwrights, such as Heiner Müller, whose work has exercised such an influence on him. As has been observed, several Belbel plays have been premiered outside Spain. Copenhagen has been the location of his two latest premieres, and it might be the case that writing for a non-domestic audience affords him a freedom that he has lost in Catalonia.

Be that as it may, Belbel continues to be a key figure in the development of new Catalan drama, although the emphasis has now shifted more to his work as a facilitator. He is doing much to encourage young writers from his position as Artistic Director of the TNC through the T6 scheme. During Belbel's early career, the Sala Beckett was the main outlet for new writing in Barcelona. One of his more recent achievements has been to open up the TNC, a large, mainstream theatre, to such writing, broadening the remit of a theatre that was perceived not to nurture living and emerging Catalan writers. He has helped a number of theatre practitioners, including directors, actors, designers and composers, to develop their careers. Building on the professionalism associated with the Teatre Lliure since the 1970s, Belbel has ensured the existence of a solid team of specialists at the TNC, in which no one component dominates another, a situation that is so different from the tradition of the all-powerful actor-manager in Spain. Belbel has, thus far, demonstrated a pragmatic attitude to his work as Artistic Director. The issue of language is inevitably a major one in the National Theatre of a nation without a state, like Catalonia. Belbel has steered what one might term a middle path through these difficult waters. He clearly supports the view that Catalan has to be the number-one language of performance, but is open to staging productions in Spanish when necessary or in other languages as the need arises. He has encouraged co-productions with Madrid: for instance, Lorca's *La casa de Bernarda Alba*, premiered at the TNC during the 2008–09 season, played at Madrid's Teatro Español during the autumn of 2009. It was a huge critical and commercial success in the Spanish capital and was probably the hit of the season at the Español.

So what has Belbel's overall impact on Catalan theatre been? As a writer, he not only helped to restore the primacy of the text in the late 1980s but also created a recognisable style that influenced many of his contemporaries. Along with Lluïsa Cunillé he was the leading member of the generation that emerged under Sanchis Sinisterra's guidance at the Sala Beckett. Of course, that process took place over twenty years ago, and a whole new generation of playwrights has emerged since then, with writers such as Pau Miró, Victòria Szpunberg, Marc Rosich, Gemma Rodríguez and Ricard Gázquez coming to prominence, and among whom Belbel's influence is not so pronounced.

As Chapter 5 made clear, the TNC has attracted fierce criticism from some quarters. Belbel is the Artistic Director of a powerful entity within Catalonia, and there is always the danger that anyone in this position can start to lose touch with the grass roots. While emerging writers have been given opportunities at the TNC (Pau Miró is an obvious example), this is, of course, in no way the only outlet for new talent. The Sala Beckett (where Belbel cut his teeth) continues to nurture new writing, not least through its Obrador Internacional de Dramatúrgia, a project dedicated to permanent training and research, aiming to combine theatrical theory and practice.[4] The alternative

---

4 For further information on the role of the Sala Beckett, see Sharon G. Feldman, 'The Sala Beckett and the Zero Degree of Theatricality: From Lluïsa

theatre sector continues to struggle with financial difficulties, and, indeed, it appears that the T6 will no longer be a collaborative venture. Some of these new initiatives have been modest and low-cost, a world away from the grandiose edifice of the TNC. One of the most ingenious of these has been the 'Càpsules a 1€' and Plataforma AREAtangent. Situated in the working-class, immigrant Barcelona district of the Raval, this initiative by a group of young practitioners involved the weekly presentation of a short rehearsal piece, for which one euro was charged. It became a kind of laboratory for an emerging generation of practitioners, launching a number of them into a professional career. This sort of initiative in no way negates what Belbel is doing at the TNC (or Rigola's work at the Lliure, for that matter), but it does demonstrate that there is another world beyond that of the publicly funded theatres, one, indeed, in which the young Belbel first came to prominence.[5]

As Chapters 4 and 5 respectively demonstrated, Belbel has received criticism from a variety of quarters over the years, both for the perceived quality of some of his plays and for his TNC role. However, nobody can deny that he has been a highly significant figure in the transformation that Catalan theatre has undergone since the 1980s. He has led the way as writer, director and facilitator, and the dynamism of the Catalan theatre scene today owes much to his multifaceted talents.

Cunillé to Carles Batlle', in *Catalan Theatre, 1975–2006: Politics, Identity, Performance, Contemporary Theatre Review*, 17:3 (2007), 370–84.

5 For further information, see http://www.areatangent.com/. See also a special number of *Pygmalión* dedicated to contemporary Catalan theatre, which contains articles on new writers and performance groups, as well as one on Catalan theatre politics by one of the younger generation of writers, Ricard Gázquez, 'El teatro catalán en los inicios del siglo xxi', ed. David George, special issue of *Pygmalión*, 1 (2010). Young theatre director Iban Beltran has an article on the Càpsules a 1€ and Plataforma AREAtangent in the forthcoming proceedings of a conference on short theatre that was held at Sueca (Valencia) in December 2009.

# APPENDIX:
# PLOT SUMMARIES OF SELECTED BELBEL PLAYS

## *Minim.mal Show* (co-authored with Miquel Górriz) 1987

Like all of Belbel's plays, *Minim.mal Show* does not possess the conventional three-act structure of the well-made play, but is constructed around a succession of scenes. These are named, as follows: Passarel·la (Catwalk), Monòleg (Monologue), L'Altre (The Other), La Causa (The Cause), 'Nem', Sil·logisme (Syllogism), La Conseqüència (The Consequence), Pòdium, Soliloqui de Dos (Soliloquy for Two), Bolero, L'Exemple (The Example), L'Escena (The Scene), Solema, Galeria (Gallery), Aparador (Shop Window), Diàleg (Dialogue), Nessuno, Síncope (Syncopation), Discòpula (Discopulation), Nessuna, Pentàgon, Pista (Trail, Clue or Cue).[1] Some of these scenes have more than one version (for example, there are five 'Pòdiums' and 'Nems') and many of the titles are humorously ironic. The scenes are really a series of sketches, and, despite the lack of a plot as such, a certain pattern develops in those scenes that are repeated. For instance, each Syncopation is a satire of a frustrated attempt at an encounter between B and Y. Dialogue is often clipped and unconnected, while some scenes (such as the Syncopation sequences) are wordless and depend on movement and sound to evoke action. An example is the representation of sexual intercourse through guttural sounds in the Discopulation sequence. Metatheatre is strong in this early play, while the interaction between actors and audience reinforces its ironic humour. As in many

---

[1] I am uncertain of the meaning of 'Pista' that is intended here. It may be most appropriate to take it as indicating a cue to come on stage: as Pista is the title of the play's final scene, this meaning would accord well with the playful irony of the work.

Belbel plays, the characters are unnamed – a feature taken to an extreme in *Minim.mal Show*, in which they are denoted by a single letter of the alphabet.

## *En companyia d'abisme* (*Deep Down*) 1988

The action takes place in a stark, bare zone in the abyss where two men (Man and Young Man), whose relationship is never clearly defined, meet unexpectedly, or so the text initially leads us to believe. Their ambiguous and evasive conversations become a battleground in which each man attempts to establish a dominant position over the other. In the absence of physical action (each character executes only three brief movements, although each inflicts damage on his still adversary), words become the primary weapon through which status and power are established. The meticulous body positions, which Belbel details in his stage directions – excruciatingly difficult for an actor to maintain and gruelling for an audience to watch – are far removed from the demands of the pseudo-naturalistic play, yet they fulfil a central role in creating the tense stage environment in which the characters' mysterious inter-actions take place. From an atmosphere of eerie stillness, Belbel creates a devastating commentary on the pain inflicted by human beings on each other.[2]

## *Tàlem* (*Fourplay*) 1990

The action unfolds in an empty room, bereft of doors or windows, where the only item of furniture is an enormous bed. This is the focus of the action as the elder married couple attempts to persuade a young couple to sleep in it. Through a series of short episodic scenes the char-acters lure themselves and each other into compromising (emotional and physical) positions. Transcending its literal significance, the bed becomes both a visual metaphor for the sexual undercurrent which is ever present in the play and a manifestation of the characters' deepest

---

[2] The above summary is based on Maria M. Delgado and David George, 'Sergi Belbel', in *Modern Spanish Dramatists: A Bio-Bibliographical Sourcebook*, ed. Mary Parker (Westport, CT/London: Greenwood, 2002), pp. 75–85, pp. 77–78.

fears and hopes. Tantalisingly, desire exceeds the means through which it can be consummated, for circumstances conspire to ensure the bed remains unused.

## Carícies (*Caresses*) 1991

The play's structure is based on Austrian writer Arthur Schnitzler's *La Ronde* (1900), and, like its predecessor, consists of 10 interlocking scenes, each between two people, one of whom reappears in the following scene. These are, respectively, a young couple (Scene 1), the same young woman and her mother (Scene 2), the mother and an old woman whom we presume had once been her lover (Scene 3), this old woman and her brother, who is a tramp living rough on the city streets (Scene 4), the tramp and a boy who steals from him (Scene 5), this boy and his father (Scene 6), the father and his mistress (Scene 7), the mistress and her father (Scene 8), the father and his rent boy (Scene 9), and a mother and her son (Scene 10). The play concludes with an Epilogue, in which the young man from Scene 1, who has been badly beaten by his partner, is lovingly tended by a neighbour, who turns out to be the mother from Scene 10.

## Després de la pluja (*After the Rain*) 1993

The action of this play, which may be linked to the office TV drama and 'Smoking Room' films, takes place on the flat rooftop of a skyscraper in an unnamed city, but which is more reminiscent of New York or Chicago than Barcelona. Staff from an office in the building (both secretaries and their bosses) escape to the rooftop in order to enjoy an illicit cigarette, as smoking is banned by their company. From the conversations between the characters, details of their own and other people's lives emerge. Most of them are neurotic to a greater or lesser extent, and some are in unhappy or broken relationships. Belbel portrays the tensions and the underlying violence of a repressive postmodern society, in which all the characters participate in restrictive surveillance.

## *Morir (un moment abans de morir) (To Die: A Moment Prior to Death)* 1993

The play is in two parts, which provide two different outcomes to the same events. In the first, death comes suddenly and violently to a series of characters (a film scriptwriter, a heroin addict, a young girl, a hospital patient, a pill-popping alcoholic mother, a motorcyclist hit by a police patrol car, and a businessman murdered by a contract killer), while in the second part, each of these characters survives. The first part is distinguished by selfishness, aggression and a lack of solidarity. The second half paints a much more optimistic – although by no means idealistic – picture of human conduct, as not only do the characters survive but a sense of neighbourliness and even personal sacrifice emerges.

The structure is more complex and less episodic than that of *Caricies*. The order of scenes in the first part is reversed in the second, a technique Belbel had earlier used in *Tàlem*. However, whereas in *Tàlem* the structure is part of an elaborate game, in *Morir (un moment abans de morir)* the idea of art as play is denied in the Epilogue. The scriptwriter is the only person to die a second time, although the ending is ambiguous as Belbel leaves open the wife's attitude to the death.

## *Sóc Lletja (I'm Ugly*; co-authored with Jordi Sànchez, with music by Òscar Roig) 1997

This humorous black musical comedy recounts the adventures of the eponymous anti-heroine, who is rejected because of her ugliness by a world obsessed with image. She wreaks her revenge bizarrely by murdering a series of those 'beautiful' people who are her antithesis.

## *La sang (Blood)* 1998

A politician's wife (called simply Woman) has been taken hostage by a group of terrorists, and is held by two of the group, a Man and a Young Woman, accompanied by a child, who was orphaned when her parents, former members of the terrorist group, were killed. The Woman is subjected to a series of amputations while the terrorists await a ransom from her husband, and is ultimately put to death. Following each amputation the terrorists package and send off an amputated body part (finger, ear, foot), the first two of which are discovered by chance by a boy and girl in a park, and a policeman and policewoman, respectively, while the foot reaches their intended target – her husband – while he is in the company of his mistress.

### *El temps de Planck* (*Planck Time*; with music by Òscar Roig) 2000

Based on the life of German physicist Max Planck (1858–1947), the founder of quantum theory, in some ways *El temps de Planck* is Belbel's most ambitious work. It is a musical drama that recounts the interaction between the dying Max Planck and his wife and daughters, and explores the subjectivity of time, which ranges from the nano-second to eternity. The play contains a mixture of the most insignificant daily actions and great philosophical concerns, and is characterised by a familiar Belbel blend of seriousness and occasionally outrageous humour.

### *Forasters* (*Strangers*) 2004

Subtitled a 'family melodrama in two periods',[3] the play takes place in an unnamed city. The two time periods in question are the 1960s and the beginning of the twenty-first century. The play concentrates on one specific family, and the relationships between them and their neighbours. They are, in many ways, a typical Catalan bourgeois family, and the neighbours are from the south of Spain (the 1960s) and North Africa (the start of the twenty-first century). The play opens in the second time period, with the young immigrant boy from the 1960s – now a successful businessman, referred to as Home (Man) – surveying with the Son the family's property, which he has just purchased. The remaining scenes (ten in Part One, and four in Part 2) alternate between the two time frames and build up a picture of a dysfunctional family and their interaction (or lack of it) with their neighbours. The Mother from the 1960s and her daughter in the 2000s suffer from cancer, which eventually kills them both. The Son has a traumatic relationship with his mother, who is a domineering matriarch, reminiscent of a long line

---

[3] Sergi Belbel, *Strangers*, p. 107. The original direction is 'melodrama familiar en dos temps' (Sergi Belbel, *Forasters*, p. 27).

of dominant female characters in Spanish theatre, from the Celestina to Bernarda Alba. The Son runs away at the hour of his mother's death but, by the 2000s, has learnt to face up to death and is able to accompany his sister at her final hour. The Epilogue clarifies the identity of the Man who is to purchase the house, and an exchange between him and the young orphan boy from the twenty-first century reinforces a link between them that has been suggested earlier in the play.

### *Mòbil* (*Mobile*) 2007

This play consists of 29 scenes, which take place in a railway station, in cars, an airport, and the entrance, suite room and exterior of a hotel: hallmark locations in any modern city. In this play, Belbel uses a terrorist attack in an airport to deal with such themes as the dysfunctional family, the verbal violence to which we subject our fellow human beings, and the discovery of tenderness and affection between strangers. There are four characters: Sara (55) and Rosa (30) (mother and daughter), and Clàudia (49) and her son Jan (27). Family relations are wounding and aggressive, just like those within couples. Sara's husband has left her, as has her daughter's partner, while Jan has problems with his girlfriend. Sara and Clàudia are to travel by plane: Sara – whose daughter has just bought her first mobile – travels to the airport by train, while Clàudia (a businesswoman) gets there by car. A terrorist bomb explodes in the airport, activated, as the audience learns in the penultimate scene of the play, by a mobile phone. The explosion is heard by both Rosa and Jan on their mobiles while they are speaking to their mothers, although the children, of course, do not realise what is happening. The two mothers survive, and, thanks to a series of coincidences, Jan meets Sara and they instantly fall in love. Although this appears to be a highly improbable situation, the discovery of love and tenderness between two strangers has parallels in other Belbel plays, for instance, in *Carícies*. Sara changes as a result of this sudden sexual encounter, becoming calm and relaxed, in contrast to the other two women, who retain the hysterical behaviour that characterises a number of Belbel's female characters.

## *A la Toscana* (*To Tuscany*) **2007**

Set in the first decade of the twenty-first century, *A la Toscana* deals
with the mid-life crisis suffered by a successful architect called Marc,
which seems to have been exacerbated by what was supposed to be a
rejuvenating holiday in Tuscany with his wife Joana. She counterbal-
ances him in that she simply wants to enjoy the little things in life,
whereas he is obsessed by 'big' issues, and sees problems where none
exist. The couple are friends of Marta and Jaume, but the relationship
between these two is unclear. The spectator is never sure whether
events are real, or Marc's dreams, or the result of his unbalanced
mental state, nor whether Tuscany is anything more than a symbol of
the world of illusion that Marc inhabits. Thus, much of the play takes
place in the blurred space between waking and dreaming. The doubts
extend to issues of illness and death. A number of deaths seem to occur
in the course of the play, although it appears that the only actual death
is that of Jaume, whose real physical illness contrasts with Marc's
imagined sickness.

# BIBLIOGRAPHY

**Plays by Belbel***

Belbel, Sergi. *En companyia d'abisme i altres obres*. Els Llibres de l'Escorpí/Teatre El Galliner, 116. Barcelona: Edicions 62, 1990
———. *Deep Down*. Trans. John London, in *Modern International Drama*, 26:2, 1993, 5–24
———. *Carícies*. Els Llibres de l'Escorpí/Teatre El Galliner, 127. Barcelona: Edicions 62, 1992
———. *Caresses*. Trans. John London, in Elyse Dodgson and Mary Peate (eds), *Spanish Plays: New Spanish and Catalan Drama*. London: Nick Hern, 1999, pp. 1–54
Górriz, Miquel and Sergi Belbel. *Minim.mal Show*. Teatre 3 i 4, Valencia: Eliseu Climent, 1992
———. *Després de la pluja*. Teatre Català Contemporani: Els Textos del Centre Dramàtic. Barcelona: Editorial Lumen/Generalitat de Catalunya, 1993
———. *After the Rain*. Trans. Xavier Rodríguez Rosell, David George and John London (published with Klaus Chatten, *Sugar Dollies*). Methuen Drama. London: Methuen, 1996, pp. 85–178
———. *Morir (un moment abans de morir)*. Teatre 3 i 4. Valencia: Eliseu Climent, 1995
Belbel, Sergi, Jordi Sànchez and Òscar Roig. *Sóc Lletja*. El Galliner/Teatre, 158. Barcelona: Edicions 62, 1997
———. *La sang*. El Galliner/Teatre, 168. Barcelona: Edicions 62, 1998
———. *Blood*. Trans. Marion Peter Holt. Estreno Contemporary Spanish Plays, 25. New Brunswick, NJ: Estreno, 2004
———. *Hivern*. Narrativa, 191. Barcelona: Empúries, 2002
Belbel, Sergi, and Òscar Roig. *El temps de Planck*. Col·lecció Columna Romea. Barcelona: Fundació Romea, 2002


* These are ordered chronologically, followed by the corresponding English translation if available. All are by Belbel alone, unless co-authors are cited

————. *Forasters*. Col·lecció TNC. Barcelona: Proa, 2004

————. *Strangers*. Trans. Sharon G. Feldman, in Marion Peter Holt and Sharon G. Feldman (eds), *Barcelona Plays*. New York: Martin E. Segal Theater Center, 2008, pp. 107–231

————. *Mòbil*. Barcelona: Fundació Teatre Lliure, 2007

————. *A la Toscana*. Barcelona: Proa, 2007

**Other Sources**

Adams, David. *Stage Welsh: Nation, Nationalism and Theatre: the Search for Cultural Identity*. Changing Wales. Llandysul: Gomer, 1996

Astles, Cariad. 'Catalan Puppet Theatre: A Process of Cultural Affirmation', in Delgado, George and Orozco (eds), *Catalan Theatre, 1975–2006: Politics, Identity, Performance* (2007), 323–34

Aznar Soler, Manuel. Introduction to José Sanchis Sinisterra, *Ñaque/ ¡Ay, Carmela!*. Madrid: Cátedra, 1993, pp. 9–101

Bacardit, Ramon, et al. *Romea, 125 anys*. Barcelona: Generalitat de Catalunya, 1989

Batlle i Jordà, Carles. 'Contemporary Catalan Theatre: Between the Desert and the Promised Land', in Delgado, George and Orozco (eds), *Catalan Theatre, 1975–2006: Politics, Identity, Performance* (2007), 416–24

Belbel, Sergi, Guillermo Heras, José Sanchis Sinisterra, et al. 'Perspectivas dramatúrgicas: hacia el siglo XXI', transcript of panel discussion, Sitges Teatre Internacional 1998, *Escena*, 60–61 (May–June 1999): Documentos, p. 7

Benet i Jornet, Josep Maria. *Desig*. 2nd edn. Valencia: Tres i Quatre, 2000. Translated as *Desire* by Sharon G. Feldman, in John London and David George (eds), *Modern Catalan Plays*. London: Methuen, 2000, pp. 105–74

————. 'Per situar-nos', in Górriz and Belbel, *Minim.mal Show*, pp. 9–16

Bradby, David and David Williams. *Directors' Theatre*. Macmillan Modern Dramatists. Basingstoke: Macmillan, 1988

Buffery, Helena. 'The "Placing of Memory" ', in Delgado, George and Orozco (eds), *Catalan Theatre, 1975–2006: Politics, Identity, Performance* (2007), 385–97

————. 'Theater Space and Cultural Identity in Catalonia', in P. Louise Johnson (ed.), *Catalan Spaces*, special issue of *Romance Quarterly*, 53:3 (2006), 195–209

Carlson, Marvin. 'National Theatres: Then and Now', in S. E. Wilmer (ed.), *National Theatres in a Changing Europe*, pp. 21–33

Ciurans, Enric. *El Teatre Viu, una resistència cultural*. Barcelona: Associació d'Investigació i Experimentació Teatral, 2009

Coca, Jordi. *L'Agrupació Dramàtica de Barcelona: intent de Teatre Nacional Català, 1995–1963*. Monografies de Teatre, 9. Barcelona: Edicions 62/Institut del Teatre, 1978

———. 'Brossa and the Others'. Trans. Simon Breden, Maria M. Delgado and David George, in Delgado, George and Orozco (eds), *Catalan Theatre, 1975–2006: Politics, Identity, Performance* (2007), 446–52

———. 'Introduction', in Jeff Teare and Jordi Coca (eds), *Black Beach and Other Plays*. Cardigan: Parthian, 2008

Connon, Derek. 'Marivaux's *Les Fausses confidences*'. Exeter Modern Languages Tapes, no. F317 (1987)

Crameri, Kathryn. *Catalonia: National Identity and Cultural Policy, 1980–2003*. Iberian and Latin American Studies. Cardiff: University of Wales Press, 2008

Delgado, Maria M. 'Calixto Bieito: Staging Excess In and Across the Stages of Europe', in Maria M. Delgado and Dan Rebellato (eds), *Contemporary European Theatre Directors*. Abingdon: Routledge, 2010, pp. 277–97

———. 'Forum 2004 Barcelona: A Summer of Stagings in Spain's Theatrical Capital', *Western European Stages*, 16:3 (2004), 71–84

———. 'In Barcelona', *Plays International*, September 2002, 26–29

———. 'Journeys of Cultural Transference: Calixto Bieito's Multilingual Shakespeares', *Modern Language Review*, 101:1 (2006), 106–50

———. *'Other' Spanish Theatres: Erasure and Inscription on the Twentieth-Century Spanish Stage*. Manchester: Manchester University Press, 2003

———. *Ventura Pons Retrospective*. Publicity leaflet for the Institute of Contemporary Arts (London), 1999

——— and David George. 'Sergi Belbel', in Mary Parker (ed.), *Modern Spanish Dramatists: A Bio-Bibliographical Sourcebook*. Westport, CT/London: Greenwood, 2002, pp. 75–85

———, David George and Lourdes Orozco (eds). *Catalan Theatre, 1975–2006: Politics, Identity, Performance*, special issue of *Contemporary Theatre Review*, 17:3 (2007)

——— and Paul Heritage. *In Contact with the Gods? Directors Talk Theatre*. Manchester: Manchester University Press, 1996

Faulkner, Sally. *Literary Adaptations in Spanish Cinema*. Colección Támesis, Serie A: Monografías, 202. Woodbridge: Tamesis, 2004

Feldman, Sharon G. *In the Eye of the Storm: Contemporary Theater in Barcelona*. Lewisburg: Bucknell University Press, 2010

——— . 'The Sala Beckett and the Zero Degree of Theatricality: From Lluïsa Cunillé to Carles Batlle', in Delgado, George and Orozco (eds), *Catalan Theatre, 1975–2006: Politics, Identity, Performance* (2007), 370–84

Fitz-Simon, Christopher. *The Abbey Theatre: Ireland's National Theatre, The First Hundred Years*. London: Thames & Hudson, 2003

Gallén, Enric. 'Catalan Theatrical Life', in *Contemporary Catalan Drama*, ed. David George and John London. Anglo-Catalan Society Occasional Publications, 9. Sheffield: Anglo-Catalan Society, 1996, pp. 19–42

George, David. 'A Young Lad in the Arms of an Old Man – Sergi Belbel Directs Àngel Guimerà's *La filla del mar* (*The Daughter of the Sea*)', in *Spanish Theatre 1920–1995: Strategies in Protest and Imagination* (3), *Contemporary Theatre Review*, 7:4 (1998), 45–64

——— . 'Belbel Rescues a Forgotten Guimerà', *Catalan Review* (forthcoming)

——— . 'Beyond the Local: Sergi Belbel and *Forasters*', in Delgado, George and Orozco (eds), *Catalan Theatre, 1975–2006: Politics, Identity, Performance* (2007), 398–410

——— . 'From Stage to Screen: Sergi Belbel and Ventura Pons', *Anales de la Literatura Española Contemporánea*, 27:2 (2002), 89–102

——— . *The History of the* Commedia dell'arte *in Modern Hispanic Literature with Special Attention to the Work of García Lorca*. Lewiston/Queenston/Lampeter: The Edwin Mellen Press, 1995

——— . *The Theatre in Madrid and Barcelona, 1892–1936: Rivals or Collaborators?* Cardiff: University of Wales Press, 2002

——— and John London. 'Avant-garde Drama', in David George and John London (eds), *Contemporary Catalan Drama*. Anglo-Catalan Society Occasional Publications, 9. Sheffield: Anglo-Catalan Society, 1996, pp. 73–101

Hall, J. B. 'Madness and Sanity in Calderón's *El alcalde de Zalamea*', *Iberromania*, 43 (1996), 52–67

Henríquez, José. 'Sobre el difícil género de la comedia', *Primer Acto*, 315:4 (2006), 14–16

Jones, Anwen. *National Theatres in Context*. Cardiff: University of Wales Press, 2007

Klaic, Dragan. 'National Theatres Undermined by the Withering of the Nation-State', in S. E. Wilmer (ed.), *National Theatres in a Changing Europe*, pp. 217–27

Leonard, Candyce and John P. Gabriele. 'Fórmula para una dramaturgia española de finales del siglo XX', in John P. Gabriele and Candyce Leonard (eds), *Panorámica del teatro español actual*. Serie Teatro. Madrid: Fundamentos, 1996, pp. 7–21

Levitas, Ben. 'The Abbey Opens: A First Night Revisited', in S. E. Wilmer (ed.), *National Theatres in a Changing Europe*, pp. 73–83

London, John. 'Contemporary Catalan Drama in English: Some Aspirations and Limitations', in Delgado, George and Orozco (eds), *Catalan Theatre, 1975–2006: Politics, Identity, Performance* (2007), 453–62

———. 'The Theatrical Poetry of Joan Brossa', in *Joan Brossa, Words are Things: Poems, Objects and Installations*. Exhibition Catalogue. London: Riverside Studios, 1992, pp. 20–23

Madariaga, Iolanda G. 'Una fulgurante trayectoria: Sergi Belbel en la cumbre del teatro catalán', *Primer Acto*, 315:4 (2006), 8–13

Ordóñez, Marcos. *A pie de obra*. Barcelona: Alba, 2003

———. *Molta comèdia: Cròniques de teatre, 1987–1995*. Barcelona: La Campana, 1996

Orozco, Lourdes. 'National Identity in the Construction of the Theater Policy of the Generalitat de Catalunya', in P. Louise Johnson (ed.), *Catalan Spaces*, special issue of *Romance Quarterly*, 53:3 (2006), 211–22

———. *Teatro y política: Barcelona (1980–2000)*. Serie Debate, 12. Madrid: Publicaciones de la Asociación de Directores de Escena, 2007

Perarnau, Esther. '*Carícies*, de Sergi Belbel', in Manuel Aznar Soler (ed.), *Veinte años de teatro y democracia en España (1975–1995)*, Cop d'Idées. Barcelona: CITEC, 1996, pp. 177–81

Potter, Nick. '*The Merchant of Venice*', in Graham Holderness, Nick Potter and John Turner (eds), *Shakespeare: The Play of History*. Basingstoke and London: Macmillan, 1988, pp. 160–79

Puchades, Xavier. 'Renovación teatral en España entre 1984–1998 desde la escritura dramática; puesta en escena y recepción crítica'. Uunpublished doctoral dissertation, University of Valencia, 2005

Pujol, Anton. 'Ventura Pons y la crónica de un territorio llamado Barcelona', *Arizona Journal of Hispanic Cultural Studies*, 13 (December 2009), 61–81

Ragué-Arias, Maria-José. *El teatro de fin de milenio en España (de 1975 hasta hoy)*. Ariel Literatura y Crítica. Barcelona: Ariel, 1996

———. *¿Nuevas dramaturgias?: los autores de fin de siglo en Cataluña, Valencia y Baleares*. Madrid: Instituto Nacional de las Artes Escénicas y de la Música, 2000

Salvat Ferré, Ricard. 'Les aportacions del Teatre Viu, l'EADAG i la Companyia Adrià Gual dels anys cinquanta i seixanta', *Assaig de teatre: Revista de l'Associació d'Investigació i Experimentació Teatral*, 37 (2003), 111–22

Shellard, Dominic. *British Theatre Since the War*. New Haven and London: Yale University Press, 2000

Welch, Robert. *The Abbey Theatre (1899–1999): Form and Pressure*. Oxford: Oxford University Press, 1999

Wilmer, S. E. (ed.). *National Theatres in a Changing Europe*. Studies in International Performance. Basingstoke and New York: Palgrave Macmillan, 2008

Zatlin, Phyllis. 'From Stage to Screen: The Adaptations of Ventura Pons', in Delgado, George and Orozco (eds), *Catalan Theatre, 1975–2006: Politics, Identity, Performance* (2007), 434–45

**Press reviews, interviews and articles, and webography**

Anon. 'A la Toscana', viewed at http://horitzons.blogspot.com/2007/12/la-toscana-sergi-belbel.html, accessed 31 December 2008

———. 'El teatre català es diu Sergi Belbel', *Avui*, 4 January 1989, p. 34

———. 'Gähnen der Geschlechter', *Tribüne*, 20 March 2008

———. Interview with Sergi Belbel, *El Observador*, 8 October 1992, p. 55

———. 'Liebesspielwiese im modernen Remix', *Zett*, 16 March 2008

———. Review of *Nach den Regen*, *Der Tages Spiegel*, 15 November 1995

———. 'Un brillante Belbel', *El Periódico*, 26 November 1993, p. 2

———. 'Una tragèdia de Guimerà abre el Romea', *El Periódico*, 27 October 1992, p. 55

———. 'Unausgesetztes Lust-Stöhnen', *Oldenburgische Volkszeitung*, 1 October 1996

Antón, J. 'Belbel monta Marivaux al estilo de las comedias clásicas de Hollywood', El País, 15 November 2005, p. 44

Armengol, Joaquim. 'Contumàcia', *El Punt*, 7 October 2007, viewed at http://www.teatrebcn.com/critiques/critiques2.asp?Id=4315, accessed 31 December 2008

Barrena, Begoña. 'Entre Hollywood y la Italia del XVI', *El País*, 25 November 2005, p. 4

Bassett, Kate. Review of *After the Rain*, *The Times*, 4 April 1996, p. 36

Batlle Caminal, Jordi. 'Forasteros', http://www.fotogramas.es/Peliculas/Forasteros/Critica, accessed 16 December 2008

Bäuerle, Inge. 'Die Rituale der fleißigen Telefonierer', *Stuttgarter Zeitung*, 30 June 2007

Becker, Peter von. 'Geile Welt, heute Welt', *Theatre Heute*, June 1995, p. 4

Benach, Joan-Anton. 'Dramaturgia de las neurosis urbanas', *La Vanguardia*, 30 October 1993, p. 36

———. 'El malicioso método Galceran', *La Vanguardia*, 1 May 2003, p. 35

———. 'Una lamentable confusión', *La Vanguardia*, 1 January 2007, viewed at http://www.teatrenacional.com/critiques/mobil.html, accessed 17 September 2008

Benet i Jornet, Josep M. 'Guimerà sin naftalina', *El Correo Catalán*, 30 June 1974, p. 14

Blumenstein, Von Gottfried. 'Hochform, wohin das Auge auch blickt', *Lausitzer Rundschau*, 10 December 2001

Bombí-Vilaseca, Francesc. 'L'escriptura surt quan trobes que la forma va lligada amb el contingut', *Avui* (Cultura), 25 November 2004, pp. x–xi

Burguet Ardiaca, F. 'Una carícia pot ferir la sensibilitat dels rosegaaltars', *Diari de Barcelona*, 1 March 1992, p. 37

Cánovas, Ana Rosa. Interview with Sergi Belbel, *La Vanguardia*, 20 April 1990, p. 56

Casas, Joan. 'Els perills de l'amanerament', Mirador, *Diari de Barcelona*, 23 April 1990, p. 3

Centeno, Enrique. 'Caricias como zarpazos', *Diario* 16, 27 May 1994, p. 34

Coca, Jordi. 'Don Joan a l'exili', *Avui* online, 23 November 2007, http://paper.avui.cat/article/cultura/106640/don/joan/lexili.html, accessed 28 June 2008

Conrad, Peter. 'But You'll Have to Wait for Godot', *Observer*, review section, 24 May 2009, p. 20

Corbella, F. 'Grec 97 (I). Antes del próximo milenio', *Reseña* I, 286, September 1997

Croggon, Alison. 'After the Rain', http://theatrenotes.blogspot.com/2005/02/after-rain.html, accessed 21 December 2008

———. 'Caresses', http://theatrenotes.blogspot.com/2004/08/caresses.html, accessed 19 December 2008

Doria, Sergio. 'Bombillitas a todo taco', ABC, 1 January 2007, viewed at http://www.teatrenacional.com/critiques/mobil.html, accessed 17 September 2008

———. 'Los espejos de Belbel y la ley de la herencia', *ABC*, 24 September 2004, p. 82

––––––. 'Viaje a ninguna parte', *ABC*, 20 November 2007, viewed at http://www.teatrebcn.com/critiques/critiques2.asp?Id=4315, accessed 31 December 2008

Flatt, Molly. 'Theatre of the Underdog', http://www.guardian.co.uk/stage/theatreblog/2008/apr/16/theatreoftheunderdog, accessed 22 December 2008

Fondevila, Santiago. 'Una intrigante comedia', *La Vanguardia*, 7 October 2007, viewed at http://www.teatrebcn.com/critiques/critiques2.asp?Id=4315, accessed 31 December 2008

––––––. 'Viuda rica, hombre pobre', *La Vanguardia*, 15 November 2005, p. 39

French, Philip. 'An Actor of True Genius and a Man of Great Decency', *Observer*, 29 September 2008, pp. 2–3

Gallén, Enric. 'Desig', consulted at http://www.pencatala.cat/ctdl/autors_catalans/josep_m_benet_i_jornet/obra/desig.php, accessed 25 March 2009

García Garzón, Juan I. 'El síndrome de la felicidad', *ABC*, 20 March 2008, p. 57

Gardner, Lyn. Review of *After the Rain*, *Guardian*, G2, 4 April 1996, p. 9

Gschleier, Kathrin. 'Erwartungen und Erkenntnisse', *Dolomiten*, 6 March 2008

Haro Tecglen, Eduardo. 'Da bastante asco', *El País*, 28 May 1994, p. 31

Hartig, Klaus. 'Alles ist, wie es ist', *Tageszeitung*, 14 March 2008

Haydon, Andrew. Review of *Fourplay*, *Time Out*, 10–16 April 2008, p. 150

Helfer, Christine. Review of *Tàlem*, *MiMa*, 13 March 2008

Hera, Alberto, de la, 'No es nuevo', *Ya*, 4 June 1994, p. 32

Jarolin, Peter. 'Ein verbaler Spiegel der Lust', *Kurier*, 27 September 1997

Labbert, Astrid. 'Wir reden gern – aber nur am Handy', *Weser Kurier*, 6 March 2007

Ley, Pablo. 'Un clásico bien montado', *El País (Cataluña)*, 23 September 2000, p. 15

––––––. 'Un reloj mal montado', *El País*, 15 November 1999, p. 51

Lladó, Marçal. 'Sergi Belbel, nou director del TNC', *Lamalla.cat*, 18 March 2005, http://www.lamalla.cat/actualitat_cultural/teatre/article?id=98481, accessed 13 October 2008

López Rosell, César. 'El TNC a examen', http://blogs.que.es/6527/2006/11/11/el-tnc-fa-10-anys-amb-repte-d-assentar-dramaturgia accessed 13 October 2008

López Sancho, Lorenzo. '*Caricias*, la muestra y el modelo en la Olimpia', *ABC*, 4 June 1994, p. 98

Marx, Heike. 'Vom dach die Tiefe, vom Leben in den Tod', *Die Rheinpfalz*, 3 March 1997

Massip, Francesc. 'Camí de crancs', *Avui*, 1 January 2007, viewed at http://www.teatrenacional.com/critiques/mobil.html, accessed 17 September 2008

Miret, Albert. 'Sergi Belbel parla sobre *Les falses confidències*', http://www.teatral.net/asp/traientpunta/cos.asp?idtraient=41, accessed 3 December 2008

Molins, Manuel. Interview with the Associació d'Actors i Directors Professionals de Catalunya (AADPC), which appears on their website, http://www.aadpc.cat/publicacions/revista-entreacte/arxiu/155/article.html, accessed 19 June 2009

Monedero, Marta. 'El TNC obrirà la temporada amb un Calderón en castellà', *Avui*, 13 July 2000, p. 30

Negrín, Florentino L. 'Eso de las vanguardias', *La Clave*, 14 March 2008, p. 95

Oberhammer, Margit. 'Keen Sense of Rhythm', translation of 'Sicheres Gefühl für den Rhythmus', *Dolomiten*, 13 March 2008

Ordóñez, Marcos. 'Koltès, siempre hacia el oeste', *El País*, Babelia section, 3 August 2002, viewed at http://www.elpais.com/articulo/arte/Koltes/siempre/Oeste/elpbabart/20020803elpbabart_9/Tes, accessed 3 March 2009

———. 'La novela de un joven pobre', *El País*, Babelia section, 7 January 2006, p. 14

———. 'Sin cobertura', *El País*, Babelia section, 20 January 2007, p. 21

Pérez, Xavier. 'Un prolífic investigador', *Avui*, 26 April 1990, p. 36

Pérez de Olaguer, Gonzalo. Interview with Sergi Belbel, *El Periódico* (Catalan-language edition), 16 September 2000, p. 47

———. 'Patinazo del Teatre Lliure', *El Periódico*, 1 January 2007, viewed at http://www.teatrenacional.com/critiques/mobil.html, accessed 17 September 2008

Ragué, María-José. 'La espectacularidad del TNC', *El Mundo*, 25 November 2005, p. 70

———. 'La inalcanzable utopía', *El Mundo*, 14 November 2008, viewed at http://www.teatrebcn.com/critiques/critiques2.asp?Id=4315, accessed 31 December 2008

———. '*Tàlem*: una comedia de Sergi Belbel', *El Mundo*, 27 April 1990, p. 38

Sàbat, Núria. '*Tàlem*, el poder de la sugestión', *El Periódico*, 23 April 1990, p. 45

Sala, Jordi. 'Belbel del segle XXI', *Diari de Girona*, 7 October 2007, viewed at http://www.teatrebcn.com/critiques/critiques2.asp?Id= 4315, accessed 31 December 2008

Sagarra, Joan de. 'Mal rollo', *El País*, 1 March 1992, p. 39

———. '¿Quién le paga el mármol?', *El País* (Edición Cataluña), 13 September 1997, p. 31

Salvà, Bernat. Interview with Sergi Belbel and Ventura Pons in *Avui*, 24 November 2008, viewed at http://www.avui.cat/article/cultura_ comunicacio/47155/ventura/pons/sergi/belbel/excl·lim/tot/nomes/ falta/la/gent/ho/sapiga.html, accessed 5 December 2008

Santos, Care. 'El honor con sangre se limpia', *El Cultural*, 20 September 2000, pp. 46–47

Sardà, Zeneida. 'Sergi Belbel, dramaturg i director del Teatre Nacional de Catalunya', *Serra d'Or*, 570 (June 2007), 54–58

Savall, Cristina. 'Belbel firma una superproducción cinematográfica', *El Periódico de Catalunya*, 29 September 2008, viewed at http:// www.elperiodica.com/default.asp?idpublicacio_PK=46andidioma =CASandidnoticia_PK=545481andidseccio_PK=1013, accessed 13 October 2008

Schaake-Burmann, Nicole. 'Immer erreichbar, stets einsam', *Weser Report*, 7 March 2007

Schönfeldt, Heinz von. 'Viel Qualm auf dem Dach', *Mannheimer Morgen*, 3 March 1997

Schnackenburg, Alexander. 'Handyempfang im Brauhaus', *Kreiszeitung*, 7 March 2007

Schutt, Hans-Dieter. 'Einsam gemeinsam', *Neues Deutschland*, 20 June 2007

Sotorra, Andreu. 'Belbel a la Tarantino', *Avui DDD*, 17 April 1998, viewed at http://www.andreusotorra.com/teatre/entrevista3.html, accessed 20 October 2008

———. Interview with Sergi Belbel, *El Temps*, 31 May 2005, viewed at http://www.andreusotorra.com/teatre/entrevista118.html, accessed 27 March 2009

———. 'Sergi Belbel reprèn per quarta vegada la direcció d'una obra pròpia amb *Carícies*', *Avui*, 24 February 1992, p. 21

Spencer, Liese. Review of *After the Rain*, *What's On*, 10 April 1996

Thomson, Helen. 'Floodgates Open After Bleak Look at Corporate Nightmare', *The Age*, 1 March 2005, p. 11

Trancón, Santiago. 'Provocadores de la nada', *El Mundo*, 9 June 1994, viewed at http://www.elmundo.es/papel/hemeroteca/1994/06/09/ cultura/718602.html, accessed 6 March 2008

Tugues, Pep. 'Sergi Belbel i *El temps de Plank* [*sic*]', http://www. teatral.net/enrevista/belbel-plank.html, accessed 20 October 2008

Turpin, Adrian. Review of *After the Rain*, *The Independent*, Section 2, 1 April 1996, p. 27

Villán, Javier. 'Lo catalán triunfa en Madrid', *El Mundo* (Cultura), 11 March 2008, p. 57

———. 'Virtuosismo y frustración', *El Mundo*, 12 January 1991, p. 38

Villena, Luis Antonio, de. 'Teatro de texto y realidad', *El Mundo*, 27 May 1994, viewed at http://www.elmundo.es/papel/hemeroteca /1994/05/27/opinion/716496.html, accessed 6 March 2009

Villora, Pedro. 'Belbel, En la Toscana', *El Mundo*, 6 March 2008, viewed at http://www.elemunda.es/papel/2008/03/06/madrid/234 0900.html, consulted 31 December 2008

———. ' "No veo por ningún lado al Calderón de la Barca reaccion-ario" ', *ABC*, 20 December 2000, p. 77

Wengierek, Reinhard. 'Sie küssen und sie kloppen sich', *Welt.de*, 24 January 2006

# INDEX

Play titles are included only when they are written or directed by Belbel; plays written by Belbel are listed as separate individual entries; plays directed by him are entered under their respective authors. The names of academic critics are included only when they appear in the main text, but not in footnotes. Only selected theatre critics from Barcelona – where Belbel is based – are included, and, again, only when they appear in the main text.